Jesse Fink was born in London in 1973. He has variously been an editor, journalist and columnist but is best known for the books *Laid Bare* and *The Youngs*.

He lives in Sydney, Australia, with his daughter.

KU-523-718

PRAISE FOR *THE YOUNGS*

'The best book I've ever read about AC/DC.'
– Mark Evans, bass player of AC/DC, 1975–77

'An essential read for fans of the band. Most important, *The Youngs* gives a full portrait of just how significant a role George Young, Malcolm and Angus's older brother, played in AC/DC's development.'
– *The New Yorker*

'Fink's ability to overcome the Youngs' code of Scottish Australian omertà is impressive . . . a cut above other AC/DC tomes, and Fink knows it.'
– *Classic Rock*

'It's extraordinarily well written and presents a fascinating view of the band and the people that helped make it happen . . . a great piece of research.'
– Phil Carson, former vice-president of Atlantic Records who signed AC/DC

'A largely untold, much more controversial story . . . anything but a hagiography. A fresh, incisive take on the band.'
– *MOJO*

'I loved it.'
– Jerry Greenberg, former president of Atlantic Records

'A great job.'
– Tony Platt, engineer of *Back In Black* and *Highway To Hell*

'I love the insight Jesse Fink has given us with *The Youngs*.'
– David Thoener, engineer of *For Those About To Rock (We Salute You)*

'I loved it. Fink did an amazing job.'
– Doug Thaler, former booking agent of AC/DC and manager of Mötley Crüe

THE YOUNGS

THE BROTHERS WHO BUILT
AC/DC

⚡

JESSE FINK

BLACK & WHITE PUBLISHING

First published in the UK 2014
This edition published 2015
by Black & White Publishing Ltd
29 Ocean Drive, Edinburgh EH6 6JL

First published 2013
by Ebury Press, Random House Australia Pty LTD

1 3 5 7 9 10 8 6 4 2   15 16 17 18

ISBN: 978 1 84502 966 1

A CIP catalogue record for this book is available from the British Library.

Typeset by RefineCatch Limited, Bungay, Suffolk
Printed and bound by Nørhaven, Denmark

*For Tony Currenti and Mark Evans
and in memory of Michael Klenfner*

'Violence and energy . . . that's really what
rock 'n' roll's all about.'

– Mick Jagger

TRACK LISTING

AUTHOR'S NOTE
'Gimme A Bullet'

We all have a story when it comes to this band.

I can't put a date or a time on mine. My memories of the occasion are blurred by the whisky fog that eventually wiped me out that dismal eve. Home alone on another Saturday night, wondering how I'd ended up in an untidy room in a damp, shitty, below-street-level flat in inner-city Sydney, Australia, when for so long I'd had it *all*: the comfortable suburban home, the happy family, the beautiful wife, even a scrawny pound dog with a waggy tail. And now I'd been reduced to sorting black socks to pass the time before it was late enough to safely go to sleep and not find myself waking up at 4 am. If being up at 2 am is lonely for a newly divorced man, 4 am is unbearable.

Wanting to go out and be with a woman, any woman – just to hold and touch someone; and I'd done enough emergency 'dating' to get through such nights – but paralysed by the fact that the one woman I still loved and wanted to be with was with someone who wasn't *me*. I felt powerless, angry and, more than anything, stuck. I was totally depressed. My situation was quite pitiful.

And then – it was as simple as 'then' in this tale of wretchedness

– I grabbed my battered old MacBook, opened up iTunes and put on some AC/DC.

The song I chose wasn't 'Back In Black', 'Highway To Hell', 'Thunderstruck' or any of the Australian band's catalogue of arena standards. (Aussies still claim AC/DC, even if Angus and Malcolm Young have gone out of their way in recent years to effectively disown their antipodean heritage.) It was 'Gimme A Bullet', a largely forgotten track off a release that had somehow slipped through the cracks of mainstream acclaim and bypassed mass album sales, 1978's *Powerage*. Their fifth album, the last studio album produced by the ex-Easybeats duo of elder brother George Young and Harry Vanda in AC/DC's golden period of 1975 to 1980 and the band's unshowiest, most artistically realised recording. There isn't a bad track on it.

Oh, she hit me low.

Yes, Bon, my woman did. Was this band reading my mind? I'd heard AC/DC before, of course, but that night, sitting on the end of my bed, I was utterly transfixed by what I was hearing. The flinty tone. The rising power. The delineated but somehow enmeshed guitars. No Angus flourish to speak of – rare for AC/DC. Just the Youngs interlocking with a driving groove from their rhythm section. And the words: lyrics that were a balm to the part of my soul that had been torn open by my wife's leaving. Finally, I was *getting it*. When it was over, I had to listen to the whole album – and then all over again.

More than anything they did before then or have done since, *Powerage*, clocking in at under 40 minutes, is a sonic Polaroid of real life, in all its domestic ordinariness, as seen through the lens of a group of disreputable-looking men that can lay serious claim to being the greatest rock 'n' roll band of all time.

Knocked together in a handful of weeks in a studio on the fifth floor of the now-demolished Boomerang House in Sydney,

Powerage isn't an album about fucking, drinking, guns or inclement weather. Mercifully there are none of the juvenile sexual double entendres with which the band's third and final singer, Brian Johnson, managed to spoil some of the Young brothers' best guitar work in the 1980s. It's an album true listeners (an important distinction from true fans) of AC/DC's music can relate to because, thanks in no small part to the input of Bon Scott, it's about human frailty.

It's this glimpse of humility and pathos in *Powerage* that separates it from the rest of the AC/DC catalogue. Other albums feature the same wrecking ball of Gretsch, Gibson, Music Man and Sonor, but the nine songs of *Powerage* (10 on the European LP release) explore themes that rarely get celebrated in hard rock. Abandonment. Yearning. Dispossession. Aspiration. Hardship: emotional and financial. Getting dealt a bum hand. And, most electrifyingly, risk. The majestic Scott wouldn't have lived a life by any other credo.

The chorus of 'Rock 'N' Roll Damnation', the disc's opener, says it all: *Take a chance while you still got the choice.* I eventually did, leaving that room, the whisky bottle and my unsorted black socks to run off to New York City to hook up with a burlesque dancer who looked like Scarlett Johansson. I wasn't going to die wondering. I wrote a book. I fell in love again. I got my life back on track.

But it was 'Gimme A Bullet' that knocked me sideways first and still does every time I hear it. When Cliff Williams's bass breaks through the ramparts of the Youngs' guitars and Phil Rudd's beat at around 1:17, the song soars to another level of rock perfection altogether. It's probably the closest thing the workmanlike 'plugger' Williams, as Rose Tattoo guitarist Rob Riley laconically describes him, has ever got to a solo in over 30 years of playing with AC/DC.

He hasn't done much else creatively. By most reliable accounts, the hard-nosed Youngs won't let him. It's not his band. It's not his *place*.

But was it even Williams's guitar? Mark Evans, the Englishman's predecessor in the band, later told me: 'My understanding of the situation is that George played bass on the whole album.' Which might just account for why *Powerage* is so good. Such mysteries abound in any discussion about AC/DC. In any event, the effect it had on me was the same, whoever was playing.

Hearing 'Gimme A Bullet' and being swept up by it gave me resolve and determination to stop feeling sorry for myself. I played it in my car, when I was jogging on the streets around Sydney or pumping iron in the neighbourhood gym. My then seven-year-old daughter, normally into Selena Gomez, Taylor Swift and Ke$ha, loved the song so much she'd dance around the room to it. I felt a surge of paternal pride when she presented me with a drawing of a big heart with florid patterning around its edges and some scribble underneath where she'd written, 'My dad loves AC/DC and The Rolling Stones.' To be able to connect to your child through music you love is a beautiful thing. At 37, after half a life spent listening to good, melodic but comparatively anodyne music, I'd finally grasped the meaning of AC/DC.

I can only liken the impact 'Gimme A Bullet' had on me that night to the scene in the movie *High Fidelity* where John Cusack's character confesses he arranges his records not chronologically or alphabetically but autobiographically. Anytime I hear that song it takes me back to that moment when I thought I'd lost everything, could have easily walked outside and in front of a garbage truck but didn't. It restored my mood. It made me feel good. It made me feel like I wasn't alone in the world; that there were other guys out there and before me, Scott among them, who'd got through similar nights of loneliness, gritted their teeth and prevailed. And that is what the best music does. It immortalises those beautiful, private moments of existential clarity. It makes us embrace life and its vicissitudes.

When years later, back in New York, I ran across the Brooklyn Bridge in a snowstorm with 'Gimme A Bullet' on my iPod, the song propelling my legs forward like it had done so many times before, I had to stop for a moment in the frigid January air – Manhattan on my left, Brooklyn on my right, Sydney and my old life very far away – and smile for regaining my health and happiness. AC/DC's music as much as anything else had helped me get there.

Angus and Malcolm Young might shrug their shoulders and say they're only playing rock 'n' roll, be largely oblivious to the personal stories of fans for whom their music has been deeply affecting, shy away from writers and journalists who want more than the soundbites that get occasionally thrown out like burley off the side of a boat when they have a record to promote. But along with George, their reclusive elder brother, mentor and producer, they're more important than that. The music of the Youngs is about much more than drinking, fucking and rock 'n' roll. They might not believe it. They can go on protesting for all I care. No one's buying it.

For when they're gone, there's going to be a lost guy somewhere who'll hear 'Gimme A Bullet' for the first time and decide to wake up in the morning. We all have a Young brothers song that has this kind of effect on us.

And it's that special gift of theirs, not the fame, not the record sales, not the incalculable wealth, that makes them worth appreciating.

– Jesse Fink, 2015

PREFACE
'Rock And Roll
Ain't Noise Pollution'

In January 2013 I found myself in a kilometre-long queue outside the Museum of Modern Art in New York to see Edvard Munch's 1893 painting *The Scream*. The line, remarkably orderly, stretched city blocks. It was a Friday night, free admission, and bitingly cold. Well below zero. Even with layers of clothing on, I had to stamp my feet to keep warm. But the discomfort was more than worth it. I was seeing *The Scream*. An iconic piece of art. Not something you see every day. Especially for free.

After about an hour I finally made it inside and went up to the fifth floor where all the heavyweights had been collected: Dalis, Modiglianis, Cézannes, Picassos, Van Goghs, Matisses, Monets, Klees. The blockbusters. And there, just 91 cm by 73.5 cm, was *The Scream*, one of four versions Munch had made and which had recently been sold to a banker for $120 million at Sotheby's. It was hard work getting anywhere near the painting. While some of the most notable artworks of history hung in nearby rooms unloved and ignored, *The Scream* was being mobbed.

The huddle around it was a hundred thick with locals

and tourists, not absorbing it, not pondering its message, but photographing it with their iPhones to put up on Instagram or standing in front of it for happy snaps to load up on Facebook. I waited patiently to stand in front of it but when I got my chance I was disappointed. The only thing that elevated what I superficially took to be a fairly rudimentary and not that interesting pastel work were the anguished figure's famously haunted eyes. Never mind that in other rooms metres away there was much better art hanging on the walls and no one was standing in front of those to get their picture taken. This painting had just sold for $120 million. It was *important*. It was expected of me to be in total awe and then shuffle along. This was serious *art*.

I wanted to have it bore into my bones. To be swept away. To be moved. But I felt nothing. I left the building to disappear into the bustling streets of Midtown, untangled the headphones for my iPod and put on *Back In Black*, just $9.99 on iTunes. Even though by then I'd heard the album a thousand times, it took one simple riff by AC/DC to do what one of the most celebrated paintings of history could not.

Jerry Greenberg, president of Atlantic Records from 1974 to 1980, the executive who can take credit for overseeing the band's rise to the top in America, felt exactly the same when we talked weeks later: '*Buh, buh da da, buh da da* – it's absolutely incredible.' I had to pinch myself that the man who signed ABBA, Chic, Foreigner, Genesis and Roxy Music was singing AC/DC to me down the phone from Los Angeles.

The piousness of art, its inherent elitism and suffocating snobbishness is everything the Youngs – Angus, Malcolm and George – rail against but what these remarkable Scottish-Australian brothers have done is more than get lucky with a formula. What they've achieved with their music over the past 40 years through dedication, unwavering self-belief and a smattering of musical genius is no more and no less than art in its own right. But you don't find this art displayed in museums. This isn't art that was created to be bought and sold by moneyed families or hedge-fund managers. It's art that doesn't even want to be called art. It doesn't need to be called art. It just *is*.

It's this world-class talent combined with their astonishing humility that makes the self-effacing and fiercely private Youngs – three Hobbits of hard rock from a big family of eight: seven boys, one girl – so enduringly compelling.

The brothers have composed not only some of the most stirring rock music – if not music – of all time but amassed a body of work more diverse and creative than they are ever given credit for. Their impact on the history of rock and especially hard rock has been nothing short of immense. Remarkably, a fourth musical brother, Alex, who was a young man in 1963 when George, Malcolm and Angus left Cranhill, Glasgow, with their parents, William and Margaret, for Australia, stayed behind to eventually get signed as a songwriter by The Beatles' Apple Publishing and saw his band, Grapefruit, come under the wings of John Lennon and Paul McCartney.

In fact, I would argue no set of brothers, not even the Gibbs of The Bee Gees or the Wilsons of The Beach Boys, has had such a profound impact on music and on popular culture around the world as the Youngs. Their songs have been covered by superstar acts ranging from Shania Twain and Norah Jones to Santana and Dropkick Murphys. Their music has been so penetrative that Australian palaeontologists named two species of ancient arthropod after them: *Maldybulakia angusi* and *Maldybulakia malcolmi*. 'They are both diminutives,' explained Dr Greg Edgecombe of the Australian Museum, 'and are related and have gone and left the shores of Australia to conquer the world.'

Their tedious critics – and to this day there are many; they've never quite gone away, but eased off in recent years, having realised the more they complain, the more AC/DC makes fools of them – contend that all their songs sound the same. Some of them do. The Youngs don't want to fiddle with what is clearly working for them. But those critics fail to understand a very important point. It's their very lack of boundary pushing that is a form of boundary pushing in itself.

Mark Gable of The Choirboys, an Australian band given their start by George Young and best known for their hit 'Run To Paradise', gives the best description I've ever heard of what the Youngs manage to do in their music: 'Before I wrote "Paradise" I decided to use only three chords. This restriction or boundary, if you will, creates better art. If you're allowed to do anything at all, invariably you will show your weaknesses. But if you work within the bounds of what you know best, its expansion seems to go on forever.'

That AC/DC doesn't touch on different styles of music, one could argue, is a form of laziness. Then again, you could say it's a form of brave creativity of its own. Not many musicians could work within such narrow music parameters yet come up with songs that sound new and fresh every time you hear them. But the Youngs do. Consistently. AC/DC never, *ever* sounds stale.

Says former Atco Records president Derek Shulman, probably best known for signing Bon Jovi and for reviving AC/DC's flagging career in the mid 1980s: 'I agree, 100 per cent. They have no need to further push boundaries. They have set up their very own boundaries, to which no other band can come remotely close. They were and are leaders and have never been followers and this is something that 99.9 per cent of other rock bands should realise and understand if they really want to become a legend, as AC/DC surely are as a band.'

⚡

The Youngs' songs – they have written and recorded hundreds between them over half a century – have their own stories. Why have they endured and resonated with hundreds of millions of people and inculcated such fierce loyalty and outright fanaticism? AC/DC concerts are not just concerts. They are rallies held under a band logo that is as powerful as any flag. What has made 'It's A Long Way To The Top' a virtual national anthem in Australia? Why is 'Thunderstruck' routinely played at NFL games in the United States and football matches in Europe? Why, above all other bands in the world, did a festival in Finland elect in 2006 to have AC/DC's entire catalogue performed live by 16 acts (including a military band) for 15 hours straight? What prompts cities – Madrid, Melbourne – to name lanes and streets after them? Why are there legions of Angus Young impostors on Facebook? Why is 'Back In Black' frequently sampled (without permission) by hip-hop artists and mash-up DJs; used in network television, commercials and Hollywood films; licensed to gaming and sporting corporations; and played in helicopters and tanks on the battlefield? At the Battle of Fallujah in Iraq in 2004, American Marines blasted 'Hells Bells' from giant speakers to drown out the call to arms coming from the city's mosques.

What is it about AC/DC's music that is so regenerative and restorative? That transmits that power to make us change the way we feel, alter our outlook, give us the strength we need to get through our darkest moments?

There's even a tour operator in Port Lincoln, South Australia, who's found that playing AC/DC to sharks attracts them like no other music. Matt Waller told Melbourne's *Herald Sun*: 'We know AC/DC's music works best by trial and error ... I've seen the sharks rub their faces on the cage where the sound is coming from, as if to feel it.'

The answers to these questions, whatever they are, strike at the heart of what makes the Youngs' music exceptional.

↯

And it all began with the brother who rarely shows his face in public.

George Young, who turned 69 in 2015, stopped playing on his own records with Flash and the Pan, another project with longtime writing and producing partner Harry Vanda, in 1992. He has kept his hand in with production, most recently helming AC/DC's *Stiff Upper Lip* in 2000 to add to the music he co-produced for the band with Vanda between 1974 and 1978 and again in the late 1980s. Most famous as rhythm guitarist for The Easybeats, he was also co-producer with Vanda for Rose Tattoo and The Angels (aka Angel City), and co-wrote with Vanda songs such as The Easybeats' 'Friday On My Mind' and 'Good Times', Stevie Wright's 'Evie', John Paul Young's 'Love Is In The Air' and Flash and the Pan's 'Hey St Peter', 'Down Among The Dead Men', 'Walking In The Rain' (covered by Grace Jones) and 'Ayla', the latter memorably and erotically used for a dance scene in the Monica Bellucci movie *How Much Do You Love Me?*. The sight of Bellucci gyrating to it is not a memory easily erased.

'I keep many records at home and I try various pieces of music as I work on my films, which sometimes throws up surprises,' says the film's director, Bertrand Blier. 'I like "Ayla" very much.'

George is the 'sixth member' of AC/DC, the leader, the coach, the stand-in bass player, drummer, backup singer, mimic, percussionist, composer, business manager and svengali. AC/DC is as much his band as it is Angus's and Malcolm's.

Anthony O'Grady, Bon Scott's friend and founding editor of the 1970s Australian music newspaper *RAM*, spent several days on the road with AC/DC throughout 1975–76. When we meet in Sydney's Darlinghurst he's wearing a newly minted replica of AC/DC's first T-shirt, circa 1974, on which the band's name had been daubed in white house paint.

'George used everything he'd learned – mostly to his detriment – from The Easybeats,' he says. 'It's one of those stories about, "You can be in a band that has an international hit and end up in crippling debt. This time is going to be different." And it was. He would like to have done it himself, I'm sure. But, by God, he certainly programmed Malcolm and Angus to do it without surrendering control to record companies, management or agencies.

'Don't *deviate*. That's what he drilled into Malcolm. Angus was the electricity and George and Malcolm were the power station. They directed the flow. And they were never distracted by musicianship. A number of times Malcolm has said to me, "Angus can play some really clever jazz stuff, but we don't want him to play really clever jazz stuff."'

As for George's two younger brothers in AC/DC – Angus, lead guitarist, who turned 60 in 2015 and Malcolm, rhythm guitarist, who turned 62 – not much needs to be said. They are so recognised, so adored all over the world that they are almost above introduction, having come up with some of the best songs and most memorable guitar riffs in rock. It's impossible to separate them. They are, as they are with their guitars, utterly symbiotic while dedicated to very specific roles. It wasn't always so. They started out trying to outgun each other, according to AC/DC's original singer, Dave Evans.

'They always had a healthy rivalry between them on stage,' he says. 'In the beginning both Malcolm and Angus played lead and the duels on stage were great to witness as they would go head to head and try to outdo each other. Angus was finally given the sole responsibility of the lead guitar and he relished it. The early songs especially have so much energy and that never diminishes.'

Indisputably, Angus is the star. The 'atomic microbe', as Albert Productions, or Alberts, AC/DC's Australian record company, once described him in a print ad in the American music press. A diminutive talent so freakish and whose 'crunchy, humbucker-driven sound' is so distinctive *Australian Guitar* magazine anointed him the best guitar player Australia has ever produced.

As a showman he is almost without peer, one of the most enduring live attractions in rock 'n' roll. David Lewis, music writer for the late British music newspaper *Sounds*, evocatively described Angus's 'frenzied schoolboy lunacy as he traverses the stage, making Chuck Berry's duckwalk look like a paraplegic's hobble and oozing sweat, snot and slime like some grotesque human sponge being savagely squeezed by the intensity of his own guitar playing'.

Or as Bernard McGovern said in the London newspaper *The Daily Express* in 1976: 'Angus is not a schoolkid but a crazy Scots rocker. His onstage antics . . . include throwing tantrums, smashing things, tearing up school jotters, smoking, ripping bits off his school uniform and tossing them into the audience, falling down and skinning his knees, sticking pins through voodoo effigies of teachers, and playing a very effective rock 'n' roll guitar while lying on his back shrieking and kicking.'

Lisa Tanner, a former Atlantic Records staff photographer who contributed some exceptional AC/DC images from the 1970s and '80s to this book, remembers Angus putting so much into his performances that he would literally vomit.

'After or during the first song of the set he would come offstage and hang his head in a trash can and puke while still playing guitar,' she says. 'The first time I saw him do it I was with [Atlantic Records promotion executive] Perry Cooper and I was like, "Is he okay?" Perry replied, "Yeah, he does that every show."'

Even today, though quietened down by age and creaking joints, in televised interviews there remains something almost child-like about Angus. His dedication to practising and playing his guitar has been the obsessive habit of a lifetime, according to O'Grady: 'He was the precocious kid. He could express himself on guitar far better than he could express himself through schoolwork or language, and he was encouraged to do so. [It was always a case of:] "Don't bother Angus; just let him play."'

Says David Mallet, who has directed AC/DC's videos and concerts since 1986: 'Pink Floyd is about a spectacle. Each song, each number in concert has a different type of spectacle. AC/DC is about the same spectacle every time. Called Angus Young.'

But it's the middle brother who is the king of AC/DC. And he's not a benevolent one. Mark Evans, the band's bass player from 1975 to 1977, described Malcolm rather unflatteringly in his autobiography, *Dirty Deeds: My Life Inside And Outside Of AC/DC*, as 'the driven one . . . the planner, the schemer, the "behind the scenes guy", ruthless and astute'.

A description not far off an early Atlantic Records press release but for an important rider: 'Not only is he a great guitarist and songwriter, but also a person with vision – he is the planner in AC/DC. He is also the quiet one, deep and intensely aware. This, coupled with his good looks, makes him an extremely popular member of AC/DC.'

Curiously, none of the other band members had their physical appearance appraised.

Malcolm is the brother who calls all the shots, who directs the band and drives the rhythm. Even with the decision to retire in September 2014, AC/DC remains *his* band.

'Malcolm and Angus were brought up in an environment where George was a massive pop and rock star,' explains Evans, now a little thinner on top but still fit and as handsome as he ever was, over a coffee in Sydney's Annandale. If anyone had the good looks in AC/DC it was Evans. 'It's not a big jump for them to think we'll put a band together and take it overseas. It wasn't like a dream, "I want to go and play for Glasgow Rangers" or something. The dream was *inside* his house. It was a tangible thing. Malcolm picked up a lot from George. George and Malcolm are very similar in a lot of ways. Although I do believe Malcolm is the most driven of the lot of them.

'One of the things that's amazed me over the years is that Angus and Malcolm, not so much George, are portrayed as not being all that sharp – maybe because it's their persona. But, *man*. I haven't met too many guys in my life that have been sharper than Malcolm.'

Where his younger brother duckwalks, moons, spins and does whatever the hell he pleases, Malcolm, stiff and twitchy, immovable as a menhir, could be relied upon to stay anchored down the back of the stage in front of the Marshall stack.

'Live, they put on a great show but it's not flash,' says their longtime engineer, Mike Fraser. 'It's amazing for me. You sit there and watch Malcolm play. He's actually leading that whole band from standing there beside the drums. Everyone watches him for the cutoffs. "Let's do another round." He's got all these little nods. Little flicks of his hand. Everybody's got their eyes on him. Even Angus, as he's flying around, flipping around backwards. He's watching Mal for everything. It's quite awesome to watch.'

John Swan, a fellow Scot, venerable rock figure in Australia, one-time singer with Bon Scott's old band Fraternity and to this day a close confidant of the Young family, agrees: 'Everybody looks at Angus as being the man, but for me, Malcolm's the man. Take "Live Wire". He'll play the chords in that song and the dynamics he uses all the way through are really quite brilliant. And he'll change one little pattern. Rhythm players play it and then play that same pattern over. He'll change that one thing that's so subtle you have to be a fan of Malcolm's playing to be able to get into what he's actually done there. It's that one little piece that's different that makes it rock just that bit more and makes the musician who's listening to it love it a bit more. He and Keith Richards are the best rhythm players in the world.'

ZZ Top and Led Zeppelin engineer Terry Manning, co-owner with Chris Blackwell of Compass Point Studios in The Bahamas, where *Back In Black* was recorded, goes further, contending that the only comparable rhythm players are Ritchie Blackmore of Deep Purple and blues legend Steve Cropper, 'but when you look at just distilling the essence of rhythm guitar I think Malcolm has it better than anybody'.

Together, though, they don't need to be compared to anyone. The light strings of Angus's slim-necked Gibson SG and the heavy-gauge strings of Malcolm's Gretsch Firebird manage the paradoxical feat of being a single force yet remain distinct. No other pair does what they do as well as they do. For so long they were inextricable. Stevie Young's job is to maintain this synergy.

So much so that Joe Matera, an Australian rock guitarist and internationally published guitar journalist for magazines such as *Classic Rock* and *Guitar & Bass*, says the two guitar sounds would cease to be effective if separated.

'It is a chemistry where one needs the other and vice-versa for it to have such an explosive sonic effect,' he argues. 'It's such a strong combination that without the other, the result would be most non-effective.'

Georg Dolivo, lead singer of California rockers Rhino Bucket, the one band among a rash of imitators that has probably got closest to the sound of *Powerage*-era AC/DC and which even had ex-AC/DC drummer Simon Wright play with them for a time, tells me: 'The interplay between the guitars and the bass and drums is second to none. Every note counts. Angus and Malcolm both play off each other so well that it almost sounds like one massive wall of power.'

Joel O'Keeffe, frontman and lead guitarist for Airbourne, a group that live is about as close to AC/DC at the Glasgow Apollo in 1978 as it is possible to get, explains the AC/DC sound as a process of reduction and austerity: 'It's as much what the Youngs don't do as what they do. It's those precision-timed spaces in the riff, like the small space after the first three A chords in "Highway To Hell", or the "ANGUS!" chant space in "Whole Lotta Rosie" that makes the hairs stand on edge. And when they're both in it's not just two guitars, it's guitars to the power of.'

'The Young brothers are two of the best guitar players I've ever had the pleasure of working with,' says Fraser. 'Not only are they talented, they are very hard workers as well. In the studio they know exactly how to play dynamically to make the song rock. This is often hard to do in a studio, as the atmosphere can sometimes be clinical and uninspiring. It is tough to play in the studio with the intensity you would when playing live, but to make a great record that's exactly what you have to do. Malcolm and Angus have that ability down to a tee. It's truly remarkable to witness.'

⚡

Scores of bands, with varying degrees of success, have tried to replicate part of the sound and 'no bullshit' ethos of AC/DC: Guns N' Roses, The Cult, Airbourne, The Answer, Mötley Crüe, Krokus, Kix, The Four Horsemen, The Poor, Dynamite, Hardbone, Heaven, '77, Starfighters, Accept, Rhino Bucket, Jet, the hard-rockin' and French aristocrat-dressin' The Upper Crust and more. Many indulge in pastiche. Then there are the straight ripoffs. Listen to 'Dr Feelgood' by Mötley Crüe against AC/DC's 'Night Of The

Long Knives' off *For Those About To Rock (We Salute You)*. Or David Lee Roth's 'Just Like Paradise' against 'Breaking The Rules' off the same album. Or The Cult's 'Wild Flower' against 'Rock 'N' Roll Singer' off *TNT*.

Not that AC/DC didn't consciously or subconsciously pinch from others when it suited them earlier in their career. ZZ Top's 'Jesus Just Left Chicago' is all over 'Ride On' and Them's 'Gloria' (covered by Bon Scott with his first band, The Spektors, in 1965) forms the basis for 'Jailbreak', both songs off the original Australian release of *Dirty Deeds Done Dirt Cheap*. Illinois band Head East's middling 1975 hit 'Never Been Any Reason', written by guitarist Mike Somerville, also informs – if that's a polite way to put it – 1980's 'You Shook Me All Night Long'. Intriguingly, AC/DC supported Head East for one show at the Riverside Theater in Milwaukee in August 1977.

But they still make everything they do their own. As Tony Platt, mixing engineer of *Highway To Hell*, recording engineer of *Back In Black* and co-producer of *Flick Of The Switch* told me from London: 'You wouldn't believe how many AC/DC-sounding bands came along after *Back In Black* was successful, wanting me to work with them. When someone says, "Can you get me Angus Young's guitar sound?" the only answer I can give is, "Yeah, of course I can, but first of all we're going to need a vintage Marshall cabinet, a vintage Marshall head, a Gibson SG and, of course, don't forget we'll need Angus."

'You do get quite a lot of bands, especially in the rock genre, where the idea of being a rock musician is a little bit more important than getting it right. Whereas these guys were, "Let's get this right, let's make sure it's the best that it can be and if we get to be rock stars afterwards so much the better."'

Fraser, who's engineered Aerosmith, Metallica, Van Halen, The Cult and Airbourne, agrees the task of matching up to the

Youngs is futile: 'While there are bands that certainly may have borrowed elements from AC/DC's sound, I would say AC/DC's powerful simplicity would be difficult to replicate. A lot of bands will double their guitar parts to try to make them sound big and fat. The end result, as good as it may be, will be a different sound to AC/DC.'

Terry Manning, who shaped the sound of Rhino Bucket and The Angels, knows all too well the danger of too much hero worship. He was offered the chance to produce what became the *Who Made Who* sessions (recorded at Compass Point) by AC/DC's then managers, Steve Barnett and Stewart Young, but due to a scheduling clash with Fastway at Abbey Road could not commit.

'I was forced to turn that down. I will always regret that,' he says. 'No one has ever completely duplicated the AC/DC ethos. Nor should they. A good artist can certainly borrow elements, or be even heavily influenced, but somewhere along the line they must make it their own, put their own personal style and stamp on the music. I know with both Rhino Bucket and The Angels I kept this in mind at all times: never clone, but do not hesitate to accept influence. And always help the artist to be the best of themselves that they can be at that moment.'

Manning has never worked with AC/DC but they've been a boon to his business and the economy of The Bahamas. Compass Point was booked solid for years by all sorts of rock bands hoping some *Back In Black* magic would rub off on them.

'How can it possibly hurt to have what will end up being the biggest selling album of all time recorded under your banner? It had to inspire people: Anthrax recorded at Compass Point, Iron Maiden, Judas Priest.'

There's a good reason why a band that has sold over 200 million records yet slowed it down only once or twice over a 40-year period became the biggest in the world while others that looked like they might claim the mantle – Guns N' Roses chief among them, whom the late Danny Sugerman, The Doors' former manager, praised in his eccentric biography, *Appetite For Destruction: The Days Of Guns N' Roses*, for 'their devotion to the ecstatic omnipotent state of rocking' and in conjuring 'the raging sound of Dionysus resurfacing' – fell away into artistic redundancy and ongoing acrimony.

The 'Gunners', led by Axl Rose, had a lot of similar qualities to AC/DC: authenticity, vision, gang mentality, a sound pretty much their own that wasn't going to be fucked with by anyone and an almost feral hostility to the world and outsiders. They covered 'Whole Lotta Rosie' – astonishingly well – in their prime. They played 'Back In Black' over the PA in some of their shows. But they didn't have the juice in the tank to last the distance. AC/DC didn't allow the partying, drugs, sex and money to affect the music.

Matt Sorum of Guns N' Roses and later The Cult and Velvet Revolver believes AC/DC has something special 'that starts with the Young brothers' classic riffs and below-the-waist grooves . . . they know when to play and when not to'.

'Less is more with AC/DC,' he says. 'Always supporting the song is the message. The power is in the simplicity and it is subliminal in tone. Not much distortion on the guitars. The low end of the bass and groove make it swing. Each member has a job to do which makes that work perfectly. It's that old expression of "if it ain't broke don't fix it". Working-class boogie rock 'n' roll at its best. Guys dig it and girls love to dance to it. Hearing great bands go back to their roots is always refreshing. I wish more great rock bands stuck to their instinct and weren't wavered by trends.'

This coming from a man who played all those repetitive fills on 'November Rain' (one of Rose's ideas, according to Sorum). He should know. Guns N' Roses' detour into pompous balladry was really the beginning of the end for the most exciting rock band since AC/DC. Apart from the egregious miscalculation of 'Love Song' in 1975, AC/DC has never done an out-and-out ballad. They just come up with flat-out rock songs anchored in feel, melody and groove. A perfect alchemy – like AC/DC's other holy trinity of guitar, drum and bass – that anyone can understand and to which we all respond by rocking, a state Sugerman cannily describes as an 'impulse every bit as instinctual as a child putting his finger in the fan'.

'I think playing in The Cult was the closest I came to playing an AC/DC style,' continues Sorum. 'Songs like "Wild Flower" and "Lil' Devil" I would always think of Phil Rudd in my approach. Guns N' Roses and Velvet Revolver always looked to all the great bands as influences, AC/DC at the top of the list. But at the same time we were trying to do our own thing.'

Rob Riley, the Falstaff of Australian rock and a man Mark Evans anoints as Australia's greatest living guitarist (no small praise considering he played in concert and in the studio with Angus and Malcolm), is an avowed fan of the Youngs: 'Most people can understand AC/DC. It's not fucking complicated. It's people friendly. You don't have to be a fucking fantastic musician to get your head around it. It just *rocks*. And they were and still are the exponents of rock. It makes me tap my foot and bang my head.'

Says Stevie Young, the Youngs' nephew who permanently replaced Malcolm after his retirement due to illness: 'They're honest about what they do. That's why they're a great band.'

⚡

But that is still not enough for some people.

The critics, especially in the United States, long ago would have preferred these rough-looking, guitar-slinging homunculi crawled back under the Gorbals rock from whence they'd sprung.

Robert Hilburn is one. The Johnny Cash biographer and rock writer for *The Los Angeles Times* from 1970 to 2005 once cut them viciously: 'Someone ought to pull the plug on AC/DC.' But when contacted for this book he shows some remorse.

'The review was a live show and I must have been disappointed by it,' he says. 'I felt the band was slipping or something – because I wasn't an anti-AC/DC critic. I had written approvingly of them before and have them – in my mental list of bands – on the positive side, though they were in no way on my top shelf, which was reserved for bands that had more literary sensibilities and uplifting messages: The Band, Creedence Clearwater Revival, The Beatles, The Rolling Stones, The Who, The Kinks, U2, Nirvana, The Replacements, Rage Against The Machine, Nine Inch Nails, REM, The White Stripes and Arcade Fire.

'Every artist or band that I'd call truly great in rock history has pushed boundaries because the artist and/or band should reflect life's experience, and life changes as time goes by. The music should reflect those changes. Their curiosity as musicians, for instance, should lead to opening new doors – look what The Beatles and U2 did in that sense: The Beatles going from "I Want To Hold Your Hand" to *Sgt. Pepper's*, U2 going from *The Joshua Tree* to *Achtung Baby*. Similarly, the lyrics and themes should change to reflect new ideas and emotions.

'AC/DC deserves credit, most certainly, for not simply recycling its music; it didn't just play the same record or song over and over again, like lots of big commercial forces. But I think the group's history would have been better served if they moved from their early energy and fun to something more substantial . . . as it is, they are a band you think of fondly, but don't hold in awe – a band of its time, so to speak, rather than a band of the ages.'

Dave Evans concurs with Hilburn. He claims he's never owned an AC/DC record since splitting with the band – and is perhaps well entitled to have completely turned his back on them, given the treatment he received when he was sacked in 1974 and the disparaging comments made about him since then by the Youngs. The fact is, though, he has a healthy career out of his association with the band and plays it up for all it is worth.

'They have kept to the original and unmistakable AC/DC simple sound and it's amazing that it has been so popular for so long,' he says. 'I like music to give me different feels and messages even though the band will still have its own style. It's like rap, which is the same-old, same-old but is highly popular, and hip-hop, which all sounds the same to me and is also huge. I don't understand it. Being an avid Beatles fan, what I loved about them was that they kept evolving and exploring music and feels and took the whole world for a fantastic musical ride with them and influenced so many bands and their audiences too with new and exciting sounds without losing The Beatles sound. Whatever it is, AC/DC is the most popular rock band in the world today.'

In 1976, the year a repackaged *High Voltage* featuring the killer chugalong single 'It's A Long Way To The Top' hit American record stores, *Rolling Stone*'s Billy Altman slagged off AC/DC as 'Australian gross-out champions' who had 'nothing to say musically (two guitars, bass and drums all goose-stepping together in mindless three-chord formations)' and a singer, Scott, who 'spits out his vocals with a truly annoying aggression which, I suppose, is the only way to do it when all you seem to care about is being a star so that you can get laid every night. And that, friends, comprises the sum total of themes discussed on this record. Stupidity bothers me. Calculated stupidity offends me.'

Altman, still a music journalist but now also a teacher in the Humanities Department of the School of Visual Arts in New York, doesn't back down when I ask him if he thinks he was too tough on the Australian band.

'I didn't think I was being tough,' he says. 'Just doing my job. And in the context of 1976, that is exactly how they struck me. So, yes, I'd certainly stick by what I wrote – at the time.' He then proffers a review he wrote of *Stiff Upper Lip* for MTV/VH1's website in 2000 as an example of coming to the party. 'It's all a matter of perspective, yes?'

Once feral against AC/DC, the American music press has come to begrudgingly accept that this band won't go away and started to tolerate its existence, even given praise to albums that really aren't a patch on the product they mercilessly slagged in the 1970s and early '80s. Damn the good stuff. Praise the crap: *Stiff Upper Lip* is one example. *Black Ice* another.

Altman's new review was hardly a music critic's mea culpa, though he'd managed to detect that Angus could play guitar a bit. A degree of contempt for AC/DC is still there, but it's disguised through caveman metaphor ('pointy little arrested-development heads') and intellectual ridicule ('recalcitrant yokels').

What was once 'calculated stupidity', Altman now recasts as 'organic rock ... as in two-guitars-bass-drums, verse-chorus-verse-chorus-solo-verse-chorus-chorus, screaming banshee-vocals, stoopid lyrics, riffs-from-Stonehenge rock'. AC/DC, he posits, 'can now probably lay claim to the title of longest playing broken record in the entire history of rock. All their songs sound the same – yes! – and what a damn good song it's been.'

The same begrudging charity didn't extend to 'It's A Long Way To The Top', one of the greatest rock songs of all time, when it mattered. Not nearly enough, way too late.

Like most critics, Altman and, to a lesser degree, Hilburn just don't recognise the cleverness of AC/DC.

It's a shame that Angus never cut a jazz or blues record, sure.

But AC/DC is not in the music business for the purpose of pushing boundaries, even though that's what they do so well by not giving in to trends and fashion. It's a primal thing. Catchy hooks and boogie rhythms are essential for primal music. But primal doesn't sit well with critics.

Clive Bennett in *The Times* used the very same word in a review of one of AC/DC's shows at the Hammersmith Odeon in late 1976: 'My objections are to their music, not their words, which simply express without inhibitions what most of us have discussed innumerable times with equal frankness in private. Music of any sort must surely require more from performers than just the capacity to mindlessly bash their instruments into oblivion. It is in this primal state that AC/DC exist.'

So. The. Fuck. What.

Says Tony Platt: 'If you manage to strike the seam of that, the last thing you want to do is go messing it up or covering it up or confusing it by dressing it up in any different way. You've got to keep returning to that really raw, primal core. The critics are not really understanding the essence of AC/DC; what's at the core of the music.'

Mike Fraser also shares that opinion.

'As long as I have known the band, they have always played their music as they wanted to do and are never worried about what critics think. As Angus once said to me: "We play music that we like and want to play. If the fans like it and want to buy it, that's just a bonus." So I think it is very important to the boys to do work in a vein they love. In all of the records they've done, they have never done a song trying to keep up to an era or fad. No keyboards, no disco beats, no horn sections. When you buy an AC/DC record you know what you're getting and I agree with your argument: this is really them pushing a boundary. And I think only AC/DC can pull it off because they never get boring to listen to. Who could get bored of the passion they play with?'

Their hundreds of millions of fans don't, as Angus once pointed out.

'We've got the basic thing kids want. They want to rock and that's it. They want to be a part of the band as a mass. When you hit a guitar chord, a lot of the kids in the audience are hitting it with you. They're so much into the band they're going through all the motions with you. If you can get the mass to react as a whole, then that's the ideal thing. That's what a lot of bands lack, and why the critics are wrong.'

Says John Swan: 'I don't think AC/DC are capable of changing their format because they have no desire to. It's a work in progress. As long as my arse points towards the floor, AC/DC will be AC/DC and they will never be anything else.'

It's really as simple as that.

⚡

One man who understands what AC/DC are about, *Sounds* journalist and later band biographer Phil Sutcliffe, wrote in 1976: 'The rhythms hit your heart like a trip-hammer ... the two Youngs' music is like a forge in a black night, beating heat and energy together into something almost beautiful it's so strong.'

There's an exceptional passage in Mark Evans's *Dirty Deeds*, to this day the only autobiography written by a member of AC/DC, which perfectly conjures the palpable, totally unique energy of the band. They'd arrived in London in 1976 after packing pubs in Sydney and hadn't played for a month. The five members – Angus Young, Malcolm Young, Mark Evans, Bon Scott and Phil Rudd – were busting to play and landed a booking at the Red Cow in Hammersmith. A free gig in a tiny pub in front of maybe 30 punters, soon to be blown away.

'We opened with "Live Wire",' Evans remembers. 'My bass intro drifted in the air, Mal's ominous guitar chords joined in, Phil's hi-hat cymbals tapped away and then the song exploded when Angus and the drums absolutely fucking erupted. I felt like I was lifted off the ground, it was that powerful. It just sounded so much like AC/DC. That may seem a ridiculous thing to say, but we hadn't played a gig for ages and we were ready to make a statement. There was that great feeling of power; not the chaotic, noisy, out-of-control power that is very common in bands, but the AC/DC brand of power. Loud, clean, deep, menacing and full of rhythm. We were back and firing and Bon hadn't even opened his trap yet.'

Evans was *lifted off the ground*. That's what the music of AC/DC is supposed to do – and he was playing it.

Says Barry Diament, who mastered a suite of their albums for compact disc: 'I think it is precisely in the relative simplicity of the music that Malcolm and Angus achieved the power of their music. I'd use the word "primitive", not in any pejorative sense but as a positive attribute, describing the rawness I hear in their music. It is an "in the gut" experience the listener can feel immediately.'

⚡

There's nothing wrong in what AC/DC does or with the music they make. They've just been victims of lazy journalism and, at a base level, class prejudice. The music of the Youngs, and more generally, rock 'n' roll, deserves to be spoken of in the same breath as any great painting, book or example of architecture, because it is a form of art – which I would define as any craft elevated to another plane because of skill, creativity, talent and imagination – that makes you feel *alive*. That it is considered lowbrow, beneath serious appreciation, because so many of AC/DC's devotees get around in black T-shirts, drink cheap beer and buy their CDs at

Wal-Mart, is contemptuous bullshit. No other act on the planet has brought as much good music into stadiums, arenas, bars, cars, truck stops, nightclubs, strip clubs, bedrooms, living rooms and sports fields than AC/DC.

Says Phil Jamieson of Grinspoon, who performed on the remake of the Vanda & Young song 'Evie' in 2004 to raise funds for victims of the Boxing Day tsunami: 'The Youngs are tenacious. They don't lie down. Among the great hits, the great songs, it's their ability to just get up without any sort of embellishment, plastic surgery, strobe lights, smoke machines – they don't need any of that. They just need four amplifiers, a voice and a drum kit. That's what makes me adore them. They don't play the backing tape. This is a true rock 'n' roll band. Nothing really beats it, in my opinion, when you witness something that powerful. That's what it does for me. It makes every guy with a guitar amp and a drummer and a mate believe maybe they can do it. It's not defined by people that go to music conservatoriums and can read sheet music; it's for everyone.'

'As a rock producer you're looking for the human reaction,' says Mark Opitz, engineer on *Let There Be Rock* and *Powerage*. 'The emotional reaction. The connection. Lyrics are incredibly important but melody and rhythm, that's the secret. It makes you dance. It's a release of energy. It keeps you going. The tempo's perfect for your heartbeat in most cases. It doesn't push you too far, not like thrash. It's got intensity. It's got that fucking "heart feel" rhythm. And by dance I don't mean dancing. I mean *moving*. Stamping your foot like an African. Just moving side to side. Nodding your head. That's "guy dancing". That's testosterone being put out. When you add all that together that's what happens from it. What is the chemical reaction in the brain that adds it all up? I'm not quite sure. But I know what the result is. Melody and rhythm.'

Tony Platt agrees with the thrust of Opitz's hypothesis but makes an important observation: AC/DC's music is also steeped in humour, joy and light.

'There's a lot to be said for this notion that it's the resonances of our own body. It's something that gets the endorphins going. It's the same as drinking a nice glass of wine or going and doing exercise. It gets right to the core of you and lifts you. AC/DC's music is not depressing music. It's fun. It doesn't take itself too seriously. You take, for instance, Iron Maiden. One of the things I've always found quite bizarre about Iron Maiden is how seriously they take themselves, for starters. It's very difficult to stop laughing some of the time. Their fans take it really, *really* deadly seriously as well.

'And then there are a lot of those kind of darker heavy-metal bands. You look at how many of those darker heavy-metal bands have had accusations that they've been the catalyst that's caused some poor young adolescent to end his life, and there have been lots and lots of circumstances like that. There is music that has this darkness at its heart. AC/DC's music doesn't have that darkness at its heart. It doesn't take itself too seriously but, by the same token, it's going to make you jump about a bit.'

There is some credit to that argument, but it has holes. No one could ever claim AC/DC advocated violence, but their disingenuous explanation in the wake of the Richard Ramirez 'Night Stalker' murders in the mid 1980s that 'Night Prowler' off *Highway To Hell* was just about a bloke sneaking into his girlfriend's bedroom in the middle of the night convinced very few people. As Joe Bonomo writes in *Highway To Hell*, his excellent book-form essay on the album, 'Bon Scott's more treacherous imagery pushes the song into regrettably mean places. I'm not sure that the band can have it both ways.' Ramirez, a fan of the band whose name has unfortunately come to be associated with the song, died of natural causes in June 2013 while awaiting execution.

But what Terry Manning tells me cuts to the secret of AC/DC's success and is a testament to the intelligence and brilliance of the Young brothers: their capacity to edit themselves.

'I think that somehow, whether they know it at the top of their brains or not, they innately know what just the basic, most simple rhythm of humanity is. It's something gut level, primitive almost. It goes right to the human condition. Basic fight-or-flight emotion. They somehow tap right into that. It never gets too fast. So many bands are too fast, too full, they try to do too much. I don't ever hear AC/DC try to do too much. They just do what's *necessary*. And that's such an amazing talent that is so hard to find and so overlooked.

'To me it's like a tom roll or a guitar solo. If you had the toms playing a roll through the whole song, they don't mean anything. If you have a guitar solo from beginning to end it doesn't mean anything. It becomes garbage, unlistenable. But if you have the toms come in with a loud, simple roll at the very right spot it just lifts everything. It excites you. If the solo comes in only in the middle or the end of the spot that it's really needed it lifts everything up; it just takes it to another level. So you have to learn the ability to put the embellishments in the right place. And AC/DC are the masters at doing that.'

When the band played its first Bristol concert in 1976, at Colston Hall, even the venue's owners were dismayed by just how much AC/DC's music had an unstoppable effect on its patrons.

'The management were rather perturbed to find a normally passive audience leaping out of their seats,' wrote a snippy local reviewer.

⚡

Bon Scott never got the fame and riches he was due while he was alive, but the Youngs have achieved more financially and in terms of celebrity than even they would ever have dared to imagine and perhaps even wanted. As far as your standard rock-star narrative goes, their success has been counterintuitive. They're by most reasonable measures unattractive, short, eccentric and highly combustible and good taste has been known to frequently desert them: for some reason they have approved or been behind some of the worst album-cover designs in the history of music (*Fly On The Wall*, *Flick Of The Switch*, the original *Dirty Deeds Done Dirt Cheap*). For so many reasons they shouldn't be as big as they are. But they're going to get bigger, even after they've stopped playing music.

It's almost a contradiction of their enormous drive to make it that they are private, almost obsessively so. One could make an argument it's a form of aggression born of inferiority complex because of their stature, modest background and lack of formal education; the Youngs spent a lot of time in their early days fighting among themselves and with others and telling anyone within earshot to fuck off. In the public realm, only a few photos exist of all three of them together; one of those is from 1978's *Powerage* sessions by Australian record-company executive Jon O'Rourke, at the time a music journalist who'd been invited into the Youngs' private realm by Alberts' house drummer Ray Arnott. A number of O'Rourke's photos are published for the first time in this book. The most ubiquitous picture of the three, by Philip Morris in 1976 and the cover image for *The Youngs*, was taken during the *Dirty Deeds* sessions.

'I didn't realise at the time the significance of it,' says Morris. 'I haven't seen any photos that have got them together that close. It was hard to get.'

Four decades later, nothing much has changed. They are frustratingly inaccessible to anyone outside their super-tight circle of trust.

Unlike the relatively amiable Gibbs of The Bee Gees (only one of whom remains alive), the Youngs have a reputation for being brusque and as short with their temper as they are in their stature. George, who's been characterised as 'very volatile' by his own music partner, Harry Vanda, and 'a genius with the extreme character that goes with that' by Mark Gable, is a recluse who rarely speaks to the media. So reclusive that for years an Australian man was able to impersonate him and swindle gullible concert promoters and investors. But he remains active in the affairs of AC/DC. One anonymous insider described his work to me as 'the equivalent of being the chairman of the board of whatever network of structures is in place to maximise the revenues to the band and the Young family . . . he has an extremely canny business brain'.

'George is definitely a recluse. Not a recluse from everything, but a recluse from the past,' says Mark Opitz. 'He's a recluse from things he doesn't need to be involved with any more or that aren't interesting to him. Before Pete Wells from Rose Tattoo died in 2006, they had a concert for him at the Enmore Theatre in Sydney, and George was in the third row, standing down the front by himself. Came out of nowhere and disappeared just as quickly. I wouldn't say he'd be a recluse from anything that's interesting to him because he's got too big a brain and values his life too much.'

Gable's first encounter with George lasted just about as long as the great man's appearance at 'the Enmore'.

'When I first met George I was in awe of him; I had idolised him for years,' he says. 'Even though he was short in stature he was a giant creatively. As I got to know George I realised there was a dichotomy: unbelievably talented with amazing business acumen on one hand and yet there was this other side. There's more to him than meets the eye. It's something that I only understand now that I'm older.

'I remember going to the Bondi Lifesaver either in late 1978 or '79 and a very young Sam Horsburgh [the Youngs' nephew] came up to me and said, "My uncle George is at the back; come up and say hello." I trotted up to the back of the room to find George at a table by himself holding what looked like a glass of scotch. At this time I was a complete teetotaller, so alcohol did not impress me at all. It wasn't so much that George had a glass of scotch in his hand; it was that he seemed to have maybe 20 in his guts. As I approached he lifted both his right hand and the glass in recognition of me. As soon as he had half-lifted his hand, it and his upper body collapsed forward onto the table.'

Reclusive or with 20 scotches in his guts, he remains a pivotal figure in the direction of AC/DC, according to Opitz.

'They're brothers. The older brother is the older brother and always shall be. Particularly when you get a close-knit family of Scots. They're like Italians. Family is everything. When you're struggling in Glasgow and your father's working down the mine you have a fucking shitload of respect. The women work hard at home, cleaning or doing other things, and the kids do it tough. Running around in the streets. The brawls. These guys came out here for a fresh break and they walked into fucking sunshine, thinking, "Can you believe *this* is here? Can you believe this? And all these fucking fat Aussies aren't doing anything about it because they're so used to it. Fuck that." Just like the Italians and the Greeks who got out here and went, "Fuck. I can't believe it. Let's go." It's a hard choice to take in life to follow your dream. But that was something they did because they came from nothing. And when you come from nothing you want to go to somewhere.

'I can remember walking into the A&R offices of Atlantic Records in New York, at that time the biggest record company in the world with the Stones and whatever else on its roster, and talking to the head of A&R and I said, "How big are AC/DC to you?" and he said, "Who do you think pays the fucking rent for the Rockefeller Plaza?"'

♯

As for George's younger brothers, their aversion to any form of public exposition outside what they can dictate is legendary.

Clinton Walker, who wrote *Highway To Hell: The Life And Death Of AC/DC Legend Bon Scott* and got no cooperation from the Youngs, was damning: 'A closed shop, uniformly suspicious, paranoid almost, possessed of the virtual opposite of Bon's generosity, prone to sullenness. Just as nobody can find a bad word for Bon, few of the people who have had dealings with the Youngs can find a good word for them . . . Angus and Malcolm had this incredible tunnel vision where no one else counted . . . insularity bordering on paranoia. Malcolm and Angus were not blessed with many social skills.'

Evans was scarcely more charitable in *Dirty Deeds*: 'Mal and Angus were very guarded guys, almost to the point of suspicion . . . there was a coldness about them that I hadn't experienced before. It did have me wondering about them; matter of fact, still does.' Most of the time, though, they were 'morose, grumpy, sullen and generally not too much fun to be around'.

So what kept Evans looking so happy all the time? There's scarcely a photo from those halcyon days of the band where he isn't smiling or having a lark with Angus or Malcolm.

'That was one side of them,' he says. 'They could actually be a lot of fun. There was a sense of humour around that band. While we were all very serious about it, for God's sake: you're playing in a band with some fucker up the front dressed as a schoolboy. We're not trying to be Pink Floyd here. There was a certain attitude – a lightheartedness – to the band when Bon was in it, owing to his lyrics. There were a lot of fun times in AC/DC and to be around was a lot of fun. But by the same token there were darker times too.

'It was just a normal relationship. Being in a rock 'n' roll band on the road playing with that intensity is never going to be a bowl of cherries. I think in all great bands there's a fair amount of internal angst. The Stones. The Who. Aerosmith. Metallica. There's a friction inside the band that becomes believable.'

But in his dealings with the brothers, Atlantic Records president Jerry Greenberg didn't find them difficult, instead finding them 'kind of, like, shy'.

Jay-Z's and Justin Timberlake's engineer Jimmy Douglass, who got his start as Atlantic's in-house engineer, remembers them being 'cordial and responsive . . . freaking cool human beings'.

It's a softer side of their personality few people get the privilege of seeing.

Opitz recounts a story of Malcolm delivering 'four or five quick jabs to the head' of a much taller concert promoter over a dispute in Detroit in the late 1970s.

'They were tough customers, the Youngs,' he says. 'They knew what to expect and weren't afraid of it. You didn't cross Malcolm. Great guy. No question about it. He's a strong-minded fellow. He's like George. He's got that determination – I can move mountains if I so wish – without the bullshit attached to it, because they're working-class Gorbals boys, so they've got that innate toughness that gets born into you if you're Glaswegian.'

That aside, though, Opitz also describes the Youngs as a regular family unit: 'I remember going to a Christmas party at the family's place in Burwood. Playing table tennis. Having a few beers out in the sun. A barbecue. Normal as bloody anything. Just great. I remember thinking, "How well has this migrant family done that's just popped up, stuck together, stuck it out and they've had success in ways they couldn't have imagined?" And this was in the '70s.'

Says John Swan: 'Margaret [the Youngs' sister] was like a big sister to all of us. She would have a big pot of soup on and she'd always make sure you had a feed and a bed to sleep in. They were much more family-oriented than most other musicians were. Most other musicians would do that if it were you *and* your girlfriend, but they wouldn't do that if it were just you. [The Youngs] took *everybody* in.

'That's why you'll find not just for AC/DC but for the Youngs they certainly lived the Glaswegian style of family communication. Everybody lives together. If it's your mate, it's *our* mate. They wouldn't bring an idiot to the house. They'd bring someone who was a fellow Glaswegian or a fellow Scot or somebody who had a problem that Margaret could help with.'

They've also maintained, at least outwardly, no traces of ostentatiousness, despite fabulous, almost undreamt-of wealth. When getting around they're sticklers for the Glasgow-style 'gallus walk' – head down, hands in pockets, huddling up, a protective instinct – and it's not a rare thing wherever they are in the world to see them down at the local shops clutching a packet of smokes and wearing cheap clothes as if they're just average Joes.

Anthony O'Grady and Angels guitarist John Brewster were members of the private Concord Golf Club in Sydney's inner west. Several times they linked up with Malcolm and George for a social round. During one such outing, George told O'Grady AC/DC had sold 'over 10 million albums' with *Back In Black* and were now the biggest band in the world.

'Soon after George had said that, Malcolm, in all seriousness, said to me, "This is a really good golf club, isn't it? How much do you pay to belong to this in a year?" I forget what the fees were then. I said something like $1500. And he went, "*Aw*, you must be *rich*! I belong to Massey Park [a nearby public course]." And I just looked at him and he was a man that could buy half of Florida and all the golf courses on it. They were very aware of being observed not to be putting on the Ritz. Very, very, *very* aware.'

Swan relates a similar story about Angus, who was living in Kangaroo Point in Sydney's southern suburbs. He was driving around in a Mercedes that had plenty of miles on the odometer and Swan, living in neighbouring Sylvania, had bought a new Jaguar. Swan asked Angus why he was driving something so 'fucking old' when he could afford anything he liked.

'He said, "There's nothing wrong with that car. What are you talking about? It's a perfectly good car." I said, "Yeah, but you're fucking rich now." He said, "That's got nothing to do with it. It's a good car. I *like* it." They don't need to drive around showing everybody what they've got. Same goes with their shoes. They used to take the piss out of me for wearing flashy runners because they wore Dunlops. Seventeen bucks a pair. And I'd walk in with a $200 pair of fucking shoes on. And they'd go, "Ah! *Look!* Somebody's in the money!"'

'They're really good people,' says Opitz, 'but they're very private people.'

$$\maltese$$

For those readers seeking a conventional biography, the Youngs' life stories have been dealt with (or at least *attempted* to be dealt with) adequately in books such as Walker's *Highway To Hell*, Evans's *Dirty Deeds*, Murray Engleheart's *AC/DC, Maximum Rock & Roll: The Ultimate Story Of The World's Greatest Rock Band*, John Tait's *Vanda & Young: Inside Australia's Hit Factory*, Phil Sutcliffe's *AC/DC, High-Voltage Rock 'N' Roll: The Ultimate Illustrated History*, Susan Masino's *Let There Be Rock: The Story of AC/DC* and Mick Wall's *AC/DC: Hell Ain't A Bad Place To Be*. There's a bunch more of them, in different languages, of varying quality, mostly straightforward chronologies or illustrated guides with little or no critical examination (some verging on journalistic fellatio), even less actually written about the music and why it works the way it does, and most containing some major howlers.

For instance, in the Wall book, there's a photo of an old man in a schoolboy uniform hanging out with AC/DC in London in 1976. It's from Dick Barnatt's well-known sequence of photos in which Angus Young is drinking milk straight from a bottle. The mystery man is captioned as being Phil Carson, one of the most important figures in the AC/DC story: the man who signed them. So it's a crucial detail to get right, especially when he's interviewed for the book. But the man in the photo is in fact Ken Evans, an Australian who was program director for Radio Luxembourg and formerly of pirate radio stations Radio Caroline and Radio Atlanta. He'd recorded an interview with AC/DC to help promote their music and they were there to help celebrate his birthday. When I spoke to him in early 2013, he remembered little of the day but confirmed it was 'the one encounter' with the band he had. Evans passed away a year later.

In a brief email exchange, I remarked to Stevie Young, who first filled in on rhythm guitar for the American leg of 1988's *Blow Up Your Video* tour, when Malcolm stood down to get on top of his drinking, that there was a lot of misinformation out there in books and fan sites about the band. I fell victim to it myself, thinking Stevie's father was Alex Young because of what I'd read. He replied: 'There is. But I like it . . . my dad was Stevie Young, their eldest brother.' Stevie Sr was the first of eight siblings in the Young family, born in 1933. Alex's son, he says, is called Alex and lives in Hamburg.

There you go. Like father, like son. Hopefully I have avoided making a few mistakes of my own.

So familiar details don't need to be rehashed here; retelling the already-told story is not what this book is about. Bigger is not necessarily better. I didn't want to relentlessly plunder old music magazines for secondhand quotes to fill pages or go over old ground with people who have been interviewed already ad nauseam or those who were sick of talking and would only open up under sufferance. Nothing is more dull, and so many books written about AC/DC have been just that, even the mercifully shorter ones such as *Why AC/DC Matters* by Anthony Bozza. The American writer says of Australia that the band was 'raised there and imbued with the idiosyncratic cultural confluence that makes that island unique', ventures 'theirs is a wild-eyed cry of unruly youths from a country founded by convicts', that 'AC/DC came from the trenches' and that the band 'have not reinvented the wheel – they've spun it like a motherfucker'.

You get the drift. Even a slimline 160 pages is hard going with that amount of fanboy guff. The well-intentioned Bozza later admitted he'd done the book in the hope he'd be anointed as AC/DC's official biographer. It reads as such: verging on hagiographical. All the same, the title of the book deserved answering. Bozza can be commended for having a crack.

The thing is, and it's a point that needs to be strongly made, not everything AC/DC has done has been good. In fact, some of it has been downright crummy (from individual songs such as 'Hail Caesar', 'Danger', 'The Furor', 'Mistress For Christmas', 'Caught With Your Pants Down' and 'Safe In New York City' to forgettable albums such as *Fly On The Wall*, *Blow Up Your Video* and *Ballbreaker*). Some of it has been crass ('Let Me Put My Love Into You', 'Cover You In Oil', 'Sink The Pink'). But even when the lyrics are bad or in dubious taste the music always manages to sound good – the riffs never let you down.

For a group that Bon Scott once described as an 'album band' it's ironic that of AC/DC's 16 originally released, non-compilation studio albums at time of writing, only four (*Let There Be Rock*, *Powerage*, *Highway To Hell* and *Back In Black*) are truly essential. Their last great album was recorded in 1980.

As the Australian music critic Robert Forster writes in his book *The 10 Rules Of Rock And Roll*: 'The reduction that goes into an AC/DC song, and the tight palette of influences the band has always worked with, gave the early work precision and power, but three decades later it acts less as a liberator and more as a noose.'

Tony Platt agrees they've got themselves stuck in a musical corner of sorts from which there can be no escape: 'Their biggest strength, the simplicity and directness of their music, is also their biggest weakness because there's only so much you can do with that. Where do you go? If you're David Bowie you can reinvent yourself on a regular basis and nobody bats an eyelid. But if AC/DC reinvented themselves, they would lose their fans overnight. You'd be hearing the outrage from millions of miles away.'

That said, the Youngs might not be reinventing themselves with each new AC/DC record, but that has never been the point of what they do. It's sticking to a basic palette.

Phil Carson, who signed them to Atlantic Records in 1975, says: 'I guess that the Youngs had a realisation that rock music should be a driving force that shouldn't be overburdened with complexity. AC/DC has a unique sound, and the space within it was created by the Young brothers as musicians and producers.'

Says Mike Fraser: 'Everybody kinda says, "Well, they never change." Yeah, but that's hard to do. [They'll do] B, G, C; three, four chords in a song. They play it in such a way that it's simple but it grabs you and really sounds powerful. I find with a lot of other bands – Van Halen, Metallica, for instance – they're different types of bands in that they create a *soundscape*. A very nice, complex picture. Great songs. But with AC/DC, it's red, white, black and that's it. I think your brain absorbs it better.'

Sure, it's possible. But then there is the view that trying to divine the secret of what they do is simply pointless.

'I've never heard a band so tight in my whole life,' says David Mallet. 'Never *anywhere*. They play and they are tight and the subtleties of rhythm in those riffs and the way they are put together, you could analyse them from now for the rest of your life and you'd never know the way the riffs are played. It's certainly beyond what 99.9 per cent of the population can begin to understand.'

But, hell, it's worth a shot.

⚡

As *The Scream* was to the history of modern art – redolent of what had come before it, but just a bit *heavier* – those AC/DC albums released between 1977 and 1980 were to hard rock. No other band has come close to what AC/DC achieved during that four-year period and nobody has been able to replicate the fury of the Youngs' guitars. When they come in together – *whoomp* – it's like a spark igniting a bushfire.

'I don't think there's been a better guitar duo ever,' says Mark Evans.

Perhaps only Guns N' Roses or Nirvana came close to matching AC/DC during those years in blowing apart the rock paradigm. But AC/DC are still in their own league. They delivered four absolute belters in a row and even in the lean period that followed released the occasional knockout track, like 1990's 'Thunderstruck', not to mention a slew of unappreciated gems off 'lesser' albums: 'Spellbound', 'Nervous Shakedown', 'Bedlam In Belgium', 'Who Made Who', 'Satellite Blues' and 'All Screwed Up', among others.

Rob Riley, who should have conquered America with Rose Tattoo but instead inspired Guns N' Roses to do what his band of illustrated bad boys could not, says he has 'nothing but respect and fucking love and admiration for the boys from Acca Dacca'.

'Most people I know reckon, "Oh, but that fucking album sounds the same as the fucking last and they sound the same all the time" and I go, "No, I don't think that at all." I think they're fantastic just for the simple fact that they can come up with that fresh sound. I think they're great. I love "Riff Raff", "Thunderstruck", "Ride On", a shitload of stuff. Great stories. Like "It's A Long Way To The Top".'

Even one of their most strident critics, Radio Birdman guitarist Deniz Tek, pays them respect: 'I think AC/DC's strength was singlemindedness and unwavering adherence to a signature sound that millions of fans loved. They stayed true to it, within a narrow operating range. Most bands veer off course after the first few recordings, usually not in a good way. AC/DC never went off the track.

'It's not my taste in music but their incredible success and worldwide impact cannot be overstated. I appreciate their sticking to their vision and doing what they do best, giving their fans all over the planet exactly what they want over an amazingly long period of time. They certainly are great at it. They obviously worked very hard for their success and they clearly deserve it. They are one of the few handful of bands that have put Australia on the map as a centre of uncompromising hard rock.'

George brought a similar lack of compromise to shaping his brothers' musical and financial destiny. He made it plain very early on that AC/DC should not fall into the same trap The Easybeats did by stretching themselves too thin into different styles of songwriting, muddying their identity and confusing the message of their music.

'Malcolm and Angus were born to be in that band,' says Mark Evans. 'A lot of it has to go back to being exposed at a very young age to what George went through. Without The Easybeats I don't think you'd have AC/DC.'

As Doug Thaler, AC/DC's first American booking agent, who went on to manage Mötley Crüe and Bon Jovi, puts it succinctly: 'The Easybeats were a world-class group but they didn't have world-class results.'

George, the mastermind, made sure his little brothers were never going to fail in that regard and was happy to get them horribly tangled up in Forster's 'noose' in the process.

It was a price all three were willing to pay for the riches that would follow.

The Youngs wouldn't cooperate with Clinton Walker for his pioneering book about Bon Scott, just as they haven't for the shelf of AC/DC books that followed and I set out writing this one fully expecting not to be given any help at all. It seems anybody who's wanted more out of them than a few far-from-enlightening soundbites for magazine or TV interviews and goes the official route to contact them gets short shrift from their minders, who are notoriously protective.

'You're setting yourself a hard task, as you know,' Walker warned me before I'd even started.

Emails were exchanged between myself and Fifa Riccobono and Sam Horsburgh, the trio's gatekeepers in Australia. Riccobono poured cold water on my chances from the outset but at least asked me to send through some written questions for George Young and Harry Vanda. But it didn't get me anywhere. Nor did an approach to Vanda's new studio, Flashpoint Music. I even walked past Vanda on Sydney's Finger Wharf one day but as he was sitting down to lunch with his family and it being a public holiday, I thought it best to leave him alone.

'I have sent this through several times but it hasn't been picked up,' Riccobono wrote back to me after a long hiatus. 'I'm sorry I can't be of help . . . I told you in the beginning that it would be a long shot.'

Horsburgh, the point man for Angus Young and Malcolm Young at Alberts, replied: 'I will forward your request explaining that you are approaching [your book] from a different angle but they – Angus, Malcolm and George – usually decline book requests.'

Nothing eventuated. I made a follow-up enquiry and got no response. How to explain the shutout?

'Once AC/DC became a printing press, they really closed ranks around the family,' is how one insider explains Alberts' almost paranoid protectiveness of the band.

In New York, I emailed then called the office of their manager, Alvin Handwerker, and explained what I was doing. Again, there was no response.

Which is not necessarily a bad thing. Musicians, even the best of the lot, aren't always terribly articulate about what it is they are doing in their work. The Youngs, though fantastically astute operators and smart men, even if Angus and Malcolm were once described by their former British booking agent and now One Direction manager Richard Griffiths as 'thick', aren't renowned for their erudition. They like a bit of blue language and got to the top amid a whirl of stewed tea, groupie sex, bar fights and a few too many long drags on cigarettes. As Melbourne's *The Age* said in its review of the Engleheart biography of AC/DC, when not enclosed in their 'famous dome of silence' Angus and Malcolm deal in 'foul-mouthed, grammatically garbled quotes' and are 'hardly the most eloquent commentators for this legend'.

'AC/DC remain as guarded and uncooperative as ever, leaving their loathed biographers to join the dots with old magazine interviews and whichever witnesses dare talk.'

Conversely, though, there is the argument that music doesn't need explaining. It's a fair call yet one I have tried to resist. But writing this book was made doubly difficult by the fact that many people still within or that used to have a place in the AC/DC universe outside of the Youngs are either dead, declined interviews, didn't respond or eluded contact, didn't feel they had anything worthwhile to contribute or won't talk to anyone. Formal approaches were made to interview the three non-Young members of AC/DC but I didn't get anywhere through Handwerker. Trying the backdoor approach, I got a typed letter personally presented to Brian Johnson through a friend in Barcelona. It had to be printed out or he wouldn't read it. Again, no dice. As my disappointed mate had warned me beforehand, 'If he doesn't do it, it will be the Young issue.'

The Young issue. It became abundantly clear to me that not everybody who's worked with the Youngs wants to talk about them, for a variety of reasons. Even members of their own band.

As for the Switzerland-based Robert John 'Mutt' Lange, the great thinker/obsessive behind the megaplatinum success of Foreigner, AC/DC, Def Leppard, Shania Twain, The Cars and Maroon 5, it was futile to approach him, according to two of his friends, Terry Manning and Tony Platt. Like Guus Hiddink, the Dutch football manager, Lange subscribes to a very particular style of dealing with the media: say nothing, ratchet up your mystique and increase your asking price. It's paid dividends. He's worth hundreds of millions of dollars. Yet the producer of *Highway To Hell*, *Back In Black* and *For Those About To Rock* is the elephant in the room of the Youngs' story, the one they'd probably prefer you didn't know yet the one who was fundamental to the development of their sound and their fortunes. The fact is AC/DC *did* develop a sound. They weren't static from the outset.

'It won't happen; I can tell you that for sure,' laughed Manning when I told him I wanted to interview Lange. But I went ahead anyway and emailed Manning some questions to forward on.

A few weeks later, Manning got in touch.

'I know for absolute certain he will not answer the first three, but perhaps I might get a comment on the next to last one; maybe the last one as well. Will let you know when and if.'

The first three were about working in the studio with AC/DC. Months rolled by. Nothing came back.

'As I suspected,' Manning eventually informed me, 'he preferred not to answer questions in a public way.'

⚡

Fortunately, though, I spoke at length with five men who between them have engineered AC/DC's best records, worked with them at close quarters and know their sound perhaps better than anyone else alive outside Mutt Lange and George Young himself: Mark Opitz (*Let There Be Rock*, *Powerage*), Tony Platt (*Highway To Hell*, *Back In Black*, *Flick Of The Switch*, *Let There Be Rock: The Movie – Live In Paris*), Jimmy Douglass (*Live From The Atlantic Studios*), David Thoener (*For Those About To Rock*) and Mike Fraser (*The Razors Edge*, *Ballbreaker*, *Stiff Upper Lip*, *Black Ice*, *Backtracks*, *Family Jewels*, *Iron Man 2*, *Rock Or Bust*). Their humour, technical insight, knowledge of music and generosity to me during what often felt like a quixotic project won't be forgotten.

Other people involved with the project proved to be illuminating or vital: Easybeats icons Stevie Wright and Gordon 'Snowy' Fleet; rock producers Terry Manning, Shel Talmy, Ray Singer and the late Kim Fowley; AC/DC mastering engineer Barry Diament; AC/DC's first vocalist, Dave Evans; AC/DC, Marcus Hook Roll Band and Stevie Wright session drummer John Proud; AC/DC and Stevie Wright session drummer Tony Currenti; AC/DC bassist Mark Evans;

AC/DC managers David Krebs, Steve Leber, Ian Jeffery, Michael Browning, Stewart Young and the late Cedric Kushner; Australian rock musicians Rob Riley, Bernard Fanning, Joel O'Keeffe, Tim Gaze, Chris Masuak, Phil Jamieson, Allan Fryer, John Swan, Mark Gable, Joe Matera, Deniz Tek and the late Mandawuy Yunupingu; rock journalists Billy Altman, Robert Hilburn and Anthony O'Grady; rock photographers Lisa Tanner, Dick Barnatt and Philip Morris; rock promoters Sidney Drashin, Jack Orbin and Mark Pope; Guns N' Roses, The Cult and Velvet Revolver drummer Matt Sorum; Back Street Crawler vocalist Terry Slesser; John Wheeler of Hayseed Dixie; Dropkick Murphys frontman and bassist Ken Casey; Rhino Bucket lead singer and guitarist Georg Dolivo; record-company executives Phil Carson, Chris Gilbey, Jon O'Rourke and Derek Shulman; and, most of all, the indefatigable Jerry Greenberg: at one point in the 1970s arguably the most powerful man in music by virtue of his position as president of Atlantic Records.

Greenberg in particular was exceedingly generous with his time and his black book and, even after several phone calls from Sydney and New York, went out of his way to meet me in the bar of the Beverly Wilshire Hotel in Los Angeles. Greenberg now promotes and tours tribute bands of old Atlantic acts such as ABBA, AC/DC, Led Zeppelin and The Rolling Stones. It's a growth industry. Through him I got privileged access to a part of the AC/DC story that had hitherto been locked to outsiders and almost completely untold. I am in his debt.

To my knowledge this is the first book that has got both Leber and Krebs of the extinct but powerful Contemporary Communications Corporation (aka 'Leber-Krebs') together on the record about AC/DC; the first to get a comment from Jake Berry, AC/DC's production manager in 1980, about the events immediately after Bon Scott's death; as well as the first with the input of Cedric Kushner, Jerry Greenberg and a cast of important

Atlantic staffers: Steve Leeds, Larry Yasgar, Nick Maria, David Glew, Jim Delehant, Mario Medious and Judy Libow. For different perspectives, I also talked to decorated American war hero Mike Durant, whose incredible rescue in Somalia in 1993 (with a bit of help from AC/DC) formed part of the story for the film *Black Hawk Down*, and Australian war photographer Ashley Gilbertson, who was on the ground with US forces in 2004 when 'Hells Bells' ripped through the Fallujah night to drown out Iraqi insurgents.

There are so many gaps and holes in the AC/DC story and in what has been written about them previously that even though I purposely set out not wanting to write a biography there were biographical elements that could not be avoided and which deserved exploration. There were details that needed to be filled in, mistakes that needed to be corrected, accepted stories that demanded being pointed out as flat-out wrong or required challenging, as well as unsung figures who were well overdue some credit and recognition: radio identities Holger Brockmann, Bill Bartlett and Tony Berardini; designer Gerard Huerta (the man who came up with AC/DC's logo but has never received a dollar in royalties from merchandise featuring his graphic masterpiece); late Atlantic Records senior vice-president Michael Klenfner (whose upset over his sacking was revealed to me generously by his widow, Carol Klenfner); neglected session drummers Proud and Currenti; and Doug Thaler, who it would appear from his own and various testimonies worked hard behind the scenes to connect the Youngs with Mutt Lange, a working relationship that would change the course of rock history and bring untold wealth to everybody involved with *Back In Black*.

⚡

The Atlantic Records side of the story, AC/DC's early American adventure, was of particular fascination. New York-headquartered

Atlantic gets a bum rap in a lot of accounts and from the Youngs themselves but it's an undeniable fact that Atlantic made the band. They also made plenty of mistakes. But without the label and the unrecognised efforts of people inside it AC/DC might well have ended up like Rose Tattoo: a band that could have been and should have been but never quite got there.

This, in my opinion, is what has been missing from previous tellings of the AC/DC story or at least different parts of that story. The Youngs' success was not achieved in isolation. Their music and their collective drive weren't enough just on their own. It required the beneficence, vision and separate talent of a whole host of forgotten and unheralded people who saw something in them when others didn't. This faith in and loyalty to AC/DC hasn't always been returned.

When I met David Krebs at a diner in the Upper East Side of Manhattan, he was wearing a navy-blue scarf, navy-blue sportscoat and New York Yankees cap. At his peak, Krebs had managed Scorpions, AC/DC, Ted Nugent, Aerosmith and Def Leppard. Apprehensive about being interviewed and wary of the voice recorder on the table between us (he asked me to turn it off after about 20 minutes), he compared managing a rock band to Akira Kurosawa's *Rashomon*, in which four separate witnesses to a rape and murder give accounts that contradict each other. No matter the kind of book I was going to write, he said, there were always going to be people who saw the same event in a completely different way. There was no truth, no definitive AC/DC story, there were many different versions, and I shouldn't try.

Days later, with *Back In Black* on my iPod, I went for a jog in Central Park. Hopelessly underdressed for the weather – it had begun to snow – I cut back down East 96th Street to seek refuge in the subway and ran into Krebs again, walking down the street.

He was dumbstruck: 'You and I could be living on the same block in New York for 20 years and never see each other. How's that?'

Krebs hadn't seen the Youngs for three decades.

⚡

For all of AC/DC's Aussie pub posturing, their resistance to backup singers, symphony orchestras, samples and greatest hits albums, their anthems against greed ('Money Made' off *Black Ice* and 'Moneytalks', an insipid song from *The Razors Edge* that broke into the top 30 in the *Billboard* Hot 100, a singular feat for a group that has never seen itself as a 'singles band'), the reality is that they own and control one of the most commercial and money-geared brands in the world, right up there with Nike and Coca-Cola.

They do exclusive deals with Wal-Mart. They license their music to game companies, iOS apps and sports franchises. They remaster old records with new packaging – and truth be told don't sound any better for it. But who cares when they can outsell The Beatles' back catalogue? On 19 November 2012, they finally released their albums on iTunes (plus two iTunes-only box sets: *The Collection* and *The Complete Collection*), something they previously refused to do – just like they'd said no to Live Aid in 1985 and big charity gigs in general but turned out for the SARS benefit concert in Toronto in 2003. It was a change of heart with a big payoff. 'Highway To Hell' and 'Back In Black' entered the British Top 40 singles charts a week later, more than three decades after their original release dates.

The move surprised many, failed to impress others. Anthony O'Grady, for instance, will only listen to them on vinyl.

'AC/DC were made for vinyl. Because vinyl has the bass,' he says, with a wistful look in his eye. 'They were a band that used to go into stores and rearrange the racks so that their albums were up the front.'

There will be a time soon, no doubt, when they will give in to hip-hop artists and license samples of their music. It brings the catalogue back. It introduces a whole new demographic and market to their music. Public Enemy, Beastie Boys and other acts have tried to use AC/DC's music officially but been knocked back. Jimmy Douglass, for one, is puzzled by their continued holding out against the inevitable.

'Without a doubt sampling, when it's done right, is the ultimate flattery,' he says. 'It's a new form of art. That's all it is.'

They use huge stage sets with bells, cannons, Angus statues and inflatable fat ladies. They repackage greatest hits albums in the guise of box sets and soundtracks. Paramount Pictures used 15 of their songs on a compilation for *Iron Man 2*.

But O'Grady argues that they haven't sold out: 'They're always very aware of *context*. So they would sell their songs to *Iron Man* because there's a shared context between *Iron Man*'s audience and their audience. They wouldn't sell them for any movie that would use them in an ironic context, for example. If Woody Allen had have come up to them and asked, I think they wouldn't even answer his letters.'

⚡

Go to eBay, type in 'AC/DC' and you're confronted with branded merchandise ranging from light-up red devil horns to baby bibs. AC/DC have their own range of wines, both whites and reds. They have their own self-branded German beer, each can of which contains an 'individual code that fans can use to buy attractive devotionalia or bid for prizes'. (The company behind the beer also released an accompanying 'High Voltage' energy drink.) They have their own line of Converse Chuck Taylors, their own Monopoly board game and their own high-end headphones. Their most recent tour grossed nearly $450 million, making it the second-highest earning concert series in history, behind only The Rolling Stones. In 2011, they were the first musicians to ever make Australian *BRW* magazine's Rich 200 list. In 2013, in the same magazine, they were adjudged the 48th richest family in Australia, with a combined fortune for the previous year of $255 million – the only entertainers on the list.

For brothers who pride themselves on a 'no bullshit' philosophy, the reality of what the Youngs do and the mountains of money they make does jar. But like the way ZZ Top and Aerosmith reinvented themselves from loose, raw, 'rough and ready' beginnings in the 1970s to become commercial behemoths in subsequent decades, Tony Platt sees AC/DC's transformation into an arena band as a sign of their character.

'That's the strength of the guys,' he says. 'They reacted to a developing music market. As the audiences' penchant for bigger, more bombastic, and so on and so forth grew, as good artists, as perceptive artists, they developed to take full advantage of that.'

Phil Carson, who's put his neck on the line for them several times over his career, doesn't begrudge their success for a moment, even if it has come at the expense of some relationships: 'AC/DC have found a real connection with their fans, and for the Young brothers it has always been paramount that the fans come first. That's why they kept ticket prices low while all the other bands of their ilk were charging more and more. Musically, they found a formula that worked, and they funnelled their creative energy into staying within those parameters. They kept going even through the difficult periods of *Flick Of The Switch* and *Fly On The Wall* and emerged at the end of it stronger and better.'

⚡

But left a trail of blood in their wake.

Witness the way the Youngs have handled some band members, producers, engineers, managers and anyone else who rubbed them up the wrong way for whatever reason: Dave Evans, Mark Evans, Mutt Lange, Phil Rudd (absent the first time after an almighty blue with Malcolm over a personal matter during the sessions for *Flick Of The Switch*), Chris Slade, Michael Browning, Ian Jeffery, Peter Mensch, Steve Leber, David Krebs and a bunch of others, including a small army of forgotten drummers and bass players from their early days in Australia. The names Colin Burgess, Peter Clack, Larry Van Kriedt, Ron Carpenter, Paul Matters, Russell Coleman, Rob Bailey, Noel Taylor and the late Neil Smith only function in the AC/DC story as index entries or band trivia. When Smith died in April 2013, he didn't even rate a mention on AC/DC's official website (30 million 'likes' on Facebook at time of writing – and counting).

The body count was not always to the brothers' advantage. The losses of Mensch, AC/DC's manager at the height of their fame, and Lange, the best producer the band ever worked with, were for many years catastrophic commercially and artistically.

It strikes me that AC/DC bang on about how much they do it for their fans because the fans, unlike some band members, managers and journalists, don't give lip. They don't say no. They don't ask tough questions. They swallow the hype. Buy the merchandise. Don't challenge the Youngs' authority. AC/DC, anecdotally, is as welcoming to outsiders as a Mongol's yurt. As Mick Wall says in his book, 'the heart of the AC/DC story' is that they are 'more of a clan than a band'. Yet when an American filmmaker and AC/DC superfan called Kurt Squiers decided to make an affectionate film called *Beyond The Thunder*, about how their music connected with fans, they didn't want any part of it. There is an inherent contradiction at play here. At time of writing, the documentary, some years in the making, hasn't been released. Squiers and his partner, Gregg Ferguson, are hoping to go into a partnership with AC/DC's management and get the band's blessing for a worldwide distribution deal.

Dave Evans paints a picture of insularity: 'The Youngs were always tight knit and I remember George telling me that when he was with The Easybeats they were millionaires on paper but ended up broke because of being ripped off by management. The brothers closed ranks and none of us were privy to the meetings they often had which did not go down well with the rest of us.'

Anthony O'Grady, who'd been to singalongs at the Youngs' family home in Burwood, what he called 'a genuine, "Knees Up Mother Brown" sort of situation', also shares this view: 'I think the band was representative of the Young clan. I don't think there's any doubt at all that AC/DC are the frontline troops of the Young clan and that Malcolm is the general of the band and Angus is the strike weapon of the band and everything else fits around that.'

He saw this at close hand, being asked to leave the house at one point and sit in a car outside with a passed-out Bon Scott to 'listen to the pelting rain on the roof' while band business was being discussed inside with their then manager, Michael Browning. O'Grady sat the sozzled Scott upright and patted him on the back a few times when AC/DC's legendary frontman sounded as if he were choking. (If only he'd been with him in that Renault 5 in South London in 1980.)

But this is a family steeped in the rules of the Glasgow mean streets, in Protestant/Catholic rivalries. A band that started out playing roughneck pubs in front of crowds of 'Sharpies'; that right from the beginning attracted the street element and a working-class audience.

John Swan, who was living in a migrant hostel in Adelaide when he met George and saw The Easybeats when they came through town, explains the Glasgow mentality: 'Mine is the same philosophy as theirs: if you put it on me or mine, I'll get you back. It doesn't matter when. *I will get you*. If you beat me today I'll be back tomorrow. That was given to us by generations before us in Glasgow. You're brought up like that. So you bring that to this country and you tend to live that out. In Australia the average guy that was in a band would come from a fairly stable family, who had reasonable parents who didn't believe that one's a Catholic and one's a Protestant and they should fucking kill each other. If you fuck with someone in our family, then you will wear it.'

Another Glaswegian, Derek Shulman, was struck by how much George continued to play a crucial role in the decision-making of the band. Shulman had performed in his own group, Gentle Giant, with brothers Phil and Ray before becoming a record-company executive and launching the commercial juggernaut known as Bon Jovi into American arenas.

'When I worked with the guys, I realised that the fraternal bond was extremely close knit,' he says. 'Having been in a group with my brothers I understood that this "bond" was one that needed trust from all three brothers. Also being born in Scotland myself I knew instinctively where, how and why the Young brothers kept their distance – as the Shulman brothers did in the past. Their "clannishness" really was intrinsically part Scottish reticence and part fraternal insularity.'

Yet this clan loyalty didn't stop Angus and Malcolm agreeing to ditch George as their producer after *Powerage* stiffed, even if they did so with his blessing. As long as he continued to pull the band's strings behind the scenes, it was a compromise they could live with. They are nothing if not pragmatic.

But all of these intrigues are peripheral. They're a job for AC/DC's biographers or for the person who writes the Youngs' inevitable official biography. This is not it. It does not attempt to be. Their personal and family lives are their own business, even if there are some journalists who fail to respect their privacy. This is a book, ultimately, about the power of their music and how they built the colossus of AC/DC. It's an appreciation of three brothers whose journey with the two greatest rock groups to ever come out of Australia appears to be coming to an inevitable end, with the announcement in April 2014 on AC/DC's Facebook page and website that Malcolm was 'taking a break from the band due to ill health'. Months later, that break became permanent. His dementia, though, has not stopped AC/DC. A new album, *Rock Or Bust*, a new guitarist in Stevie Young, troubles for Phil Rudd, and another world tour suggests there is plenty to come in the AC/DC story.

1

THE EASYBEATS
'Good Times' (1968)

It took a teenage vampire movie and nearly two decades for 'Good Times', The Easybeats' maracas-driven thunderclap off 1968's *Vigil* album, to break into the charts, reaching #2 in Australia, #18 in the United Kingdom and #47 in the United States. The only other song by the band to break the top 50 in all three markets was 'Friday On My Mind', and that had happened round about the time it was supposed to: in 1967, not 1987.

There has never been any rhyme or reason to success in the music business, especially the fortunes of The Easybeats, and this confirmed it. The movie was *The Lost Boys*, starring Kiefer Sutherland and directed by Joel Schumacher, and easily the best thing about it was the Australian song, a duet for Jimmy Barnes, former lead singer of beer-soaked pub giants Cold Chisel, and the late Michael Hutchence of INXS, featuring the backing of his five bandmates.

Containing three talented Australian brothers of its own – Andrew, Jon and Tim Farriss – INXS was on its way to becoming an arena act with 1987's megaplatinum *Kick*, while Barnes was pushing hard to do the same thing with the self-titled and radio-geared *Jimmy Barnes*, a repackaged version of the *For The Working Class Man* album that had gone to #1 in Australia.

But unlike INXS, he had failed to fire in the States. Now, though, the Glaswegian shrieker had an accidental American smash on his hands. A hit no one involved with the recording saw coming, 'Good Times' having been initially covered to promote Australian Made, a loss-making Australia-only summer concert series conceived by Barnes's manager, Mark Pope, and INXS manager Chris Murphy as a means of showing that a homegrown festival featuring homegrown acts could compete with big international tours for bums on seats.

That all changed when Ahmet Ertegun got personally involved, as he had with AC/DC in the late 1970s. With his elder brother Nesuhi, the urbane Turkish-American co-founder of Atlantic Records came to belatedly get behind AC/DC, even after the band's second US album, *Dirty Deeds Done Dirt Cheap*, had been rejected by his own artists and repertoire (A&R) department.

Ertegun heard the INXS-Barnes cover by chance in February 1987 and was bowled over. 'They don't make rock records like this any more,' he said. Accordingly a 'softened up' US radio-friendly remix was put on *The Lost Boys* soundtrack and went on to sell a couple of million units.

'Good Times' was a shrewd choice by Pope and Murphy: a four-on-the-floor ripsnorter begging for the sweat and spittle of Barnes but which also managed the feat of transforming the normally effete, slightly soft Hutchence into a figure so ballsy and cocksure with the microphone it was like the ghost of Jim Morrison or Bon Scott had entered his body. Mark Opitz, who produced the single, could see similarities with AC/DC's late figurehead, at the time only seven years dead: 'Like Bon, Michael was a real gypsy. A singer in a band that wasn't necessarily the same as the rest of the band.'

But beyond the two impressive lead singers, then at the height of their powers, and the not-too-shabby group of musicians behind them, the choppy guitar riff was the star. It felt familiar, almost AC/DC like. For good reason, hinted at by the mysterious credit. This remake of a forgotten Easybeats song was the first time much of the MTV generation on both sides of the Pacific had heard something composed by George Young, the Jor-El of AC/DC.

⚡

When it was released as a single in 1968 under the US title of 'Gonna Have A Good Time', having been recorded and produced the year before by Englishman Glyn Johns, 'Good Times' sank without a trace, not even the backing vocals of Steve Marriott of Small Faces or the piano of Rolling Stones session pianist Nicky Hopkins able to cut the Australian band some chart slack. The only love it got in the States was an obscure but totally rocking, organ-scorched 1969 cover by a group of previously uncorrupted Mormon sisters from Utah, The Clingers, a cleancut rival act to The Osmonds. Looking for an image buster, they recruited Michael Lloyd and Kim Fowley as producers and released it under its US title.

'Michael and I found it on an Easybeats album,' said Fowley, a notable songwriter for Kiss, Alice Cooper and Warren Zevon, among others, who went on to create, manage and produce the greatest female rock band of all time, The Runaways, and would guide Guns N' Roses before they exploded on the rock scene in 1987. He died in 2015. 'We played The Clingers the song and they learned it and we recorded it.'

Like so many bands, The Easybeats were just too far ahead of their time. The spate of covers of the song – some 40 of them and counting – was mostly to come in later years. Before 1970 had rolled around they broke up, 'Friday On My Mind' both their biggest hit and their albatross.

'The good thing about that Easybeats version is the high backing vocals,' says Mark Opitz. 'Marriott just happened to be in the next studio. I was a schoolkid when I first heard The Easybeats' "She's So Fine" on the radio. I just thought, "*Fuck*, what's this? This is great. That's just brilliant." I was blown away.'

Doug Thaler, keyboardist/guitarist for Ronnie Dio and the Prophets and later AC/DC's first American booking agent, heard 'Good Times' in 1967 while on the same bill as The Easybeats in upstate New York on the Gene Pitney Cavalcade of Stars roadshow. Thaler went on to record the Vanda & Young tune but couldn't replicate the same swing.

'It really grooved,' he says. 'I thought it was pretty funny that 20 years after The Easybeats played that song every night on tour over here somebody finally had a hit with it.'

Now intoxicated kids around Australia, England and America were throwing up on front lawns, down stairwells and in sand dunes as it shook the walls of house parties or reverberated from parked cars in makeout spots. 'Good Times' was exactly as its title suggested: the kind of song you played on a Friday or Saturday night as a gee-up before you went out on the town. An unapologetic boozing and shagging song: exactly what it was intended to be in 1968.

But back then it couldn't resurrect The Easybeats' toxic career. There were rumours of drug use – heroin, no less – by one member (and it wasn't lead singer Stevie Wright) tearing the band apart. This and the band's failure to write another hit of the calibre of 'Friday On My Mind' and the fact that for all their success they couldn't rub two pennies together cut George Young deep. He went off cursing under his breath about managers and record-company swindlers, hung around in London playing and recording music with Harry Vanda and older brother Alex Young, then returned to Sydney in 1973 from a 'four-year binge' of creativity that his two pimply younger brothers were fortunate to absorb by osmosis and which ignited the beginnings of AC/DC.

Some of the best work of this 'binge', as George called it, is found on Marcus Hook Roll Band's *Tales Of Old Grand-Daddy*, a 1973 album he started in London with Alex then finished in Sydney with the help of Malcolm and Angus. 'Quick Reaction' and 'Natural Man' are steeped in the sound of AC/DC. The bass line and power chords on 'Natural Man', especially, are replicated almost note-for-note two years later on *TNT*'s 'Live Wire'.

Martin Cerf, reviewing 'Natural Man' for the Los Angeles-published *Phonograph Record Magazine* in 1973 when it was just an import on the Regal Zonophone label from England, described it perfectly as a natural progression from 'Good Times' and saw the revolution that was coming when no one else did, not least a bunch of record companies in the United States that didn't know what to do with Marcus Hook.

'If you can imagine what The Easybeats would have sounded like four years on should they have stayed together, then you know what "Natural Man" is all about,' he raved. 'It's got a snare that tears speakers. It's got protest lyrics. It demands you dance. It's got Beatle harmonies. It's got a riff the best this side of The Hollies' "Long Cool Woman" and "Heaven Knows" by The Grass Roots, and a hook, well, now I know the reason for the group's name.'

Marcus Hook, incidentally, is a town outside Philadelphia.

Declared John Tait in *Vanda & Young: Inside Australia's Hit Factory*: 'The album is pure power rock – a prototype for the sound that was to become the signature of AC/DC.'

※

In *Why AC/DC Matters*, Anthony Bozza writes that nothing in The Easybeats' catalogue 'touches the musicality of "Friday On My

Mind". It is their most innovative track, and the only one relevant to a discussion of AC/DC.' Which is wildly wrong and underscores just how little some American critics really know about the music of The Easybeats, outside of AC/DC the most important Australian band of all time.

Wrong because three other songs – 'Sorry' (1966), 'Good Times' (1968) and especially 'St Louis' (1969) – set the tone for and laid the musical path of AC/DC. You can hear AC/DC in George's rhythm guitar in all of them, the violent swipe of a claw across the strings. The same riffs that have become the signature sound of Malcolm Young and the bedrock of everything AC/DC does.

The Australian music website Milesago describes the 'killer hook' in 'Sorry' as emblematic of 'George's innovative (and much-imitated) guitar technique, in which he scratched the pick across the stopped strings to create an arresting percussive effect' while 'St Louis', The Easybeats' last single and which scraped into the *Billboard* Hot 100 in the United States, is 'an unmistakable signpost of the direction AC/DC would take a few years later'.

'I was pissed off it didn't do well chartwise,' says Ray Singer, who produced it.

The riff of 'St Louis', a true companion piece to 'Good Times', was so infectious it got the attention of Motown's creator, Berry Gordy Jr.

'The following year I went to the States with my then-business partner [future Marc Bolan and Wham! manager] Simon Napier-Bell. We were invited to Motown, which was still in Detroit in those days, and introduced to Berry, who had just launched a subsidiary label called Rare Earth Records. They were releasing white rock music – quite something for an all-black label like Motown. One of their first releases was "St Louis".'

Stevie Wright, who lived for a period with the Youngs, remembers 4 Burleigh Street being a hive of creativity.

'I can remember seeing Angus practising and I said, "Jeez, he's dedicated. He'll be a great guitarist one day." And he sure enough is. [Angus and Malcolm] started getting it together early when The Easybeats were chasing women and drinking. I thought the Youngs would do okay. I didn't know just how well.

'I've never had such a good time as I did living with them. They spoiled me. It wasn't long after I met George that I was over there at Burwood writing songs with him. I was just too tired to go home one day and George said, "Stay here" and I never left. George was the first to invent the *chooga chooga chooga chooga choo*. That was in "Sorry". Since then there's been many imitators. The Easybeats were a rock band as much as we were a pop band. I'm really proud AC/DC continued the job we set out to do.'

American producer Shel Talmy, the man behind The Who's 'My Generation', The Kinks' 'You Really Got Me' and The Easybeats' 'Friday On My Mind', agrees: 'I always considered The Easybeats as a rock band and not a pop band with all those negative connotations attached to being one. So with all those [Young] connections, I hear some of The Easybeats in AC/DC.'

But it was a sound that was also rooted way back further: to the music of Chuck Berry and piano player Winifred Atwell.

'I've said it for years and people have said it to me for years: AC/DC got our recipe and stayed with it,' says The Easybeats' first drummer, Snowy Fleet. 'It's that basic 12-bar boogie rhythm that they come down on and then they work around it. They don't deviate from it.'

⚡

Enigmatic producer Glyn Johns, renowned for his work with The Faces, The Who, Eric Clapton and Eagles, wouldn't be drawn on 'Good Times' for this book, saying he didn't recall anything about the 1967 sessions that ended up on 1968's *Vigil* and offered only this: 'The Easybeats were a great band and I enjoyed the sessions I did with them enormously. "Friday On My Mind" was easily the best track I cut with them.'

But Shel Talmy, who actually gets the producing credit for that timeless song (Johns was his engineer), is more generous: 'The Easybeats were very important and should have been more recognised for their contributions and should have achieved a much higher status. I thought when we were doing "Friday On My Mind" that it was a natural and knew it was going to be an instant hit.'

But he has nothing kind to say about the boss of Alberts, Ted Albert, and in actual fact blames him for sowing the seeds for the demise of The Easybeats. According to Talmy, suggestions that there was a falling out between himself and the band over 'musical direction' – alleged in the Stevie Wright biography *Hard Road* by Glenn Goldsmith – are a crock. It was about money.

'I hope Ted Albert brought some sunblock with him. He's gonna need it where he went,' he says. 'I was young, naive and stupid enough to think the person I was dealing with was honest and trustworthy. He wasn't, as I discovered to my chagrin. Unfortunately, I signed a contract to produce The Easybeats directly with Ted, one of the biggest mistakes I ever made, and one I never repeated, albeit that most everybody else I dealt with was not like Ted, but he sure as hell permanently soured my attitude toward trusting so-called managers or any others purporting to rep a band.

'Ted screwed me. He refused to pay me and I have never received one penny in the royalties I'm due for "Friday On My Mind" or any of the other tracks I produced. The fact that he'd pissed off back to Australia [from England] made it financially impossible to sue him and his company as I also knew what a big man he was there, so I realised I stood a snowball's chance in hell of succeeding and decided not to spend a fortune proving how right I was.

'Ted could get away with it as he rightly concluded I wasn't going to go to the expense of trying to collect what was owed to me on the other side of the world. History was on his side as other scumbags like [Beatles and Rolling Stones accountant] Allen Klein, [Roulette Records founder] Morris Levy and [Small Faces manager] Don Arden had been getting away with it forever.

'I'm guessing [he did it] because of a massive ego and jealousy because when he came to London and started producing The Easybeats, [their record company] United Artists told him to stop as it sucked: the reason why I was approached. So my producing an international hit first time out of the box had to be a huge blow to his ego. That's my pop-psychology take on it.

'After he kicked off [in 1990], none of his associates jumped up to declare, "I'll make it right." [Easybeats manager] Mike Vaughan was just a stooge who was no help, as he was more interested in covering his butt. Bottom line is lots of my bread is sitting in Australia with Alberts and I hope they've been choking on it, as obviously none of the legatees had the decency to redress an egregious wrong.'

It's an extraordinary outburst and casts the history of The Easybeats and Australian rock music in a whole new light. It also jars with the reverence in which Ted Albert is generally held in the Australian music industry.

As former Alberts A&R vice-president Chris Gilbey says: 'I always thought that Ted was a real gentleman in his business dealings. If anything, far too generous, and willing to take things on trust.'

But Talmy's is not an isolated sentiment among people I spoke to for this book – Alberts is not held in universal high regard – and it prompts a question that begs asking: Had Ted Albert actually set in motion the demise of The Easybeats and unwittingly created the incendiary, us-against-the-world atmosphere that would give rise to AC/DC?

⚡

How did George Young, a Scottish-Australian multi-instrumentalist who could bridge musical and social barriers enough that one of his songs was picked up by the founder of Motown, not get the recognition and material success he deserved while he was still a young man?

'You could put any kind of instrument in front of George and he had that kind of determination that he could play it within half an hour,' says Mark Opitz.

Mark Evans was equally mesmerised by George's talent. His own bass playing couldn't compare to that of AC/DC's producer: 'They're night and day. While George can play straight, he's capable of being quite busy on the bass. Which is something you wouldn't necessarily relate to the AC/DC style. The single "High Voltage" – that's George playing. You listen to that; it's very notey. He's a little bit similar to how Ronnie Lane was with The Small Faces. Very loopy and very notey, but he always picks the great lines. My style is based on how he nurtured me.'

Not only was George versatile and talented. He was crafty.

Anthony O'Grady relates a bizarre story about Bon Scott that involved George: early in AC/DC's recording career Scott had laid down a vocal track and gone on tour with the band for a couple of weeks only to return to Alberts to listen to the finished product and find lyrics had been added by George to songs he'd already recorded.

'Bon said [*putting on his best impression*], "You know what? They changed some of the lyrics . . . and it really *worked*!" And I went, "Bon, that means they would have had to change the vocal as well." And he said, "Yeah!" I took that to mean Bon was saying George would actually replace Bon's original line.'

How would he do that?

'Punching in's no problem. It's the imitation. Bon was saying George could sing just like him.'

Says Mark Gable: 'When I first heard The Easybeats I was astonished at the songwriting standard; George was largely responsible for this material. I knew at an early age that this guy was world class and if this band had been from England they would have been much more successful than they were. The Youngs' complete understanding of pop, blues, soul and rock is beyond compare. I remember sitting down and playing a couple of tunes with George on one occasion while he was playing bass and it was without a doubt one of the most magical moments of my life. All three know how to swing, how to take their time and when to beat the living shit out of things.'

Indeed, George was 'every bit as talented as John Lennon', according to Liverpudlian emigrant Snowy Fleet, but didn't get the same exposure because he was Australian. Like the Youngs, Fleet comes from a big family. Six sisters, four brothers. He met George in the Villawood migrant hostel in Sydney.

'The connection was straight away; it was right there. George is a very deep sort of bloke, a nice guy. He was always a quiet, shy loner but he was a little fireball. I didn't realise how talented he was back then until recently. The guy has written over 300 songs. Malcolm Young used to say to me, "George is a frustrated Beatle."'

Fleet hasn't seen George since 1986, when The Easybeats came together for a reunion tour. But even back in the 1960s George was loath to do any publicity; Fleet and Stevie Wright would go to radio stations to do interviews. Since then, he's more or less shut up shop completely.

'These days George is what I've heard is an "angel",' says Opitz. 'The Youngs have made a lot of money and what George likes to do is look at projects that need funding and come out of nowhere and help fund them as a silent partner. I believe he lives in Sydney and London a lot.

'When we were mixing "Love Is In The Air", both Harry and George told me how much they hated mixing. They basically *hated* music. They were just over it. I couldn't believe it. And they said, "One day you'll understand."

'I think it was significant when Alberts held their 100th birthday party – when AC/DC were in Sydney – that George didn't go. AC/DC didn't go. I didn't go. I wasn't invited. It probably said a lot about what they thought, even if Alberts is still their publishing company. But [the Youngs] weren't ever ones for bullshit. It was arranged as a photo opportunity rather than as a genuine family reunion; as it should have been, because Alberts was always a family company from day one. You always felt that when you were in there. It was us against the world.'

A mentality George took straight into AC/DC.

Mark Opitz made a pretty penny off Ahmet Ertegun's executive decision to plant 'Good Times' on *The Lost Boys* soundtrack. The first time he got a royalties cheque for the single from Atlantic, he saw more zeros than he was expecting. He still gets payments to this day. He'd visit the record company's headquarters in New York to be 'treated like fucking royalty' and was offered all sorts of projects – some balm for turning down Guns N' Roses' *Appetite For Destruction*, one of his enduring regrets.

But relations were tested between INXS and Jimmy Barnes, who'd come to a deal for a 50:50 split of royalties (Barnes: 50 per cent; INXS with its half-dozen members: 50 per cent) in Australia, having thought 'Good Times' was only ever going to be released there and not anywhere else. But when Ertegun went nuts over it, the split arrangement was farcical. This, remember, was 1987.

INXS, who'd gone to #1 with 'Need You Tonight', was huge in America. Barnes didn't even register on the radar.

In Barnes's authorised biography, *Too Much Ain't Enough*, there's a brief and cryptic mention about the behind-the-scenes horse trading that went on over royalties: 'Difficult negotiations took place as a song recorded for fun made its way into the international arena.'

'It didn't end well,' laughs Mark Pope, who managed Barnes from 1984 to 1987 and says those were 'the most interesting *eight* years of my life, the four years of managing him'.

What is most extraordinary, though, about this resuscitated and re-energised Easybeats classic is that it almost didn't happen, even before Ertegun heard it.

'INXS wanted to do "Turn Up Your Radio" by The Masters Apprentices, which wasn't a bad song, and we'd go up on a weekend to Rhinoceros [Studios] and record it,' says Opitz. 'Jimmy and I lived in Bowral [in the Southern Highlands outside Sydney]. I remember the night before, Mark Pope came down and he'd got [Australian rock historian] Glenn A. Baker to put together a bunch of songs to listen to, and of course Baker being a sycophant for The Easybeats had of stack of them on there.'

When Pope heard 'Good Times' he knew it was a no-brainer: 'I thought to myself, "Well, that's a fucking killer." A standout. It evoked the whole feeling of what [Australian Made] was about. Nothing serious. Just a song of fucking celebration, I guess. There was something about "Good Times" that was calling it.'

'So by the time we got to the studio,' continues Opitz, 'there's INXS, with Jim Keays from The Masters Apprentices, and as the producer I called a meeting with both camps and said, "We should do 'Good Times'. 'Turn Up Your Radio' is a good song but it's a bit too awkward. It doesn't flow as well as 'Good Times'. And a good time is what we want to have at this fucking thing."

'Mark, Jimmy and I felt it was better. We were able to convince

Michael Hutchence pretty quickly. And once we had Hutch the rest followed on. Jim Keays sat out there for hours and finally went home. I had the unfortunate task of telling him that we weren't doing it. That we'd give it a shot if we got around to it. But we didn't.'

What Opitz had learned working on *Powerage* with AC/DC he brought to bear on 'Good Times'.

'I hadn't lost the Vanda & Young ideology. Feel and rhythm are so important to me. I used tons of acoustic guitars, just thrashing it, distorted acoustic guitars – *chunka chunk chunk* – and I still play the "Good Times" version without Jimmy's and Michael's vocal in the studio, all the time, just to listen to it. The way Jon Farriss comes out of that drum fill in that first verse, it's *unfuckingbelievable*.'

The best result, though, for Opitz, INXS and Barnes, beyond making a damn fine record and reaping the royalties that would flow from it, was getting a seal of approval from the notoriously po-faced George Young himself.

'At the time I was recording Hoodoo Gurus' *Blow Your Cool* at Alberts, and with great dread and trepidation I took an acetate over in the morning before I started the sessions to play it to George and Harry,' remembers Opitz. 'In the past I'd played them David Bowie's cover version or Rod Stewart's cover version or whoever's cover version of Easybeats songs, and they'd go, "Nah, that's crap, that's crap, that's crap. No, it's *crap*. That's fucking *shit*." So I took my cover version to them and both of them were sitting in Fifa Riccobono's office and they said, "Oh, g'day, mate." And I'm very sheepish. So they're treating me as such, lounging back, looking at me. "*Yeah*, what do you want?" I said: "I've got this cover version of INXS and Jimmy Barnes." I played it to George and Harry and I sat with them, played it once, and they went, as if they were unimpressed, "*Mnnn mnnn*." And I said, "Well, I'll just leave my copy with you."

'At eight o'clock that night, I was doing a guitar overdub with my engineer, Allan Wright, and in through the door stumbles a very drunken George. I never saw George pissed, at all, ever in my life before that time. He goes past Allan and shoves his hand in my face. "I just want to shake your hand. It's the best fucking recording of any of our covers. *Ever!*"'

Nearly 50 years after laying down the song's original vocals for The Easybeats, Stevie Wright remains nonplussed.

'I liked our version,' he wheezes, his body and voice, if not his mind, paying a heavy price for all those years lost to heroin and alcohol addiction. 'It's now become a standard rock 'n' roll song. If you can't cut your teeth on that, you shouldn't be playing rock 'n' roll.'

Ahmet Ertegun is dead. Mark Opitz continues to produce music and get cheques in the mail but his heyday is behind him. Jimmy Barnes is still performing, though his voice has diminished. INXS, the greatest band to come out of Australia since AC/DC, is no more, having called it a day in late 2012 after conspicuously failing to quickly record an album of new songs with a new singer when their charismatic frontman unexpectedly passed away.

George Young, of course, made sure his two younger brothers didn't make that mistake. As always, he was far too clever by half.

2

STEVIE WRIGHT
'Evie' (1974)

The Youngs get a bad rap from some people who've come into their orbit. There's no denying it. But if you wanted an example of how kind and selfless they can be, there's no looking past George Young and what he did for two members of The Easybeats who were dealing with personal tragedy.

The first recipient of George's kindness was Harry Vanda. In 1966, just 20, newly married and the father of a baby boy, he'd come home and found that his young wife, Pamela, had overdosed on sleeping pills.

'When The Easybeats went on their very first tour of England, Harry's wife committed suicide the night before,' says Mark Opitz. 'And George put his arm around him and said, "Don't worry, son, you're with me." And that's the way it always was. From that day on, George had his arm around Harry's shoulder the whole time. And that's not to say Harry wasn't a valuable part of their partnership. I like to call George the heart and Harry the soul of that situation.'

The second was his old writing partner Stevie Wright, who, concealing a hidden drug addiction and stuck in a career lull after the disbanding of The Easybeats (at one point he sold men's apparel), was gifted probably the best song Vanda & Young ever worked on in their lives, the 11-minute and eight-second, three-part epic 'Evie'. It was written (according to legend) about George's own daughter, Yvette, and Chris Gilbey confirms this is true: 'George talked at that time about Evie being inspired by his daughter, yes. But I tend to think that it was more about attaching a name with two syllables to a brilliant song idea.'

In an interview with *The Age* in 2004, Vanda would not be drawn on its meaning: 'Over the years, everybody keeps asking what the song is about, and we've never answered it, and we're not going to now.'

It was a song, though, that was never intended to run so long. It started life originally as three separate songs but it became one organically in the studio.

Like 'Good Times', then, 'Evie' was effectively a hit by accident. But it was a much more significant one in the context of Vanda & Young's songwriting career, having been offered to their old bandmate under the benevolent watch of Ted Albert. Their selfless gesture went some way to make up for the hurt Wright had felt in being shut out as a songwriter for The Easybeats, when Vanda had emerged as George's go-to creative partner.

Opitz says it was the song where 'George and Harry really stretched their legs'. Doug Thaler thinks it's 'unbelievable, an amazing piece of songwriting'. Shel Talmy says it was 'very reminiscent of things I did with The Who and The Kinks'. While Snowy Fleet says it still touches him so much he gets 'a lump in my throat' when he hears it.

'It's a damn good song,' says Wright, confirming it's the song he's most proud of but, all the same, he was never convinced about the slower Part II.

'I said, "George, they'll think I'm Engelbert Humperdinck or something." But it turned out as usual I was wrong.'

So wrong that it went to #1 in Australia for six weeks and stayed on the charts for half a year.

$$\lightning$$

In 1974 the flamboyant Queen was just starting to get big. Rock operas such as *Jesus Christ Superstar* (a local production of which Wright had starred in), *The Rise And Fall Of Ziggy Stardust And The Spiders From Mars*, Lou Reed's *Berlin* and The Who's *Quadrophenia* were all the rage. Wright's comeback album, *Hard Road*, made up of six of his own original compositions and three from Vanda & Young, required ambition and a grand vision. 'Evie' was to be a song that showed that Australia could write rock sagas with the best of them.

And it was a crucial chapter in the AC/DC story, with a young Malcolm Young, not far out of his teens, contributing the solo to the rocking Part I.

'It started the whole thing,' says Opitz, 'where Malcolm's confidence – being the elder of Angus – would have grown and with George being the mentor: the successful older brother. Malcolm just wanted to be in a rock band. I think you have to take that maturation process into account.'

Wright's influence would also extend to Bon Scott. The AC/DC icon admitted as much in 1978: 'The Easybeats were the last rock band that I really liked. We're taking over where they left off.'

Two years later, according to Wright, he was asked to front AC/DC for the second time.

'They asked me to join AC/DC after Bon Scott died. I said, "No, I can't do that. I haven't got the range that Bon had. I can't see a change to my key." That's what happened. George asked me. There used to be a café on the corner in Kings Cross [in Sydney]. He took me around there because they were playing a seedy sort of bar. And he said, "Now I'll tell you something." So I sat down. And he said, "Say no if you want; you know I'll understand completely." And I said, "Well ask me." And he asked. And I said, "Are you all right?" But for reasons to do with choice of key I declined. I had nowhere near Bon's range.'

On the surface, the story seems unlikely. AC/DC wasn't playing any seedy bars in Kings Cross in 1980. They did have a residency at the Hampton Court Hotel on Bayswater Road in early 1974. More likely is that Wright has his memories mixed up.

'That incident did happen in the early '70s,' says Wright biographer Glenn Goldsmith. 'That was before Bon joined and they were looking for a replacement for the original singer. AC/DC were actually playing a gig in Kings Cross.'

In 1979 Wright was a clean but recovering heroin addict. AC/DC's aversion to hard drugs is well known and Wright had been caught using smack in the studio during the making of his 1975 album, *Black Eyed Bruiser*. The comeback was over as quickly as it had started.

'That was the end of Wright's recording career with Alberts,' writes Jane Albert in *House Of Hits: The Great Untold Story Of Australia's First Family Of Music*. '[Ted] Albert, [George] Young and Vanda knew there was no point continuing once they realised heroin was involved. They had turned a blind eye to Wright's other addictions, but heroin was a different matter.'

As it was for Angus and Malcolm.

In *Highway To Hell* Clinton Walker tells the story of Scott's heroin overdose in the company of sisters Judy and Christine King in Melbourne in 1975. Mick Wall rehashes it in his 2012 biography of AC/DC with more than enough descriptive licence. AC/DC's former manager Michael Browning tells Wall: 'It's news to me that it was heroin . . . the brothers experienced the fall of Stevie Wright, who got addicted to heroin, so it was a huge no-no.' Yet no current or former member of AC/DC has confirmed the story and that it was heroin. Until now.

'When I found out about it I'd say it would have been down the line a bit,' says Mark Evans. 'We were in Canberra, playing a place called The Harmonie Club, a German beerfest place. I remember sitting on the bed when I got back to the hotel. The tag was the Banjo Paterson Motor Inn; this squarish tag, emerald green. I remember looking at it and saying to Phil [Rudd], "What's going to happen?" There were some doubts about Bon at that stage. He'd had a problem or he'd had an OD, very early on. It was just a dabble . . . Bon just made a bad decision. It was only *one* bad decision.

'It's not something I'm particularly comfortable talking about, I've got to be honest with you. But from what I was led to believe and came to believe, it was a very, *very* isolated incident. I never saw any evidence of anything remotely like heavy drugs [when I was in AC/DC]. I remember when it happened. It was all very in-house. That was it.'

But Evans also confirms something more shocking: that because of the overdose there was talk about dropping Scott from the band – even before they got to America.

It was something he couched in vague terms in Walker's 1994 book: 'I think [Angus and Malcolm] viewed Bon to be ultimately disposable. In hindsight, it seems preposterous, but at the time he was always in the firing line. And there was a lot of pressure, mainly from George and record companies. I think within that camp, there's been a certain rewriting of history about how they felt about the guy. No, that's wrong: how they felt about the guy professionally. Because there was no way you could spend more than 30 seconds in a room with Bon and not be completely and utterly charmed. The guy was captivating; he was gentlemanly, but he had a rough side to him, and he was funny.'

Nearly 20 years later, he's more forthright.

'There was a moment of madness. That's all I can put it down to. There was disquiet. I have to put this into perspective here: in any decision like that I had absolutely fuck-all influence. It was just something that filtered through the band: that things weren't looking good [for Bon]. There was mention of another singer. But it never got to that point.'

What were the Youngs saying?

'There wasn't a lot said at the time. It was [a case of]: "There may well be a change coming."'

So when you say Scott overdosed, you're talking about heroin? 'Yeah.'

Could Wright have been that 'change' Evans spoke about? It's an intriguing possibility. But there are other factors to consider in Wright's claim that he was asked to replace Scott, regardless of whether his recollection of events is scrambled by years of drug abuse, deep-sleep therapy and alcoholism.

Members of AC/DC did like to stay at the Hyatt Kingsgate above the Coca-Cola sign in Kings Cross. Wright would wow the 2SM Concert of the Decade at the Sydney Opera House in November 1979, just months before Scott's death. By reliable accounts Wright had been clean for two years up until that show, was jogging in the mornings and wasn't going anywhere near heroin, contrary to the statement in Wall's biography that he was 'in the midst of a full-blown heroin addiction'. According to Goldsmith, he'd been offered a job as a product manager by Alberts and started on the same day Scott died: 19 February 1980. It's also well known that Ian 'Molly' Meldrum went on ABC-TV's *Countdown* touting Wright as a replacement for Scott.

But Alberts still categorically denied any such move was afoot: 'We don't know where he got that from. There's absolutely no truth in the rumour. Stevie's got his own thing to do and AC/DC have theirs.' Additionally, in the Goldsmith book, which carries a co-writing credit to Wright, no mention is made of any approach. In fact, Goldsmith writes: 'Stevie was never in the running and the thought had never crossed his mind. Bon had a high tenor voice and Stevie a high baritone. The vocal style of the track "Black Eyed Bruiser" was very AC/DC, but Stevie could never have kept that up all night.'

I ask Goldsmith if it were possible Wright was considered for AC/DC in 1980.

'If that's the [interview] transcript clearly he is mixing up the two stories,' he replies. 'Can you imagine AC/DC playing a seedy bar in Kings Cross after Bon died?'

Mark Evans is also reluctant to give it any credence: 'I'm not sure about that. George at that stage wouldn't have had the power to offer him the gig.'

As is Chris Gilbey: 'I would suspect that this would not be true. George was really, *really* down – and rightly so – on drugs. Drugs caused the break-up of The Easybeats, reputedly. They were absolutely Stevie's downfall. There is no junkie that you can ever trust, and Stevie was a junkie. So I can't imagine George ever doing more with Stevie than having a nice conversation.'

All the same, Rob Riley says there is no doubt in his mind 'Bon got some of his performance characteristics from Stevie', though Wright himself, displaying characteristic humour even in poor health, bats the suggestion away.

'A lot of people have said that,' he says. 'I find it hard to believe because he was so good that I admired him. It's funny because I pinched a lot off Bon.'

⚡

These days Marcus Hook Roll Band, Stevie Wright and AC/DC session drummer John Proud lives in Lismore, on the New South

Wales north coast, and manufactures handmade, solid timber snare drums and drum kits for a living. He doesn't get a whole lot of calls about his time with AC/DC, even with a passing resemblance to Phil Rudd.

Best known for his fusion jazz work with Crossfire, Proud came into the Youngs' fold while doing a residency in a 'kind of semi-acoustic rock, Eagles type of thing' in an Indian curry house in North Sydney, where he was clocked by George Young. Three or four months later, Proud got the call from George to sit in on the Marcus Hook sessions at EMI Studios that produced *Tales Of Old Grand-Daddy*. He only heard the record for the first time in 2011.

'I never got a copy,' he says. 'I don't think I got any credit on the album. I saw one secondhand copy in Ashwood's record shop in Sydney many years ago and stupidly I didn't buy it. A friend burned it for me off the internet and gave it to me and I put it on and I went, "*Fuck!* That's pretty good." After 30-odd years, because I'd never heard the finished tracks and never heard anything played on the radio from it, it was quite a pleasant surprise.'

It was during these sessions that Proud was asked to join AC/DC by Malcolm Young. Proud remembers a fearsome rapscallion.

'He was a little bit of a toughie, a street punky kinda kid. You wouldn't want to have a few drinks with him and say the wrong thing or he'd fuckin' give you the Glasgow kiss. You wouldn't want to cross him. It's like a terrier, you know. You see a Jack Russell going for an Alsatian.'

Mark Evans laughs at the description: 'There's no doubt about any of the Youngs' tenacity. Thank goodness none of them are six foot tall. There would have been bits and pieces of people all around the place.'

Proud never actually met Angus in the studio.

'When we finished, Malcolm said to me, "Look, I'm going to get a band together with my little brother." So I went out to the family house in Burwood and met Angus, who was still a young schoolboy. He used to just hang around and play guitar all the time and smoke. I think he was a chain smoker back in those days, from memory. And they played me a couple of tunes that they wanted to do; I can't recall if they were covers or originals. But, as I was more interested in being a studio drummer and had a fair bit of work doing residencies in Sydney and was a few years older than Malcolm and married, I didn't fancy living in Melbourne for $50 a week. I believe that was what each of them got as a wage when they first moved down there. I was also keen to play black American music. You could say that I might have missed the chance of a lifetime. *C'est la vie.*'

He laughs and takes a moment to reflect properly. It's not every day you turn down AC/DC.

'I was a few years older than them and I don't think I would have been able to handle the social aspects of it.'

Did he ever stop and think 'what if'?

'Oh yeah, but I didn't for many years. I don't listen to the radio much. I didn't realise how big AC/DC were internationally. I probably would have died a death like Bon Scott. I just wasn't interested in playing a lot of that really loud music. To me, it was a little bit too straight. A bit too hard rock.'

Too straight is not a barb you often hear directed at the Youngs. But this is coming from a man who enjoys playing eight-minute prog-jazz songs and lives in hippie-friendly Lismore. However, after working on *Hard Road* with Wright, Proud did go on to record drums for AC/DC's debut 1975 album, *High Voltage*, an association that will forever see him listed as a former AC/DC member on some zealous fan sites.

He only recalls playing on one song.

'They couldn't get this one track. I was in the studio recording for George and Harry and they asked me if I would have a crack at doing an AC/DC thing. And I don't even know what tune it was. So I don't even know how I even got paid, mate.'

I play him 'Little Lover', the song he's reputed to have cut.

'It sounds vaguely familiar. It sounds like my style, but there might have been some overdubs put on top. I can't remember what I put the drums down to. It was always just a guitar with George and Harry. We used to do all the recording sessions dead straight. There was no alcohol or drugs or anything.'

An interesting observation considering Mick Wall's contention that the studio was 'stocked with booze and dope and cigarettes'.

'We used to sit around for half the night drinking coffee, telling stories – or mostly them telling *me* stories. I think Malcolm and Angus were lucky to have brothers like George and Alex.'

That Alex again. The 'fourth Young' is a mysterious figure and was 'very talented; all the brothers thought so', according to Stevie Young. Grapefruit band member John Perry will say only 'after the split we lost contact' and that he believes Alex died in Germany in 1997. (Alex's wife, Monica, is alive and well.) But curiously, as 'George Alexander', he wrote a song for AC/DC, 'I'm A Rebel', which was recorded as an eight-track demo by the band during a break in Hamburg in 1976 though never released. It ended up finding a grateful home in 1980 with Accept, having been offered the unwanted song by Musikverlage Oktave, owned by Alex's music publisher, Alfred Schacht.

But the German heavy-metal band weren't so impressed with Alex when he came into the studio. Guitarist Wolf Hoffman told Canadian website Metallian in 2002: 'This George Alexander guy came in and coached us a little bit how he wanted it and we played it. In fact, we didn't really like the guy. I don't think he really cared. I don't think he liked us very much. We didn't like him pretty much.

In those days we didn't know what he meant when he was talking about terms, legal terms. We were too green.'

Something no Young will ever be when it comes to business.

⚡

Another Stevie Wright and AC/DC alumnus is Tony Currenti, who has had to put up with a lifetime of having his name butchered as 'Kerrante', 'Curenti', 'Ceranti' and everything in between. (To add insult to injury he's listed under 'Current' in the index to the Wall biography, though the English author at least manages to get his name right in the one mention he gets in the book.)

Currenti migrated to Australia from the *comune* of Fiumefreddo di Sicilia, Sicily, in 1967. His father bought him a piano accordion when he was five years old and he'd play drums on it (and whatever else he could bash into oblivion) with spoons.

'I got belted for breaking every chair my mother had,' he laughs over a coffee and cigarette in the southern Sydney suburb of Penshurst, where he runs a pizzeria with his son, Anthony.

Currenti never saw a drum kit before he got to Australia but one day shortly after he arrived in the country, aged 16, he was walking down King Street in Newtown and heard a band practising in a church hall and asked if he could audition. Despite never even so much as sitting down at a drum kit before, he was better than the drummer they had, who also doubled as the singer.

'Instead of playing on chairs I just transferred to a set of drums.'

It's an extraordinary story. It beggars belief that it hasn't already been told.

'Nobody's been in touch with me,' says Currenti. 'But they have mentioned my name. The first biography they wrote [Walker's *Highway To Hell*], they misspelled my name.'

In 1974 Currenti was playing drums with a group largely made up of Greek and Italian immigrants that had started out being called Inheritance, later changed its name to Grapevine and finally settled on the very Anglo-sounding Jackie Christian & Flight (but which was also known, confusingly, as Jackie Christian & Target). Constandinos Kougios & Flight wasn't going to wash and to this day Currenti believes the problem at the time for the band was prejudice. Australia has changed a lot since 1974.

'Nobody really liked wogs and that was our downfall,' he says. 'It's a gut feeling of mine but every time we went to a radio station they were happy to meet us but within five minutes they worked out we were a bunch of wogs. Didn't want to know us. I couldn't help but get that feeling straight away.'

Currenti first met Bon Scott in 1968 when the future AC/DC legend was doing 'bubblegum pop' with The Valentines. Grapevine and Fraternity shared a residency at a nightclub called Jonathan's in Sydney.

Then came *High Voltage*.

Currenti was asked by Harry Vanda and George Young to fill in for AC/DC's regular drummer, Peter Clack, who is claimed in some quarters to have done the drumming for 'She's Got Balls' but this is disputed by Currenti. He says he played on every song on the original *High Voltage* apart from 'Baby Please Don't Go', which had already been recorded before he came into the studio and, according to Currenti, took two weeks for Clack to lay down. He went on to cut the rest of the album's drum tracks in four nights, from around midnight to four or five in the morning, at the rate of $35 an hour – what his father would make in a week. He also says 'Little Lover' is one of his tracks.

'No chance,' laughs Currenti. 'No disrespect to John. But it's definitely me. There are certain rolls in there that nobody else would have done except me. If you've got a style of your own, you *know*. "She's Got Balls" is the same. It's definitely me. I think I know my style. No doubt. No doubts at all.'

With his bald head, crinkle-cut tanned face and generous girth bearing testament to decades of pasta, pizza dough, cigarettes and Chianti, Currenti is just about the unlikeliest looking ex-AC/DC player imaginable. He's been in the pizza business since 1979. But in 1974 he came under the aegis of Vanda & Young, who wrote and produced the catchy single 'Love' and its rockin' B-side, 'The Last Time I Go To Baltimore', for Jackie Christian & Flight. It's a lost Alberts classic.

'I was recording with Jackie Christian and I got asked to stay back,' he says.

Clack, meanwhile, just wasn't cutting it and soon afterwards would be axed from the band altogether.

'I did everything except "Baby Please Don't Go". All of it, *the lot* – including the single "High Voltage", which got released at a later date [and on the US version].'

A performance credited to Phil Rudd.

'I remember doing it. I remember recording it. If George and Harry rearranged it afterwards, I'm not quite sure. It's hard to tell on that song. It feels like it's been re-recorded on top, if you know what I mean. Phil might have played on top of it. It sounds like there are two lots of recordings. If you listen to "High Voltage", it feels like it's been double tracked but [the original recording has] not [been] wiped off, especially the drum sections. So whether they got Phil to play over the top or left it, I can't say for sure. All the rest, no doubts at all.'

So what about the claim it was only recorded in March 1975, four months after the *High Voltage* sessions?

'No, no. It got recorded long before then. It was held back to be released later as a single. We did a proper recording and I knew there was going to be a single out of it. The tracking – guitar, bass and drums, minus the vocals – got recorded in four nights. The first night, [AC/DC bass player] Rob Bailey was present. The other three nights it was George playing bass. It was a combined effort between the two of them. So they took another week or so to finish it off. That I remember because I was making coffee for all of us.'

He lets out a big laugh. It's a startling claim by Currenti given that 'High Voltage' is considered the first of AC/DC's classic anthems and existing accounts of the song's creation clash with his recollection.

In the Murray Engleheart biography Alberts' A&R vice-president, Chris Gilbey, who came up with the title for the album and the follow-up song, the cover art, as well as the idea for the lightning bolt in the band's name, mentions a 'rough mix' of the song being presented to him by Vanda & Young just before the album was to be released.

He confirms this to me: 'The album was recorded and George and Harry brought it in for me to have a listen. At the time there was no album title and "High Voltage", the song, had not been written or conceptualised. I suggested to George and Harry that the logical title for the album would be *High Voltage*. AC/DC and *High Voltage* seemed pretty logical as a connection. I also suggested it to Michael Browning. George came back to me a few days later and told me that the band loved the title. So it was full steam ahead with the title.

'Then literally, the week that the album was shipping to retail, George came into my office with a monitor mix of a new song that the band had recorded called "High Voltage".'

It wasn't the only time AC/DC would create a song named after an album they'd already recorded: they did it again with 1979's 'If You Want Blood (You've Got It)' on *Highway To Hell*, almost a year after the live album of the same name.

'I listened to "High Voltage" and thought it was really strong,' says Gilbey. 'All George had was a monitor mix done when they'd cut the track. It had no reverb on it. But it was more than a rough mix. George and Harry would only take out of the studio material that they were truly satisfied with. If it had just been a rough, the only people who would have heard it would have been George and Harry themselves.'

George asked if the album could be pulled to include the new track but Gilbey said it wasn't possible.

'It wasn't that it would have cost money to redo artwork or to remaster and repress the vinyl. It was getting product through the production process. You have to understand that back in those days it really took a lot of time compared with now to get product manufactured and out to retail, and it wasn't just the disc itself. It was the thought of having to explain to retailers – who were just getting to know the name of the band – that the album that was in the catalogue wasn't going to be ready for another two months. That would have been a killer not just for the band but for Alberts as a label. Not to mention the relationship with EMI and all the people working there who kept on seeing Alberts as a competitor to their own A&R output.

'The album went out and it started selling really well. Meanwhile George and Harry went into the studio to do a proper mix of "High Voltage", the song. They came in to see me and told me that none of the mixes that they had done of "High Voltage" had the energy of the original monitor mix and they wanted to get it out as is. The original monitor mix was the track that was ultimately used for the single. They may have subsequently remixed it.

'But "High Voltage" was recorded after the album of that name was recorded, mastered and in the release schedule. If you figure that an album back then took about six to eight weeks to get into the release schedule, [the song] would have been [recorded] within probably two months of the album being mastered.'

They are two wildly diverging accounts of the making of one of AC/DC's most important songs but the admission of the original monitor mix being used and being polished enough to take out of the studio and Currenti's insistence he can hear himself on the song makes his case compelling. There is, however, no questioning Currenti's contribution and his appalling lack of recognition. The man's name – when you think about it, perfect for a band called AC/DC and a track called 'High Voltage' – doesn't bob up anywhere on the Australian or international releases of *High Voltage*, *TNT*, *'74 Jailbreak*, *Backtracks* or any other releases on which his playing may or may not have appeared. The American version of *High Voltage* – featuring possibly up to three Currenti drum tracks out of a total of nine – sold three million copies. On *'74 Jailbreak*, three of the five songs contain Currenti's drumming, including the brilliant Young/Young composition 'Soul Stripper', a highlight of the original Australian LP. The cobbled-together EP, released in the United States in 1984, officially sold over a million copies. Only in occasional dispatches on the internet does Currenti get some credit. But he has no quibbles with not getting a slice of the band's fortune.

'I've always been proud to have been part of it. I'm very happy with it. The recognition is enough to say I was involved. I got paid for the sessions. I didn't expect anything else.'

In the family restaurant Currenti now runs, Tonino's Penshurst Pizzeria, there's a framed shrine to AC/DC on one of the walls, showing pictures of a younger, slimmer, hirsute Currenti from the 1970s, the cover of the American issue of *High Voltage* and various clippings from local newspapers.

'My pizzas are as good as my drumming – or my ex drumming,' he laughs.

Like Proud, he was asked to join AC/DC.

'Twice in one week. I remember being offered the job but

couldn't tell you who exactly made the offer. I felt it was a band decision; that they would have been happy for me to be part of the band. George and Harry were very keen and very happy for me to join. It was very complicated. I was already in a band and I had an Italian passport. They mentioned going to England and I couldn't go anywhere, mainly because I was eligible for the army. I would have had to have gone to Rome first and been drafted. I specifically said, and I didn't even mention Jackie Christian & Flight, being loyal to them, "Look, if your plans are to go to England I can't join the band because I can't travel with you." It was as simple as that.'

It was a decision that proved costly. While AC/DC were taking off in early 1975, Jackie Christian & Flight couldn't get off the ground and broke up.

'I would like to have joined AC/DC,' he says. 'I just couldn't travel with them overseas. They were a bunch of guys that wanted to get places. Bon and the Young brothers were very attuned to what they wanted to do. I knew they were going to make it – it was a matter of when rather than if. They were totally different to everyone else. They had the right backing. They had the right idea. They had the right gimmick.

'Working with Vanda & Young was the greatest experience I ever had and AC/DC was part of that. Even though I was never part of the band, for those four nights I felt part of the band. I enjoyed my time with them immensely. I'll treasure it for a long time.'

Currenti was asked up on stage for a couple of songs at Chequers in Sydney in early 1975 to play with them, Phil Rudd letting Currenti use his kit. Later that year Currenti also got another chance to perform with AC/DC while gigging with his new band, The 69ers, in Canberra. He claims he got a phone call to fill in for two weeks for Rudd, who had broken his hand in a fight. But this time Currenti declined because of his 69ers commitments. The job went to Colin Burgess. The 69ers broke up in 1976.

So AC/DC and Currenti were once close. But when he tried to make contact with the Youngs when they passed through Sydney on the *Black Ice* tour, he got short shrift from the band's local minders.

'I tried very hard to get in touch with AC/DC. I couldn't do it. Somehow I hit a brick wall with them every time. Sam Horsburgh was a disappointment to me. He remembered me. And when I rang up Alberts, he said, "Where the hell have you been? You don't remember me but I remember you recording *High Voltage*." I said, "Look, I'm out of the scene totally. I know AC/DC have got a concert in Sydney and I'd like to meet up with them if I could." And Sam gave me great hope of doing it. I went and saw him at Alberts.'

Horsburgh, says Currenti, told him he would do whatever he could to help arrange a meeting with the Youngs. But come concert time, nothing eventuated so Currenti went out to the stadium with his son. Despite his best efforts, he couldn't get backstage to see them. The most he could do was get a phone number for one of their aides. He was told it wasn't possible to meet them that night, it was 'too late' and the band was leaving for Brisbane the next day.

'I got the feeling no one really collaborated to let them know I was there. I'm sure if they had known, the boys would have made an effort. It's a pity. I would have been prepared to wait to see them but the manager suggested it wasn't possible. I had four blockages in my leg. An artery was blocked in four places. I couldn't walk. My son had to stop with me every 20 metres. I was in pain. Consequently, I had a little toe cut off because it went gangrenous. I have 70 per cent feeling in my right leg; my left leg is going as well. Even now I can only walk 100 metres. I don't think AC/DC got the message. But in the future I'd like to think I'll meet up with them because part of me is in [that band]. I don't want anything. I'm quite pleased and happy with the situation. There's no problem at all. I can assure you I'm not after royalties.'

It's bewildering to contemplate that a man who says he was asked to join the biggest rock band in the world can't get to meet them. After working with AC/DC, laying down tracks for *Hard Road* follow-up *Black Eyed Bruiser*, trying to form a backing band with the drug-addled Stevie Wright and coming to grips with the break-up of his other bands, the magic wasn't there any more for Currenti. He packed it in and began making pizzas instead. In April 2014, though, he returned to the stage for the first time in nearly 40 years.

'After playing with Vanda & Young and AC/DC I got no enjoyment out of it,' he says. 'It was easy to give it away. With a pizza shop it's not possible to be a musician. It's one or the other.'

The quote of a lifetime.

Nowadays, when Currenti goes back to visit his family in Italy he's feted as a hero. It wasn't always that way.

'In 1985 I took over a copy of *High Voltage* and left it there and nobody knew anything about AC/DC, especially in Sicily,' he laughs. 'If my parents didn't understand the words it wasn't any good. In 2002 I went with my kids and *everybody* knew about AC/DC. And I said, "But you've had my AC/DC album here for the last *17 years* and it's still in my mother's glory box!"'

⚡

So, with so many questions about who played what on AC/DC's first album, who sat behind the drum kit on 'Evie'?

During the recording for *Hard Road*, John Proud would do the drum tracks to guitar or piano, but never got to play on the album's masterpiece. The versatile George had got there before him (though interestingly, Tony Currenti recalls doing the drumming for Part III).

'When I first met George and Harry, they'd just come back from England,' says Proud. 'They said, "We've got this song that we recorded in England for Stevie." George told me that he played some of the drums or all of the drums on it. I think I played on just about all the other tracks. Again, I never got a copy of the finished album. Maybe I was a bit slack about it. To be honest I didn't realise that I was a part of history at the time. It was just another session. I was playing with some pretty hot players around town and I preferred to do that.'

But at Wright's free concert at the Sydney Opera House in June 1974, in front of 2500 people (and 10,000 on the steps outside) with a band featuring Malcolm and George, Proud played the song live. That day, AC/DC supported Wright. Malcolm was 21, Angus 19. A month later they signed to Alberts, who issued a press release giving their respective ages as 19 and 16. It also praised Peter Clack and his expensive Slingerland drum kit ('the first of its kind in Australia . . . underneath the pride of having that beautiful kit beats the heart of a dedicated musician'), Rob Bailey ('whose bass playing is the foundation of that SOUND of AC/DC!') and Dave Evans ('he's the VOICE that IS AC/DC!!'). All three were collateral damage within months.

'It was great,' says Proud. 'It was like being in The Beatles, if you can imagine all the screams and the volume that The Beatles would have encountered. When we went onstage, all the girls – there were a lot of teenyboppers – just went *crazy*.'

It's a day Wright cannot even recall.

Five years later at the Concert of the Decade, on a bill that included Skyhooks, Sherbet, Dragon and Split Enz, Wright performed all three parts of 'Evie' in front of a sea of 150,000 people by Sydney Harbour with a band that boasted Ronnie Peel, Warren Morgan, Ray Arnott, Tony Mitchell, Ian Miller and two unbelievably sexy backing singers in sisters Lyndsay and

Chrissie Hammond, better known as Cheetah, another Vanda & Young project. It blew everyone away. On his biggest ever stage the impish, suntanned, reborn singer – full beard, mop of unruly curls, mouthful of broken teeth – gave it everything. Spinarounds. Swinging arms. Fist shakes. Karate kicks. Cartwheels. *Jesus Christ Superstar* moves. A display of exhilarating abandon, athleticism and serious singing chops. Nothing less than the performance of his life.

Anthony O'Grady was standing by the stage: 'Stevie was so hyper he was almost levitating.'

⚡

On Boxing Day, 2004, a 9.2-magnitude earthquake in the Indian Ocean off northern Sumatra triggered a tsunami that devastated the nearby coasts of Indonesia, Sri Lanka, India and Thailand, killing 230,000 people.

The response of the international community was swift, including Australia's rock fraternity, which came together for the WaveAid charity concert at the Sydney Cricket Ground on 29 January 2005, with the aim of raising donations for charities helping victims of the disaster. One band that played that day was The Wrights, a supergroup of Australian musicians from various outfits including Powderfinger, Jet, Grinspoon and You Am I that had originally got together with producer Harry Vanda to record all three parts of 'Evie' as a way of raising money for Wright, who had fallen on hard times. It was released as a single the following month and went to #2, three decades after it had first appeared in the charts.

Phil Jamieson of Grinspoon sang Part III in the studio and recorded Part II, but couldn't nail it. In the wash-up, the 'Engelbert Humperdinck' section was performed by Bernard Fanning of Powderfinger.

'I always loved Stevie's voice and I thought that all three parts of the song showed how versatile it was,' he says. 'I was more than happy to sing the "Engelbert" section, which has that vulnerability that isn't really on display in Part I. Again it's a pretty difficult song to sing and sound as convincing as Stevie does. I remember hearing it when I was really young – along with "Black Eyed Bruiser" – pumping over the AM airwaves in the family Falcon 500, so when Nic Cester [from Jet] asked me to be a part of it I jumped at it.'

'Part III was pretty hard,' says Jamieson. 'Mind you, when Stevie performed that on the Opera House steps he was doing backflips as well, so I'm pretty sure you're going to have a bit of trouble singing and doing backflips at the same time. It was challenging. I was very nervous singing that song. It wasn't an easy song to sing by any stretch of the imagination.'

Wright has his sympathies: 'It's a hard song to sing because it's so long. But you do get a break in the slow part to get your wind together for Part III.'

'"Evie" was my earliest memory of listening to a song on the radio,' continues Jamieson. 'I remember being with my dad in the car and him turning it up. I might have been four or five. So for me it's a really formative song. Part I is quite a tricky, difficult part. For Kram [of Spiderbait], it wasn't an easy song to play on the drums. It's as straight ahead as AC/DC but it's a bit groovier. The drums are doing this crazy shuffly straight thing underneath it all. But the first part's an amazing rock song. And I think that's why it was such a hit. Nic Cester can sing the phonebook, so he did a great job vocally on it as well.'

It was the job of Tim Gaze from Wright's backing band, the All Stars, to play Malcolm Young's solo on Part I when the song was first taken on the road. He was living at Newport Beach on the northern beaches of Sydney and would drive his neighbour,

Wright, into the city with him for rehearsals. There he jammed with Angus and Malcolm.

'I always thought that solo was really funky, because it had this spontaneous throwaway thing about it I liked – the way Malcolm hit that low string and let it ring while he did the big rundown – kind of street savvy and, as history has shown, a great guitar player in the old school of bending and vibrato. I love it. As far as playing that solo goes, it would have been slightly different each night, so I guess I did it in my style at the time, which was still pretty raw at that stage.

'There is no doubt at all that "Evie" is a crafted piece of thoughtful writing, like the way it has been proffered as a song with three distinct sections or emotional journeys. And the playing by all those who are on it is just great. When George and Harry go to work on something, they sure as hell bring it out the other side just how they want, and "Evie" is a classic example of their efforts.'

$$\text{\large ϟ}$$

That this incredible song never topped the charts overseas is an injustice as much as Wright's life has been tragic and wasteful. Perhaps had it got the airplay and acclaim it deserved it may well have changed the course of that life and Wright would not be where he is today, which is living virtually broke on the south coast of New South Wales (save for the occasional royalty cheque) and using up the few favours he has left.

In February 2012, in a rare public appearance during a performance of *Stevie: The Life And Music Of Stevie Wright And The Easybeats*, a touring Australian tribute show about his life put together by the actor Scott McRae and producer Chris Keeble, Wright sang the 'Engelbert' section. (He'd later fall out with the pair, accusing them without basis of ripping him off.)

It was heartbreaking to see the shrunken, ghostly, frail man he'd become but inspiring to see how the song – and singing it, with all the sweetness and emotion he'd mustered to record it – lifted him. Like he was Stevie Wright, rock star, again. Not Stevie Wright, junkie.

'Sharing the stage with the man that had consumed the last few years of my life was an amazing experience, regardless of the fact that I had to keep my eye on him and do my best to help him shine,' says McRae. 'It was in a way a reward for all my work, a thank-you and a moment that would stay with me forever.'

Nearing his 65th birthday, Wright could still hold a tune.

'It was a moment that I knew I may never see again, and I believe the audience thought that as well,' says Keeble. 'It was unrehearsed, unplanned and an incredibly bittersweet moment. He hit every note. There was absolute silence from the crowd. He just filled the air and owned the space like the showman he is or perhaps was.'

But America just didn't get 'Evie' or Wright. Like it didn't get most things coming out of Australia at that time.

Jim Delehant was the head of A&R for Atlantic Records from 1969 to 1981 and first got wind of 'Evie' when Coral Browning, the sister of AC/DC manager Michael Browning, turned up in his office in New York with a copy of *Hard Road*.

'I loved "Evie" and *Hard Road*,' he tells me, ruefully.

Delehant signed a deal immediately and 'thought it would happen here too' but it was a dud. A promotional trip to the States had been a disaster because of Wright's heroin use. His mind was not on the job. While there he'd asked, according to Glenn Goldsmith, 'someone from the record company' for smack. Desperate for a fix, he'd flown home to Sydney early. 'Evie' and *Hard Road* bombed. Yet in a consolation of sorts, Rod Stewart had a stab at the title track and Suzi Quatro later covered Part I.

'I got it *played*,' says Steve Leeds, who first started at Atlantic in 1973 and rose to head of album promotion. He now works as vice-president of talent & industry affairs at SiriusXM, a satellite radio station in New York City. 'Atlantic got first dibs on anything Vanda & Young put out. But *nothing* happened. It was just here and there, you know. "Evie" wasn't like everything else. Radio was looking for things that were familiar and sounded the same. *Homogenised*. It didn't make waves.'

But Coral Browning's next package from Australia would do the complete opposite.

3

AC/DC

'It's A Long Way To The Top (If You Wanna Rock 'N' Roll)' (1975)

For a band that has so steadfastly forged its own brand of rock, AC/DC's influences since its beginnings in 1973 are surprisingly many: Free, Mountain, ZZ Top, Buddy Guy, Billy Thorpe, The Coloured Balls, Cactus, T. Rex, Ike Turner, The Rolling Stones and – you can hear it clearly on 'Shake A Leg' on *Back In Black* – the odd echo of Eddie Van Halen (though Angus Young was tapping before Van Halen cut a record; it's there on 1976's 'Dirty Deeds Done Dirt Cheap'). They are nothing if not a product of many outside forces, though you won't often hear the Youngs admitting to it beyond the usual, predictable nods to Chuck Berry or Little Richard.

Just as you won't hear them talking too much about their Australian roots. The Youngs' formative years in the western suburbs of Sydney are something that they seem to have gone out of their way to play down, preferring to talk up their Scottish heritage. All three brothers have spent a deal of time outside Australia at their homes in England or Europe. Those days in Burwood are long gone, literally and figuratively. AC/DC is no longer a pub band. It is now, in the words of Derek Shulman, 'the quintessential rock/punk band of the 20th/21st century'.

Yet there was a time when the Youngs embraced their past.

Malcolm was asked by a French TV interviewer in 1983 if AC/DC had opened a door or erected a bridge internationally for other Australian acts, such as INXS and Men At Work.

'Not really, maybe The Bee Gees or something,' he said, guffawing. 'We formed in Australia and it's something you can't get rid of. But we're proud of the fact we formed in Australia.'

Then there was Angus, who told an Australian TV interviewer in 2008: 'Everyone knows we started from Australia. [AC/DC] was formed there and it probably wouldn't have come out of any other country. Because the music of that time, it was the right climate, the right time, the right people. Australia's got that kind of rawness about it; it's got that kind of rough edge about it. And if anything we've always had that rough edge.'

Or *did*. When Mutt Lange took over from Vanda & Young, he filed those rough edges. What was once light, carefree and rebellious gradually became dark, bombastic and commercial. The success Angus and Malcolm desperately craved came not just without their big brother behind the mixing desk but at the expense of something intangible that had made the band unique in the first place.

And that was the sound that took AC/DC to the top, the sound that came before the Lange-shampooed *Highway To Hell* and *Back In Black*.

As much as it tries, AC/DC cannot shrug off where it came from because the music of that period doesn't lie: it *sounds* Australian. And more so than with any other band – more than Daddy Cool, more than Billy Thorpe – it is hearing AC/DC's songs from that 1974–78 period that makes Australians *feel* Australian.

In 1976 British music newspaper *Record Mirror* listed Australia's top exports thus: 'Tinned peaches, cuddly koala bears, imitation kangaroos, sheep, stuffed ducked bill [sic] platypus, souvenir boomerangs, cold lager, Rolf Harris paintings of billabongs and AC/DC.'

The sound of AC/DC's best music is Australia, in all its lack of adornment, its primitivism and its contempt for authority: on their own, appealing qualities. A sound that George Young, Harry Vanda and, to a lesser extent, Bon Scott coaxed out of Angus and Malcolm with complete singlemindedness and lack of interest in what the critics made of it.

'Bon was the biggest single influence on the band,' Malcolm once admitted. 'When he came in, it pulled us all together. He had that real "stick it to 'em" attitude. We all had it in us, but it took Bon to bring it out.'

Says AC/DC's current engineer, Mike Fraser: 'I know their roots began in Scotland, but for me their sound has always been Australian. Maybe that's because Australia was where they defined it? Hard rocking beats. Whereas American and British rock is very processed; more soundscape than honest.'

Honest. A word you cannot escape when it comes to discussion of the Youngs. And no song is more honest in their story than 'It's A Long Way To The Top'.

The subject matter is grist for any rock band's mill. But AC/DC put in the hard yards more than most. Three gigs a day at times, over a hundred gigs a year at a minimum. Just pausing to go home to Burleigh Street, shower, get a feed and then go out there and do it all over again.

'It was their lifestyle,' explains John Swan. 'It wasn't just their job. They were writing about being in a rock 'n' roll band. *If you think it's easy doin' one-night stands/Try playin' in a rock 'n' roll band*. Listen to the banter. It's just like being a fucking football fanatic, you know.'

AC/DC's first international release – it's still one of the greatest songs the two junior Youngs ever wrote, with considerable input from their older brother and Bon Scott – 'It's A Long Way To The Top' is so identified with Melbourne, where the band first took off, where the film clip was shot and where a laneway has since been named after them, that it's used before matches by Australia's biggest sporting organisation, the Australian Football League.

Touring shows, books and documentaries have borrowed its name. Most recently it was added to the Australian National Registry of Recorded Sound, a repository for 'sound recordings with cultural, historical and aesthetic significance and relevance' that 'inform or reflect life in Australia'.

It is also Fraser's favourite AC/DC song.

'The melody of it. It's got a really cool build to it and when the bagpipes kick in and start wailing it gives me goosebumps every time.'

He and millions of others, including Jack Black, Motörhead, Nantucket, WASP, Dropkick Murphys, John Farnham, Billy Corgan of Smashing Pumpkins and former Pantera vocalist Phil Anselmo (who covered it as a spoken-word poem).

Why? Because more than the crunchy opening riff – which is as good as 'Jumpin' Jack Flash' or 'You Really Got Me' – or the bagpipes or Scott's rapier-slash vocal performance or the storm of bass, drums and guitar that builds in the final stanza, it is the way 'It's A Long Way To The Top' trails off, like a car on a highway going to a place unknown, that is its true power, that uplifts.

Says the man who played bass on it, Mark Evans, it's what you don't hear as much as Malcolm's rhythm guitar that makes it so memorable.

'It's the guitar intro, it's the set-up of it, it's Malcolm, plus the actual *sentiment* of the song.'

'It's A Long Way To The Top' is one of those rare pieces of music that leaves you with a question you need to ask yourself:

What do you want and how much do you want it and how hard are you prepared to work for it?

The Youngs answered it themselves 40 years ago.

⚡

Holger Brockmann claims he was the first disc jockey on radio anywhere in the world to play 'It's A Long Way To The Top'. In 1975 he was certainly the first man to say anything on 2JJ, Australian national broadcaster ABC's youth-oriented music station, so the idea holds some water.

Now almost 70 and still working in radio, he spends most of his time on a farm in the Upper Hunter Valley of New South Wales with his wife, Marianne, and, for relaxation, blasts AC/DC into his cow paddocks.

'*Joooom*,' he says, throwing his hands into the air for effect. 'Up to 11!'

Brockmann first saw AC/DC at the Hornsby Police Boys Club in Sydney.

'It was late 1974 and I got dragged along to the Police Boys, didn't know much about it, must have been after their first record came out, and it seemed like there were 12 people there. There were probably more. I went on from night shifts to breakfast in '75 and I remember somebody bringing in "It's A Long Way To The Top" and saying, "Have a listen to this", and I just played it, and it was so fucking good that I just played it again and again. *Five* times in a row.'

Did people call the station in protest?

'Saying *more*, yeah!' he laughs.

But why five times in a row?

'Why wouldn't you if you heard it the first time? Can you imagine? The very *first* time? *Fuck*. The bagpipes got me. All of a sudden the bagpipes come and *phoooom*. *Bagpipes!* It's this fucking rock 'n' roll band and it's full of *bagpipes* and it sounds brilliant. And you put it on now and it sounds just as good.'

A comment that absolutely nails the essence of what AC/DC does so well. You can play their songs five times in a row, a *hundred* times in a row, and they still sound as evergreen as the first time you heard them. With 'It's A Long Way To The Top', it's not the bagpipes that reel you in, though they're a stroke of genius from George Young, who only recorded one take in the studio and looped. Rather, it's the second you hear Malcolm's guitar tearing through that single speaker. You're hooked. His riff propels the entire song.

'George and Harry are *really* good,' says Rob Riley. 'They have a natural ability to recognise a good song, how to write a good song, how to arrange it. George has definitely got a skill for that. He's very fucking canny and very, *very* clever. George was the studio guru. He really had his finger on the pulse. George was instrumental with the sound of AC/DC in the early days, with the way they put the songs together.

'But the boys were pretty clever themselves. They knew what they wanted. George would have helped them with any hurdles with his incredible knowledge of song, but Malcolm's contribution to the sound of AC/DC is just massive. His guitar playing is absolutely fucking crucial. He puts a beautiful, big, solid bed under Angus, which leaves him to run around the fucking shop and do what he does. Malcolm's a huge part of it.'

Terry Manning, who engineered *Led Zeppelin III* and ZZ Top's *Eliminator*, backs this critique: 'Malcolm has an absolutely perfect, amazing ability to extract the simplest, most powerful rhythm guitar elements of anyone I have ever heard. No unneeded note is ever there. Malcolm is the bedrock of the songs in my book. Then Angus, playing off what Malcolm lays down during the vocal sections, can add the extra rhythm flourishes needed. When the solos come, he has a solid bed to just explode over. He doesn't have to play as a virtuoso like Jeff Beck, or speed along like Eric Johnson. He puts his own thing in there, always doing just enough, never quite too much, and always with fervour.'

But Derek Shulman explains it best: 'Usually the rhythm section of the band – the bass and drums – drives a rock band. However, with AC/DC it is Malcolm's rhythm guitar that drives the forward movement of the songs. The drums and bass are completely spare and only play four to the bar without fills or frills. Hence the space and the ability of Angus to shine when he rips his lead guitar solos.

'Other bands can try to recreate the feel of AC/DC but only AC/DC can actually pull it off with such ease and brilliance. This way of driving the band from the top *down* rather than the rhythm section *up* is completely unique. There is no wasted chord, drum fill or notation. The complexity in its simplicity cannot be recreated by other bands.'

That doesn't stop them from trying; and that, in itself, is a tribute.

⚡

'It's A Long Way To The Top' was released in Australia in December 1975. The film clip, directed by Paul Drane, came out three months later: either an unintended or unashamed ripoff of The Rolling Stones' promo for 'Brown Sugar' on a flatbed truck in New York earlier in '75. That had been Charlie Watts's idea. As Mick Jagger explained: 'Jazz in the old days in Harlem, they used to do promotions for their gigs on flatbed trucks.'

At least the Rats of Tobruk Pipe Band was a wholly original idea. Executives from the band's future American record company, Atlantic, had not heard anything like it. They were about as stunned as Holger Brockmann had been at 2JJ.

After Coral Browning played Phil Carson of Atlantic's UK arm a film of the band, he signed them to a worldwide deal. He had no misgivings at all.

'From the moment I saw it, I knew that I could make the band work in Europe, and that was my initial goal,' he says. 'This was in the days before videos, but Coral brought along an audiovisual invention by Fairchild. It was a briefcase that opened up to reveal a screen on which I viewed AC/DC performing 'It's A Long Way To The Top', I believe, in a nightclub. It was electrifying and that's what sold me on the band.'

The clip was actually 'High Voltage', recorded at Melbourne's Festival Hall and directed by Larry Larstead, an advertising-industry friend of Chris Gilbey's who by his own account 'just happened to be in Melbourne with a crew directing for Coke' when he got the call to see if he'd be interested in shooting AC/DC.

He was and enlisted four cameramen (not five, as claimed in some accounts): Guy Furner, Ron Johanson, Paul Williams and Peter Willesee, the latter pair now deceased. They shot three clips that night: 'High Voltage' for AC/DC, Stevie Wright's 'Black Eyed Bruiser' and John Paul Young's 'Yesterday's Hero'.

'The brief was simple,' says Larstead. 'Even though we didn't have sound for our cameras, we were to get as much wild footage as we could. AC/DC was headlining and when they came on the crowd were already pumped. They were there to party and nothing was going to detract from the night becoming something special.'

But even with four cameras it didn't all go to plan.

'Larry hadn't been able to get decent close-ups of Bon Scott and needed a further studio shoot to do the cutaways,' says Gilbey. 'It wasn't expensive, so we did it, ensuring that the lighting was perfectly matched, that the amount of sweat on his face was perfect, and that he sang as hard as he could in order to make sure that the throat muscles looked like they were straining.'

Laughs Larstead: 'We had a fantastically fun time shooting all those close-ups. It ended up being an all-out contest between the guys in the band to see who could out "rage" the other guy. Angus had thrown his schoolboy hat into the crowd halfway through the live set, which we had missed on camera, so I was faced with the dilemma of only being able to use "hat on" or "hat off" footage of Angus when cutting the final images to their studio soundtrack. That was going to be hard, since I was trying to use all the great shots taken from that night.

'Anyway, Angus and I worked it out where we thought the hat should come off in the final clip and he played that particular part on his guitar and threw his hat off into the imaginary crowd in the studio with the great AC/DC attitude you can see in the final clip. We had a make-up lady on the day that was in charge of sweat continuity. Hers was a tough job, since every time she sprayed some water on Bon's face the whole band would yell for more.'

Extra special effects were to come.

'We needed audience noise,' says Gilbey. 'George Young wanted to have control of creating the audience track and went in the studio to try to put something together. It didn't really cut it for Larry, so he asked me if I would mind if he used some audio that he thought would work better. I told him to make the video as compelling as possible.'

Which Larstead dutifully did by pinching audience noise off George Harrison's *Concert For Bangladesh* live album.

'The record was a gift given to me by a friend and it turned out, with a little extra looping and doubling, to be just what I needed. I think Chris was the only other person at the time who knew about that little bit of editorial skulduggery, so don't blame it on the band. Many thanks to George Harrison, belatedly.'

⚡

Jim Delehant, Atlantic's head of A&R, says he was handed copies of AC/DC's first two Australian albums, *High Voltage* and *TNT*, when Coral Browning came back through his office a year after she'd foisted a copy on him of Stevie Wright's *Hard Road*.

'The grooves hit me like the best Stax and Muscle Shoals rhythm sections,' he says. 'Phil Rudd four on the hi-hat like Al Jackson Jr, and Angus Young's blues power simplified to the simplest. I made the deal and felt at the time it would be best to combine tracks into the Atco LP so when their second American LP came out it would have the best up-to-date material.'

Phil Carson chose the track listings.

'I went with "It's A Long Way To The Top" simply as the opening song because I thought it was the best for getting the attention of a worldwide audience. I just had to start that compilation with "It's A Long Way To The Top".'

In May 1976 *High Voltage*, a mélange of the Australian-issue *High Voltage* and *TNT*, hit UK record stores. The United States followed in September. By November 'It's A Long Way To The Top' had been released as a single.

'Because I spent so much time in America in those days, I was also sure that with the right help we could break the band on American radio,' says Carson. 'Unfortunately, the guys in the Atlantic A&R department at the time didn't agree with me and made only a minimal effort with *High Voltage*. Apart from getting a couple of great reviews, nothing really happened on that album. However, I do recall a review from Philadelphia that gave me great hope for the future. The closing line was: "AC/DC don't rock 'n' roll. AC/DC *are* rock 'n' roll."'

Bill Bartlett, a program director from radio station WPDQ (later WAIV) in Jacksonville, Florida, who has a legitimate claim to being the first man to play AC/DC on American radio, stands by Carson on this: 'When Atlantic released the US version of *High Voltage*, they were more interested in getting airplay for a band called Fotomaker. How did that work out for them?'

Contrary to the Murray Engleheart biography of AC/DC, which claims 'the first person in the United States to really jump and down about the band' was Jacksonville concert promoter Sidney Drashin, and Joe Bonomo's assertion that they got their first American airplay through disc jockey Peter C. Cavanaugh at WTAC in Flint, Michigan, AC/DC's first true champion Stateside was Bill Bartlett.

He has a letter to prove it, from Perry Cooper, dated 25 September 1979.

'We are currently melting down some gold bars to press up the gold awards for the sales on AC/DC,' writes Cooper. 'I'm hoping (and it looks real good) that we might even have to go into hock to make up a few platinum awards. This is just to show you that some of us . . . remember that you were the first person in the country to turn me on to AC/DC with their first LP. When the right time comes, the people at Atlantic won't forget either.'

That time has yet to pass. Bartlett is still waiting.

Furthermore, suggestions that AC/DC only started getting US airplay at the tailend of 1976 with 'It's A Long Way To The Top' are false. They had in fact been played for some time by Bartlett. And not just the US release of *High Voltage*. He'd been playing the Australian version, on which the song doesn't even feature, along with *TNT* and the album Atlantic kept in the vaults for five years, *Dirty Deeds Done Dirt Cheap*.

Bartlett's contribution to the AC/DC story has never been adequately recorded in all of the books written about them. As far as the band and their biographers are concerned, he might as well not exist, though Engleheart at least mentions his name once in passing and Clinton Walker, in a section of his book apropos Jacksonville, records Michael Browning talking about a 'guy from the radio station' who 'must have got hold of an AC/DC record and actually listened to it'. AC/DC's one-time manager recalls this same unnamed figure haranguing Atlantic to get behind the band and drumming up so much support before AC/DC arrived to play their first show that the city itself became 'living proof that [AC/DC] could work'. In her book Susan Masino underplays it: 'A radio station in Jacksonville programmed four or five of the band's songs into their playlist.'

Such lack of recognition is a familiar experience for scores of people who have come directly or indirectly into the Youngs' lives.

'When I moved from Jacksonville to Seattle in 1977, I also broke AC/DC in Seattle,' says Bartlett.

It's an intriguing claim given local station KISW boasts on its website that 'Steve Slaton was rocking the airwaves at night and was the first guy in America to play AC/DC on the radio!'

But Bartlett settles it: 'Steve did not know about AC/DC until I arrived [as program director in June 1977, leaving in January '78]. The general manager of KISW, Bob Bingham, chided me for playing AC/DC in the beginning. I appointed Steve as music director.'

Bartlett has retired from radio and now lives in Costa Rica.

'The ownership of WPDQ/WAIV in Jacksonville could not understand AC/DC. All I said to them was, "AC/DC will be one of the biggest bands in rock history. Trust me on this." The funny thing is nobody ever called me to promote AC/DC. It was all done on my own and I think that this information did not get to the right people in the band. Atlantic Records never recognised my efforts. I know for sure that my station was the first in America to expose Australian music and AC/DC.'

Even Sidney Drashin confirms he first heard about AC/DC through Bartlett.

'Bill got so excited he talked me into doing business and requesting live dates for AC/DC. I was glad I did. Great band. Great guys. I loved the band. The Youngs were a pleasure to do business with. Boy, did we ever get them airplay. I remember calling [Doug Thaler's agency] American Talent International and telling the president, Jeff Franklin, that AC/DC was fabulous – money in the bank for decades – on the Monday after the weekend concerts [in August 1977]. The crowds were on stun.'

So how did an unknown DJ in Jacksonville cotton on to what would become the world's biggest band even before its own American record company?

'I received the Australian version of *High Voltage* in the mail from Australia as a promo copy while programming WPDQ/ WAIV,' says Bartlett. 'It was sent to me because word got around in Australia that there was an American program director that played Australian music on the radio. Alberts sent it to me. Geoff Reynolds from EMI must have spread the word to the other labels. I had met him in Melbourne back in 1972 and in Sydney I had met Ron Tudor. Both had put me on their mailing list for items that I might expose.'

Interestingly, Tudor had signed The Valentines, Bon Scott's band with Vince Lovegrove, to his June Productions in 1968. Bartlett dutifully went back to Florida and played one of Tudor's acts, Mississippi, the core of which would go on to big things in the United States under the name Little River Band. Bartlett later recommended Beatles producer George Martin work with them, a suggestion that was passed on by EMI to LRB's manager, Glenn Wheatley. Martin produced LRB's *Time Exposure* in 1981.

'When I was in Australia in '72 I even appeared on a TV show out of Melbourne called *Happening '72*. They basically interviewed me because I was an American radio programmer whose mission was to bring Australian music to America.'

Why had he come to Australia in the first place?

'I was accepted as a foreign-exchange student at Macquarie University in Sydney. I took a leave of absence from the station in order to check it out. I went to a few rock concerts in Melbourne and saw Spectrum, Captain Matchbox and other early '70s Aussie bands but never heard them on the radio. That year, '72, was the beginning stages of "album-oriented rock" in America. I needed to find a niche that my competitors would not touch. I decided on Aussie music because it was genuine and fit into the AOR format that I was helping to develop. It also helped me brand the station and, once again, I had a commodity that I knew my competitors could not touch.

'While in Australia, I decided to visit some labels and tell them my radio story and bring back some promo items. I actually went through the phone directory and physically visited the labels, where I met some execs. What a concept, eh? I also visited Macquarie and decided that I would rather pursue a career in radio.

'I would receive new singles and albums directly from the record companies in Australia. When I received the import, I listened and played it immediately. AC/DC fit in with the branding that I was using at the station: simple, three-chord-progression rock with rebellion written all over it. It had an immediate positive reaction and there was nothing that even sounded like AC/DC out there, except for a band called Silverhead fronted by Michael Des Barres.'

Whatever Bartlett was doing was working. The late Ron Moss, 2JJ's station coordinator and Holger Brockmann's boss when he played 'It's A Long Way To The Top' for the first time in 1975, visited him not long afterwards in Jacksonville to discuss the FM format he was about to implement (2JJ eventually became 2JJJ and switched to FM in 1980) and Bartlett helped Moss develop format clocks.

There were no station visits from AC/DC.

'I only met AC/DC in the '90s. They barely remembered who I was. I met them at an arena in Worcester, Massachusetts. I knew the rep at the record company and saw them backstage for all of two minutes. I told them who I was and they acted as though it was no big deal, which was sad.'

But it was a big deal. Jacksonville was one of the key cities in the United States where the band first got some traction playing live.

'Fans had been listening to the band on the radio before they got here,' says Drashin. 'Airplay helped sell the show but the fans liked what they heard or never would have bought into it. AC/DC became headliners in record time. I thought they had made it in the middle of the first song they played.

'What set AC/DC apart were their lyrics, their show/stage presence and the overall timing. Kids were delirious about live shows and records. But I think the southeast became a stronghold for AC/DC because of the early promoters like myself. There were just a few of us and we had to make our own game plan. Getting airplay was different back then because of federal regulation [that restricted the number of radio stations a company could own]. I was able to work with local DJs that I hired as MCs for some of the shows. This gave them an incentive to play the music. It was a win-win situation. The stations played the music to promote the shows and the station and employees gained recognition at the shows.'

But not in the history books.

⚡

Remarkably, there was another unsung American radio hero working hard to push AC/DC.

His name was Tony Berardini, a programmer for KTIM, a small rock station in San Rafael, just outside San Francisco, California.

'Tony was a fanatic,' says Judy Libow, who was with Atlantic's promotion department for 16 years and started out pushing the band on college radio. 'He went on to program and eventually become the general manager at WBCN in Boston, which was one of the elite progressive rock radio stations in the country for many years. The guy would eat razor blades for AC/DC. He just loved the band.'

And still does, nearly four decades on.

'Their music was real,' says Berardini, now vice-president of talent development at CBS Radio. 'It always rocked hard – in an era of music that featured singer/songwriters and disco. They had no pretence nor made apologies for who they were or what they did and they had a great sense of humour in their lyrics; lots of tongue in cheek. I loved that about them.'

He has only happy memories of that time.

'I was managing director and a jock at KTIM and one of my jocks, Wild Bill Scott, brought the album to a music meeting, we listened to it and immediately added "It's A Long Way To The Top". It was a hard-rocking song with a bagpipe lead. Never saw that one coming. The lyrics were great; I could really relate as a jock making $2 an hour working late-night shifts six days a week. Not only does it perfectly capture the music business but in my opinion it's a damn good description of life. It will be the last song played when they finally plant me.

'This was long before the internet and social media so the only way I would know if someone was playing a band was through the trade papers. We were such a small station in the Bay Area that we didn't even report to a lot of the trade publications. All the jocks at the station loved *High Voltage* and we played it to death. We were conscious that no other stations in the Bay Area were playing the band. We really didn't give a shit what other stations were doing. We played it because it rocked.'

When he moved to Boston, nothing changed.

'WBCN was getting its ass kicked in the ratings and Charlie Kendall, the program director, wanted the station to rock more. He and I had met over the years and he knew my preference for music that rocked. The first song I played on my first air shift was "It's A Long Way To The Top". I figured that would set the tone for what was to come. The next week I added the album to our playlist, which given WBCN's history with harder music – not much outside of Queen and Aerosmith, championed by Maxanne Sartori, a great WBCN jock – I think surprised the music industry.'

With the support of Bartlett, Berardini and other unheralded believers in the band at radio stations from KMAC/KISS in San Antonio to WLVQ in Columbus, 'It's A Long Way To The Top' helped get the band its shot at the big time.

It wasn't going to let the opportunity slip.

⚡

Today, Boston is AC/DC territory. The New England Patriots play 'Thunderstruck', 'For Those About To Rock' and other AC/DC songs before, during and after games at Gillette Stadium in Foxborough. In the working-class Irish-Catholic area known as South Boston, the gritty milieu for Martin Scorsese's *The Departed* and Gus Van Sant's *Good Will Hunting*, AC/DC has taken hold because their songs are not just honest, real and aspirational, but also about not forgetting where you come from. There's no place like that place, whether you can physically step back into it or if it just remains in your heart. You shouldn't try to shake it off because it makes you what you are. Growing up in the Young family or the streets of South Boston, the bonds of family and birthplace are everything.

Boston and the outlying city of Quincy (pronounced *Quin-zee* by true locals) is also home to Dropkick Murphys, an Irish-American punk-rock stadium band that has managed to do what so many others have not: crafted a serviceable cover of an AC/DC song, taking 'It's A Long Way To The Top' and turning it into something uniquely their own. They also perform 'Dirty Deeds' and 'TNT' live.

In January 2013, at McGreevy's in Back Bay, the 'Dropkicks' perform a special free gig to celebrate the launch of an album with a very AC/DC-sounding title, *Signed And Sealed In Blood*. The bar is owned by Ken Casey, the group's vocalist and bassist. I turn up, manage to get in and join the huddle of Red Sox caps and Bruins shirts inside. There must be 200 people crammed into the tiny space, many more disappointed out on the sidewalk. When it comes time to play their anthem, 'Shipping Up To Boston', immortalised in *The Departed*, the joint trembles so violently it's like the walls are going to come tumbling down: what AC/DC were doing in small venues in Australia, England and America in the mid to late 1970s.

After the show, Casey poses for photos and signs merchandise. For all his wealth and newfound fame, he clearly connects with his fans and hasn't forgotten where he comes from. This is a man who's gone on the record as saying, 'I think our goal is to be the AC/DC of Celtic punk rock.' His face lights up when I mention I'm writing a book about the Youngs.

'Genius songwriters and showmen,' he says. 'They're just everything it is about being a real rock 'n' roll band. It's not about how you look. It's just about the music. AC/DC were a fucking man's band and they stuck to their roots and stuck to their guns. You always know what you're going to get from AC/DC and that's like what we try to be. We want our fans to know what they're getting and to be able to trust that the music's going to be what they signed on for. That's what AC/DC have always done.'

I ask Tony Berardini what it is about Boston that saw them gain such a foothold.

'The response to AC/DC on the East Coast was far greater than the West Coast,' he says. 'Outside of the city of Boston, which is relatively small, there are a lot of blue-collar, working-class towns with a much larger population than the actual city.

I think AC/DC's hard-rocking music and subject matter appealed to that working class. AC/DC are real, no-pretence, no-apologies, what-you-see-is-what-you-get, stripped-down, straight-ahead rock. I believe audiences can hear and see "bullshit" miles away. There is no bullshit in AC/DC's music or shows. Think about it: the Dropkicks are in much the same vein, in their case traditional/Irish punk, and – let's face it – who else could do a respectable cover of "It's A Long Way To The Top", including the bagpipe solo?'

Berardini himself had MCed AC/DC's first Boston gig.

'In the fall of '78 I found out AC/DC were coming to Boston to play a small club, the 500-seat Paradise Theater. I immediately called the label and said we wanted to do a live broadcast. The label was like, "Really? Sure, no problem." That was in the days when you could do something like that. It would never happen today. The club was packed; I got on stage and did the intro, which went out over the air. Unfortunately, in my enthusiasm I dropped an F-bomb and probably a couple of other expletives in the middle of the rant. The crowd went absolutely nuts and the band proceeded to blow the doors off the place.'

The Paradise still stands on Commonwealth Avenue, half a mile from Fenway Park, but has been renamed the Paradise Rock Club. The stage takes up most of the space in a tiny room. Going there, it's incredible to contemplate that AC/DC went from performing in front of a few hundred people at dives like the Paradise to performing in front of hundreds of thousands in Buenos Aires, Rio de Janeiro and Toronto and even millions at an airfield in Moscow. No other band can mobilise a mass of people like AC/DC.

'AC/DC are still rocking as hard today as they did on their first albums. They sold out the TD Garden and Gillette Stadium on their *Black Ice* tour – I went to both – and their shows are still balls to the wall, 35 or so years later. You tell me how many bands have done it that long and with that kind of integrity?'

⚡

Not everyone agrees, though, on AC/DC's mortgage on the 'no bullshit' Australian sound.

Rob Riley was just 17 when he first met the Youngs at South Side Six in Melbourne and, as he says modestly, 'had a blow with them at their joint in Lansdowne Road'. At 21 he moved to Sydney with the band Dallimore, an Alberts act that released a solitary single, 1980's 'We Are The Kids'. A year later he joined Rose Tattoo, whose first four albums would be produced by Vanda & Young after Bon Scott had championed them to Alberts, and the marriage was instantly volatile but creatively productive.

Riley says he got 'blackmailed' into joining the band. He no longer has anything to do with them, having had a spectacular falling out with frontman Angry Anderson, but will live in rock celebrity for all time for his song 'We Can't Be Beaten'. Its riff is one of Australian music's most distinctive and most loved. If anyone knows the chemistry behind a good rock song, it's Riley.

'There's definitely an Aussie sound. Everyone tries to emulate it, which is a nice thing. AC/DC have an Australian sound but they're a *world* band. They left Australia behind a long, *long* time ago and made their way in the world. The whole world finds their music accessible, the formula they've applied.'

Mark Gable takes a similar view: 'I wouldn't necessarily say that AC/DC are the quintessential Australian rock sound. The fact that Angus and Malcolm came from Scotland meant that they could create something that had never been created before because they were in Australia. If they had been *born* in Australia they would never have sounded like that. These guys were different: they looked different, they thought differently and they saw Australia in a way that Australians couldn't see it. They took pub rock and turned it into something that the rest of the world could appreciate.'

Even old enemies such as Radio Birdman's Deniz Tek have come around to appreciating what the Youngs have achieved since 'It's A Long Way To The Top', the kind of song he might have been talking about when he slagged off AC/DC as a 'lame early '70s boogie trip' in the Engleheart biography. It's the same boogie that courses through the songs 'High Voltage' and 'Rock 'N' Roll Damnation'.

But interviewed for this book, he sounds a more contrite note: 'I'm not sure where that [Engleheart] quote came from. It is certainly possible that [Birdman lead singer] Rob Younger or I said it. In our early days, in the mid 1970s, we were critical of anything we felt was aimed at mainstream acceptance or was trendy. Electric boogie rock was definitely in that category. We were pretty hard on just about every band that had industry acceptance, mainly because we were excluded ourselves.'

Time has softened that hostility.

'Regarding AC/DC at that time I recall appreciating their energy and tough stance but did not regard them as a band that was breaking any new ground. I'll stand by [what I said in Engleheart's book], generally, but if asked today I would not say "lame".

'I suppose that they were helped by their brother and by having access to Alberts management and studio facilities. I would be very surprised if that was not the case. But that does not in any way detract, in my mind, from what they achieved when they were given the chance. I would say that theirs *became* the quintessential '70s Australian rock sound. Maybe they took over where Daddy Cool left off.'

Phil Carson, for his part, doesn't buy into the argument at all: 'AC/DC is a great rock 'n' roll band with a sound that crosses international borders. I certainly don't think that their sound was indigenous to Australia. If you want to talk about an Australian sound, I would say that bands like Australian Crawl, Mondo Rock, Skyhooks, and Iva Davies with Flowers and Icehouse epitomise what I would call an Australian rock sound. I would put Cold Chisel halfway between that and a straight-ahead international rock feel, but AC/DC was full-blooded rock 'n' roll from start to finish.'

'They carved a path in Australian rock-guitar music,' says Mark Opitz. 'No question. Just like The Bee Gees did with harmony and melodic music, they carved a path. Air Supply did too. If there is an Aussie rock sound, AC/DC play a very big part, not a total part. As far as guitar sounds are concerned, we were in that period when we didn't have instant access to the rest of the world and what was happening so you more or less invented your own and what you imagined that other guitarist was doing to his amplifier. With so many pub gigs there was a lot of time to experiment with your sound and AC/DC weren't alone in having a big sound. They were maybe one of the first to go that way but a lot of other people did as well.'

There's a better way to explain it, insists Anthony O'Grady, who in any case thinks Billy Thorpe lays claim to the title. The best way of hearing the difference between an Australian and American sound is listening to Ted Nugent's old band Amboy Dukes cover Big Joe Williams's 'Baby, Please Don't Go' against the AC/DC version off the original *High Voltage*.

'The difference between the two versions is how Australians feel the blues and how Americans feel the blues. Amboy Dukes' version was like it was on tracks. Like a train on tracks. Whereas AC/DC's was like a truck revving up a mountain. You could feel the gear changes. You could feel the cam wheel underneath your feet. You could feel the rumble of the pistons.'

The rumble is unmissable to me as 'It's A Long Way To The Top' comes on the radio around midnight on a stretch of road outside Gettysburg, Pennsylvania, the heartland of America. Close to 40 years after it was released in Australia, the song has lost none of its power. The band that American radio programmers weren't so sure about in 1976 is now a radio staple alongside Journey, REO Speedwagon and Boston.

As one anonymous radio programmer told *Billboard* magazine in 1981 after the success of *Back In Black*: 'AC/DC is so "in" that their old stuff, which was "out" at the time of its release, is now "in".'

There's simply nothing like 'It's A Long Way To The Top' late at night on a lonely road on a dark highway. Those double yellow lines leading you to the life you can have if you want it bad enough. I hear it and instantly I miss Australia.

Allan Fryer, the Scottish-Australian singer who might have replaced Bon Scott were it not for Brian Johnson, calls me the next day from his home in Fort Worth, Texas, to tell me he's going into the studio to record his own version of 'Back In Black', the song.

What does he think about the Australian sound?

'It's from the heart and I'm talking from the heart here,' he says. 'It's not forgetting where you come from. When you play hundreds of gigs a year, sometimes three gigs a night, you pay your dues, you get out there, you bust your ass, and you do it for the love of what you believe in. AC/DC have never forgotten where they've come from. *Ever.* I think it's a Scottish thing, an Australian thing, a real British thing. A lot of these people never forget where they come from. I live by that myself today. And I think that's the sound. Just balls to the wall. That rhythm section. The rhythm guitar. Just pure honesty.

'There's no bullshit. There's no make-up. There's no *nothing*. It's just honest. That's what you get. You get a pair of jeans, a pair of sneakers, a T-shirt, and you get up there and you do your thing.

I think the fans know that's the truth. It's straight-ahead rock 'n' roll. And everybody can relate to every song. It's just where you come from.'

It is indeed.

4

AC/DC

'Jailbreak' (1976)

Darwin, Northern Territory, Australia, 1989. Three excited young boys from the Sydney waterside suburb of Balmain, two 16, one 17, are a long way from home: up on stage at Berrimah Prison, a correctional facility described by one criminal barrister as 'something out of Dickens, in fact it is worse than Dickens', in front of a rowdy crowd of 100 mostly Aboriginal felons.

Their band, Sooty Blotch, was there as part of the Teenage Roadshow, an initiative pioneered by a white-haired, ex-army philanthropist called Gil Weaver and funded by the Australia Council. It toured artists and musicians to outback communities and prisons in the country's disadvantaged north.

Sooty Blotch mercifully changed its name to Baby Sugar Loud and for a moment in the early 1990s threatened to break the big time but instead broke up. At one point, Brisbane rockers Powderfinger, who would go on to become superstars in Australia and had a slew of #1 albums, supported *them*.

'Virtually all the faces in the crowd were black while all the guards were white,' remembers Tom Donald, the guitarist, who now works in advertising. 'We played a set, all covers: Stones, Free, Cold Chisel, Hendrix. Rocked very hard. Had a great response. The prisoners in maximum security were shaking their doors – you could hear them rattling.

'The mood had started getting crazy-electric to the point that Gil was taken aside by one of the guards and warned: "The warden says one more song." But we were only halfway through. So Ben Quinn, our singer, announced to the crowd, "We've been told we can only do one more song."'

A few boos rang out, which became a din. The rattling in the cells was incessant. It was getting tense. Then came a cry from down the back.

'PLAY "JAILBREAK"!'

'We knew the song,' says Donald. 'I looked at Stuart Miller, our drummer. He was grinning like a fool. I looked at Ben. He mouthed, "No", as if we were taking our lives in our hands. I looked at Stu again. He clicked the sticks – *one, two, three, four* – and I launched into the riff. The place went fucking *nuts*, and there was that brief moment where we didn't know what was going to happen; that we could have made a terrible mistake. The guards made everyone sit down. We finished. The inmates went crazy. We were escorted out by the guards. One of them started screaming at Gil, telling him that the Teenage Roadshow was now banned from any Northern Territory correctional facility. Gil thought the whole thing was hilarious. It was one of the most memorable moments of my entire life.'

Six years later Aboriginal rock band Yothu Yindi did their own cover of 'Jailbreak' for the *Fuse Box* tribute album, a collection of AC/DC covers by Australian alternative acts such as Regurgitator, Ed Kuepper and The Meanies. With its didgeridoos and low, growly backup vocals, it almost betters the original: something not often said when it comes to AC/DC.

To this day, 'Jailbreak' remains a song that speaks like few others do for so much of the Aboriginal experience in outback Australia – for one simple reason.

'High rates of imprisonment,' was the straight answer of Mandawuy Yunupingu, who spoke to me before passing away in June 2013. He sang backup vocals and the Yolngu-language part of the song. 'Indigenous Australians are 10 times more likely to spend time in prison than non-indigenous Australians. Also it's simply a great song.'

But the original lyrics are also cleverly subverted. In a powerful political statement about Aboriginal deaths in custody, the words are changed at the end: *He made it out/With a sheet around his neck*.

'A sad fact but true. It's unlikely a death in custody will come from a rope. There are not too many ropes accessible to prisoners. A sheet is the stark reality of the situation.'

⚡

'Jailbreak' is not the most original of the Youngs' songs – the similarities with Them's 'Gloria' are undeniable, even though Mark Evans insists the bass line shifts and 'takes it into a different area' – but lyrically and musically it's one of AC/DC's simplest and most venomous, what Clinton Walker calls a 'virtual manifesto' for the band. It was thrown together in early 1976 and released as a single in Australia and the United Kingdom that year with an el-cheapo film clip, once again directed by Paul Drane, this time at a quarry in the suburb of Sunshine in Melbourne's western suburbs.

It starts pretty much as all AC/DC songs do: with Malcolm's riff establishing intent and driving the rhythm from the top down.

'Definitely a three-chord repetitive riff that recycles the same chordal riff to "Gloria",' says Joe Matera. 'It's on a par with Deep Purple's "Smoke On The Water" and Nirvana's "Smells Like Teen

Spirit" as one of the most popular riffs learned by guitarists when they're starting out. Yet from the moment the first strum is heard it's instantly recognisable as AC/DC.'

Then the drums and bass join in, but this time there's more of a wallop to the George Young-patented boogie than there is on 'It's A Long Way To The Top'; a kind of bounce or elasticity. Bon Scott has his snarling narration down pat; you can almost visualise his missing tooth. And it's complemented with backing vocals so blood-flecked and wretched they could be coming from a convict gang on the lam in Van Diemen's Land. But most of all 'Jailbreak' exemplifies the importance of space in AC/DC's music. The single bass note for the racing heartbeat. Angus's distortion and aggression as he mimics spotlights, sirens and firing rifles. The long pause before that lone bullet gets Scott in his *baaack*. It ends in a crossfire of cymbals, guitars and, perish the thought, even maracas: all-round AC/DC perfection.

'AC/DC will always be a live band,' says Evans, explaining the tightness. 'The four of us used to be in the studio together, recording, and that's what made it easy to mix too. There weren't any add-ons [apart from] vocals and guitar solos. So whenever you hear an AC/DC song, you're hearing sort of two Anguses. Because Angus has hidden the big chords underneath but he's also playing the solo. But ostensibly what you're hearing is the band playing live in the studio. So when you go play live, they say, "Oh gee, it sounds just like the record." It *is* the fucking record.

'This is sacrilege to some but I've seen Led Zeppelin play a couple of times and while I was a fan of the first couple of records, I went and saw them live and just went, "You fucking kidding me?" They made unbelievable fucking records and because a lot of it was so grand you couldn't produce it live with those guys. But as far as studio records go, fucking *absolutely* in a world of their own. For me, you dig a band because of their recordings and you go see them and say, "Oh fuck, that was even fucking better than the record." To me that's the greatest compliment you can give a band.'

Says Stewart Young, for a time AC/DC's manager with Steve Barnett: 'They are brilliant; still probably the best live band I have ever seen.'

Yet for some arcane reason, 'Jailbreak' fell between the cracks in AC/DC's coming assault on America. In fact, it disappeared into such a chasm of corporate ineptitude it wasn't released in the United States until 1984 on the *'74 Jailbreak* EP because the original album on which it appeared, *Dirty Deeds Done Dirt Cheap*, was shelved by Atlantic and left to gather dust. Even when *Dirty Deeds* finally hit American record stores in 1981, outrageously straight after the multiplatinum *Back In Black*, 'Jailbreak' was mysteriously left off.

'American record companies. Go figure,' says Evans.

Jim Delehant asserts somebody inside Atlantic Records, possibly Jerry Greenberg's successor Doug Morris, now chairman and chief executive of Sony Music, felt it was 'too horrific for teenage consumption'. Phil Carson, who was in charge of Atlantic's operations outside America, says he can only 'recall some discussion about that but I had turned my back on the project'.

Yet not before it very nearly claimed Carson's career. As a sign of how important he was to AC/DC between 1980 and 1981, he's the only man at Atlantic personally thanked by name on the sleeves of *Back In Black* and *For Those About To Rock*. (The latter album's cryptic mention of 'Springfield' refers to Carson's time playing bass with Dusty Springfield.)

'By the time AC/DC decided to fire Mutt Lange [after *For Those About To Rock*], Jerry Greenberg had left Atlantic and A&R decisions were being handled principally by Doug Morris and his cohorts in New York,' he says. 'I had become a little disenchanted with the way things were developing with the band. I told Doug that releasing *Dirty Deeds* [after such a hiatus] was a massive error. I told him it would disrupt what we were starting to create with Brian Johnson. AC/DC's audience had accepted more or less the unthinkable notion that Bon Scott could be replaced. What Doug did was to confuse our audience and destroy a large part of AC/DC's fan base.

'He brought an abrupt halt to the building process we had set in motion to elevate Brian. The band had to deal with yet another comparison between Bon Scott's AC/DC and Brian Johnson's AC/DC. At the time, Doug's argument was purely financial. *Back In Black* had already sold over five million copies. Because of those numbers, Doug told me that *Dirty Deeds* would sell at least two million. I told him he was right about that, but that it would also create a new sales plateau for AC/DC.'

Carson was proved correct. Certified platinum six times, *Dirty Deeds* (the one scandalously without 'Jailbreak' on it) remains AC/DC's biggest selling album in the United States post *Back In Black* and their third-biggest selling overall behind *Back In Black* (22 times) and *Highway To Hell* (seven times). *For Those About To Rock* has been certified platinum just four times. Even *The Razors Edge* (five) and *Who Made Who* (five) have outsold it.

'Doug's motivation was purely greed driven. His comment was that we would all get bigger bonuses because we had made our numbers and that I should stop thinking like an artist. To this day, I am proud of the stand that I took on behalf of the band. Releasing *Dirty Deeds* was one of the most crass decisions ever made by a record-company executive. God knows how many albums *For Those About To Rock* would have sold had Doug waited for that to come out first. He really changed the band's history with that stupid decision. I blame the lack of success of *Flick Of The Switch* and *Fly On The Wall*, to a large degree, on the inane decision of releasing *Dirty Deeds* right after *Back In Black*.'

Not only would *Flick Of The Switch* and *Fly On The Wall*

gobble like turkeys (achieving only single platinum apiece) but they would also ensure an infuriated AC/DC left Atlantic. It's not hard to imagine that it would have been particularly galling for the Youngs to hear that *Dirty Deeds*, the record considered so substandard in 1976, was enthusiastically promoted by Atlantic with beach balls.

'I remember doing a promotion with WBCN in Boston,' says Judy Libow. 'We'd decided to do a summer promotion and we took the song "Big Balls" and we had these huge beach balls made up and the station would give them away. They'd be all over the beaches. We had a great time with the band and the music.'

Why did Morris fail to appreciate what AC/DC were about?

'Doug appreciated AC/DC in his own way,' says Derek Shulman, who at sister label Atco, in one of the most magnificent intra-corporate grifts in music history, managed to nab AC/DC from Morris in a trade for The Who's Pete Townshend. 'The problem, from what I felt, was the band's slight disdain for anyone on the "record business" side. They related to musicians but not particularly well to the people who worked for them in the "biz". Doug certainly knew they were unique and fantastic sellers; however, I believe their less-than-showbiz personalities never allowed the "biz" into their insular world.'

Mark Gable got a sense of that insular world in his professional and personal encounters with the three brothers.

'My dealings were more with George on a professional basis, though I did meet Angus once and was lucky enough to have beers with Malcolm on a few occasions. Malcolm is very shy, not a loudmouth and not even the slightest bit arrogant. He's very switched on about music and in particular the business side of things. When I met Angus we chatted for a while but he didn't get my sense of humour. One thing I learned about the Youngs is that they do take themselves very seriously. Along with the huge talent comes a certain fragility. They are very careful about people they don't know. There is a sense that *we are on the inside and you are not*. That was always my impression when dealing with both Albert Productions and the Youngs.'

Shulman, however, managed to see a side of the brothers most never see.

'I haven't seen them in a while now. The last time I saw them on the road was a couple of years ago. I really love and relate to the guys. They are great people who live life by their own rules without any interference or manipulation from the outside. Just sitting in the dressing room with Angus nursing his cup of tea and cigarette and discussing issues *not* business related is completely refreshing.'

There's some irony in the fact that *Dirty Deeds*, the album that in 1981 practically destroyed AC/DC's relationship with Atlantic, was the same album that Atlantic very nearly used as an excuse to cut their ties with AC/DC five years earlier. But it wasn't going to end any other way. The Youngs' Glasgow mentality – *If you put it on me or mine, I'll get you back* – made sure of that.

⚡

After failing to convince the suits at Atlantic in New York that *Dirty Deeds* was a sellable proposition, AC/DC was in a state of shellshock. The adventure that had started in 1976 with the US version of *High Voltage* looked to be over as soon as it had begun.

'It just pissed us off,' says Mark Evans. 'The band never took criticism well. Especially coming from the record company, the guys who were supposed to be in the same tent, saying, "No, mate, it's not good enough." The band was pissed off.'

So the well-reported story goes, Jerry Greenberg wanted to drop the band but Phil Carson managed to persuade Ahmet and Nesuhi Ertegun (misspelled as 'Neshui' in the Wall biography) to keep them at the label on the condition their advance was reduced on future albums.

Carson reiterates the account for this book: 'There certainly was discussion about dropping the band at Atlantic in New York. The A&R department thought the group was going nowhere and that they were very derivative. That's why *Dirty Deeds* was never released in sequence. However, they did have the sense to consult me before actually dropping the group and, by that time, I was making very serious inroads with the group in Europe, and we were certainly recouping the $25,000 that we had to pay for each album.'

The wash-up?

'Nesuhi Ertegun was able to tell the Atlantic team that the international people were right behind AC/DC.'

Yet Greenberg remembers differently. He rejects suggestions that he didn't like the band or that he didn't care about the band. He rejects the story, put forward by Michael Browning in the Murray Engleheart book, that Carson went over the top of him to petition the Erteguns for mercy.

'I don't know anything about that,' he says. 'There was *some* conversation about [dropping the band]. But it wasn't my decision. There was someone in the A&R department, who I basically trusted, who said that we should drop them. I never, *ever* was thinking about dropping the band. The band was touring Europe at that time; they hadn't played a date in America. Phil Carson was the day-to-day person [for AC/DC at Atlantic]. What I remember basically is Atlantic – and that was *everybody*, not just necessarily me – was not that excited about that record.

'The feeling from the people at Atlantic was, "I don't know if we should put this record out." I cannot deny that. Atlantic did not want to put the record out, there's no question. That's a fact. But as far as ever wanting to drop the group, I don't believe we ever wanted to drop the group.'

So what was the true involvement of the Erteguns, the top executives at Atlantic, in the fate of AC/DC? The younger, Ahmet, told *Billboard* he'd seen the Australian band for the first time at punk club CBGB in New York City in 1977 but wasn't sold even then: 'I'm not sure I would have signed them when I first heard them . . . they were pushing the envelope . . . and very ratty-looking.'

'Ahmet wasn't really around much during those days,' says Greenberg. 'He was travelling a lot. The first tour I remember AC/DC came over and we had them at the Whisky A Go-Go [in Los Angeles]; we had them playing all those little clubs, and Ahmet wasn't very much involved [at that point].'

But when they took off, says Larry Yasgar, Atlantic's head of singles, 'Ahmet jumped right in.'

⚡

Judy Libow, who went on to become vice-president of promotion & product development at Atlantic, backs the Carson version: 'There was a point in time when there was talk of dropping the band.

'I remember going down to a WEA convention in Florida. WEA was the big distribution arm for all the labels – Warner Bros, Elektra, Atlantic. This one year [1977] Atlantic decided to have AC/DC play down there for everybody: all the labels, all the staff, all the WEA people. And most people hadn't yet seen them play. It was a small venue. I'll never forget they came out into this club that was packed with all these industry people and they did their thing. Angus was on Bon's shoulders, up and down the stage, he's mooning everybody. It was just an incredible thing to see.

'Sometime later, years later, I was on the West Coast, on a road trip in California, and I drove with our West Coast promotions guy, Barry Freeman, into Fresno; AC/DC was going to be playing there, and there was not much going on in Fresno back then. It was barely a city. And AC/DC came out and Angus pulled down his pants. We were standing on the side of the stage and the crowd started throwing garbage at them. It was crazy. They didn't expect it. They hadn't yet heard about this part of their performance. It was wild. Garbage was coming from everywhere. They just kept going. The band just kept on playing. They were very professional. They were always responsive. They always did whatever we asked them to do. Everybody who worked with them loved them.'

But offstage AC/DC was doing it tough. Nick Maria was senior vice-president of sales at Atlantic. He was with Libow at the WEA Records convention at the 4 O'Clock Club in Fort Lauderdale, the last show of the first leg of their first American tour.

'They were in the restaurant having breakfast and they didn't even have enough money to pay for it,' he says. 'I did the first allocation for them [of *High Voltage*] to ship out to the entire country. I think it was only 4000 to 6000 units.'

'The first album stiffed,' says Larry Yasgar. 'It didn't happen at all. I think it did about 50,000. We knew what we had but we didn't know how big it would get.'

By 1979, AC/DC was shifting ten times that amount.

There had been no crossed wires between Phil Carson and Atlantic's Gene Wilder-lookalike president, Jerry Greenberg, when the pair flew to Hamburg, Germany, to see AC/DC in the flesh in September 1976. Greenberg had had his own band in the 1950s, Jerry Green and the Passengers. By 1964, he was working as a record promoter. By 1974, only 32 years old, he was Atlantic's president, personally appointed by Ahmet Ertegun.

'I flew to London and Phil said, "You have to see this band",' he says.

'Every year, at least once, Jerry would come over, usually for the international meetings that took place in the autumn,' remembers

Carson. 'I seized on an opportunity to take Jerry to see AC/DC at a club called Fabrik in Hamburg. The place was packed and people were literally hanging from the rafters.'

'We flew to Hamburg. I'm a drummer. I'm a musician. I understand good musicians and rock 'n' roll,' says Greenberg. 'I *flipped out* when I saw the band. I'll never forget after the show I saw them all pile into this little truck; that's the way I started. When I was 16 years old I had a four-piece band and when we used to have to travel and do a gig 300 or 400 miles away overnight we could only afford to take one car. I used to only take a bass drum and a snare drum. I couldn't even take my full drum set. And when I saw that, with that band in Germany, all of a sudden it was like I relived my career and I said, "Man, I gotta make sure that these kids happen."

'I went back to America. We had a video of the group. I called everyone into the conference room. I said, "I want you to see what could be the next biggest band for Atlantic Records." We played AC/DC on the VHS. Atlantic was a very big rock label but we were a very big pop label, too. We had a lot of older people in marketing that didn't quite get Angus running around in shorts or on Bon Scott's shoulders. The expressions on some of the faces I can remember to this day. However, at that meeting I made a proclamation that we were going to break this band in America.'

Larry Yasgar remembers the troops being read the riot act: 'We had a meeting of all departments and were told that the group we had to bring home at that time was AC/DC. [Atlantic general manager] David Glew was the one who had to put the hammer down to everybody once the word came from the top, "You've got to bring this group in." We had a lot of pressure. A *lot* of pressure. *Really bring the group in.* All everybody talked about from that moment was AC/DC. We pounded everybody on that one.'

What of the widespread rumour that Bon Scott was firmly in Atlantic's firing line?

Alleges Anthony O'Grady: 'He was pretty lucky to survive in AC/DC because when they went over to America the first thing Atlantic said to them was, "We think you have to get rid of the singer because we can't understand him." Atlantic ummed and ahhed that Bon was not too easily understood by US boofheads. US record companies had the same problem with Jimmy Barnes and Alex Harvey – in fact, anyone with a Scottish accent. But Angus, Malcolm and George held the line.'

I put this to Greenberg and ask him if Scott's place in the band was ever an issue at Atlantic and discussed across his desk.

'No. I never did,' he says. 'I never made that suggestion.'

His UK counterpart Carson supports him: 'There was certainly no such discussion with me. Jerry is one of the most astute presidents in the entire record industry, and he got it in a heartbeat. This was just as well because all those label people in America were telling him the band had no future. Jerry saw something spectacular with his own eyes and set his people to work to come up with a plan.

'However, it wasn't until John Kalodner joined the A&R department, and Michael Klenfner came in to head up marketing and promotion, that we got any real traction. Once those two became involved, things changed very quickly for AC/DC and Atlantic.'

⚡

Who is this mythical John Kalodner figure with his flowing ginger beard, long hair and John Lennon-style wire-rimmed glasses? Go to his website and his short biography gushes about him signing Foreigner and other acts.

'John Kalodner not only finds the magic, he also helps to make the magic happen,' it blathers without a hint of humility. 'AC/DC had been signed to Atlantic in the UK, but there was resistance to picking up the band for the States. Kalodner was behind AC/DC and knew they could make it. He even physically cut and edited the band's recorded tapes together for them.'

On the fan site acdczone.com, he's also listed among key 'AC/DC personnel' alongside Bruce Fairbairn, Mike Fraser, Mutt Lange, David Mallet, Tony Platt, Harry Vanda and lighting director Cosmo Wilson. An elusive figure, Kalodner could not be contacted for this book, despite several attempts.

'I hired Kalodner in the A&R department for product management,' says Jim Delehant, who remembers the record business in the 1970s as being far removed from the corporate circus of today. 'We had some laughs.'

But a slew of others don't remember him too fondly. Prime among them is Jerry Greenberg.

'John Kalodner likes to take credit for signing Foreigner. He had absolutely nothing to do with the signing,' he says. 'Once I signed the band, John was the A&R guy who worked *with* Foreigner. In fact, at one point [Foreigner's late manager] Bud Prager wrote him a letter and he still hasn't taken it down off his website that he signed Foreigner. Understand one thing: nobody could sign anything at Atlantic without me saying, "Okay" and signing off on a memo that goes upstairs. So that's that.'

Larry Yasgar agrees with his old boss: 'Good old John Kalodner. John took credit for everything except the sinking of the *Titanic*.'

Chris Gilbey remembers meeting him one year at the music-industry trade fair Midem, in Cannes: 'He didn't know who I was, told me that he had discovered AC/DC and because of that should be respected – or some such drivel.'

'Minimal impact,' says Michael Browning. 'He pretends that he discovered them, which is nonsense. Certainly he was influential in convincing Jerry that they were worth doing something with, but beyond that there wasn't much involvement.'

⚡

Michael Klenfner was another polarising figure inside Atlantic. Where the bearded Kalodner was wiry, lean and enigmatic, the moustachioed Klenfner was sweaty, corpulent and not shy about saying what he thought, even if it put some noses out of joint. Outside of his work with AC/DC, Klenfner is best known for having turned John Belushi's and Dan Aykroyd's *Saturday Night Live* act, The Blues Brothers, into recording artists. *Briefcase Full Of Blues*, their 1978 album for Atlantic, went to #1 in the American charts.

Invited to form what one ex-staffer called the 'road artist development & touring department' at Atlantic when he left his position as head of FM radio promotion at Arista Records in 1977, Klenfner's 'bull-in-a-china-shop' style of management (a description used by a number of people interviewed for this book) eventually got him offside with Greenberg and saw him leave the company in acrimonious circumstances.

'Michael loved AC/DC,' says Judy Libow. 'He was very close to the band. He fought to keep them at Atlantic. Michael was really kind of their champion. And to whatever degree he could speak for them and work internally on their behalf he did. His influence then had an effect on the other executives, who had to make decisions that he wasn't in a position to make.'

Steve Leeds takes the same position: 'I think the people that were really responsible for championing AC/DC were Phil Carson, who signed them, and Michael Klenfner, because he believed in them more than anybody else in the company. And he was like an attack dog. He wouldn't let go. *We're going to break this band, we're going to break this band, we're going to break this band*. People at the time were ready to walk away from the project because it was just too difficult and nobody was really embracing the band.

'I didn't like Michael and we never got along. He parenthetically came into the company to disrupt the promotion department, of which I was a key person, so I'm not a fan. I tell you with total disclosure I was *not* a fan. But I have to say he really, *really* championed the band when nobody else in the company would. I'll give him that. Atlantic had a product flow of a lot of music and a lot of releases and it was easy for it to be skipped over and go to the next project. Long-term thinking, even in those days, was not really what people did.'

Carson, too, remains a believer in Klenfner's legacy: 'There is no doubt that Michael got behind AC/DC when he joined Atlantic. He visited London shortly after he came on board. I believe he was trying to sign Bay City Rollers. I told him not to waste his time with them and that he should get behind AC/DC. He took a close look at the project, realised that this band had not reached its potential and really encouraged the marketing and promotion departments to spend more time and money on AC/DC. I think that was a major part in the development of the band.'

Only Yasgar and former Aerosmith manager David Krebs sound a different note, crediting head of artist relations Perry Cooper for being the band's gamebreaker inside Atlantic.

Cooper saw himself in that way, too, going on what he told Susan Masino in her book before he died. When Jerry Greenberg had given Klenfner and Cooper a film of AC/DC to watch, Klenfner, he said, 'didn't give a shit' and asked his lieutenant to look at it for him. From that point, Cooper was under their spell.

'Klenfner was a fan,' says Krebs. 'Cooper was very much an *enthusiast* behind the band.'

'We were all behind them at Atlantic,' says a bemused Yasgar. 'I don't even know what Michael Klenfner's involvement was. The group always asked for Perry Cooper.'

Which could well be the truth. Renée Cooper, Perry's daughter, tells me: 'AC/DC and my father were really tight. After Bon died, my dad and Brian became best friends. When Bon passed, they found the emergency-person-to-contact card and it was my dad.'

'There was so much internal bullshit going on, with everybody trying to take credit for it when it broke,' says Yasgar. 'We had a ton of people in promotion that got involved and then they would come to me, "Look, Larry, it's going on in Baton Rouge, Louisiana. Make sure we get stock there." I would make sure we had stock in the area. I just had to follow all the records. That was my main job. And if they didn't have stock in an area, if it wasn't pressed yet or whatever, I would have at least 50 in my office to cover the airplay and just ship it to the stores so they would have it in.'

Bill Bartlett, however, doesn't separate the two men in his praise, which is fitting considering both came from Arista to Atlantic in 1977 as a team: 'Thank goodness for Perry and Michael for believing.'

In 1977, according to Jim Delehant, Kalodner got quietly shifted from the New York office to Los Angeles 'to keep an eye on that scene'. Two years later Klenfner also left the Atlantic building at 75 Rockefeller Plaza but, unlike Kalodner, went out all guns blazing.

$\lightning$

It's a mostly neglected detail in AC/DC biographies but the United States in the mid to late 1970s was in the grip of disco fever. Atlantic's investment in AC/DC, even after they'd decided to stick with the vertically challenged Australians, wasn't a fait accompli. Another set of Aussie brothers, The Bee Gees, was doing much bigger business than AC/DC. Their manager Robert Stigwood's RSO label had been distributed by Atlantic from 1973 to the end of 1975, Ahmet Ertegun even introducing the Gibbs to producer Arif Mardin, who reinvented their career with 'Jive Talkin''. But Ertegun didn't stop them switching labels after they received a massive offer from Polydor, owned by PolyGram.

It was a decision Jerry Greenberg calls 'a *big* mistake'; which it was, considering the *Saturday Night Fever* soundtrack would go on to be certified platinum 15 times in the United States alone. But Atlantic had other aces up its sleeve.

'In 1976–77, Atlantic was voted the disco company of the year,' says Greenberg. 'We had Chic, Sister Sledge, The Trammps. Radio was into disco. FM radio was just starting. We weren't getting that much radio play for AC/DC. So how do you break a band if they're not getting any radio play? You've got to *build* fans. How do you build fans? You need to perform. How do they perform but only get paid $300 from the Whisky A Go-Go? They've got to get money from a record company.

'I supported them not only with coming down from the presidential office to the troops [and telling them] that they needed this band but also by writing the cheques. AC/DC were very heavily in the red before they finally broke. There were times when I had to go up against corporate when it came to writing those cheques for "tour support", but I said, "Don't worry. You're going to get it back. The group's going to happen."

'We supported The J. Geils Band in the beginning, The Allman Brothers, Black Oak Arkansas, The Marshall Tucker Band. You go through the history of Atlantic and you see these rock bands that we were able to break. How did we do it? Touring. *Touring, touring, touring.*'

A logistical and organisational job that fell largely to Doug Thaler, who had met George Young while performing with their respective bands on the Gene Pitney Cavalcade of Stars, modelled after Dick Clark's travelling show.

Thaler was employed by a booking group called the Thames Agency when he first heard buzz about this band of fist-waving scruffs from Australia. One of Thames's clients was Deep Purple, whose roadies' notorious scrap with AC/DC at Sunbury in 1975 had piqued Thaler's interest. (Deep Purple guitarist Ritchie Blackmore later called AC/DC 'an all-time low in rock 'n' roll'.) He dutifully got his hands on a copy of *High Voltage*, flipped it over and saw the names 'Vanda' and 'Young'. By then 'It's A Long Way To The Top' was, he says, 'getting played like crazy' in Columbus and Jacksonville.

'I said, "You have got to be kidding me!" I'd lost track of them. So when I saw their names and saw there was the brothers [Angus and Malcolm], I got a phone number for Alberts in Sydney and I called them up. And we had some good laughs. It had been eight years by then. So I said, "I'd really like to book the guys in the United States." I think [the Youngs] were happy to have somebody involved that they knew themselves.'

Thaler made the arrangement official in March 1977 when he went to London to see AC/DC perform at the Rainbow Theatre in Finsbury Park.

'I made a deal with [UK booking agent] John Jackson and Michael Browning to represent AC/DC in America – already having received the blessing of George and Harry.'

It was a propitious deal for both parties. Having joined a new agency, ATI, Thaler ended up booking AC/DC's first five tours in the United States and rostered them on to a line-up of acts that included Cheap Trick, REO Speedwagon, Kiss and UFO. Between 1977 and 1979, roughly the two years it took for them to become an American arena attraction in their own right, there was hardly a major band AC/DC didn't headline with, support or fall under on a festival undercard: The Dictators, Michael Stanley Band, .38 Special, Nazareth, Triumph, Mahogany Rush, Foreigner, Alvin Lee, Santana, Head East, Mink DeVille, Johnny Winter, Heart, Rush, Styx, Ronnie Montrose, Aerosmith, Poco, Rainbow, Savoy Brown, Molly Hatchet, Ram Jam, Van Halen, Alice Cooper, Blue Öyster Cult, Boston, The Doobie Brothers, Journey, Ted Nugent,

Thin Lizzy and more. Future Hollywood mogul Harvey Weinstein and his company Harvey & Corky promoted their shows in Buffalo, New York. According to Nate Althoff's acdc-bootlegs. com, between 1977 and 1979 the band did nearly 450 gigs, mostly in the United States, England and mainland Europe: an average of around 150 a year. In 1976 alone, before they even got to the States in July '77, they'd racked up an incredible 183. In 1980, they did 135. In 1981, rolling in it after the success of *Back In Black*, they did just 74. Hundreds of thousands of kilometres clocked – a blur of promoters, diners and hotel rooms.

It wasn't always an easy sell.

At one show in December 1977, supporting Kiss at Freedom Hall in Louisville, Kentucky, the local newspaper's concert reviewer was so appalled by what he had seen from the two 'gross-out groups' he was moved to remark, 'It's hard to see where groups like Kiss and AC/DC can go from here.'

At another show, headlining Cheap Trick in Johnson City, Tennessee, in September 1978, one critic sneered, 'The show as a whole was little more than amplified noise loud enough to burst the eardrums of anyone who hadn't thought to bring some cotton along ... the crowd loved it, but it all only went to show that AC/DC's forte lies not in the music but in the show.

'As for that crowd, it was rowdy and young. Most of the intoxicated faces looked hardly old enough to be done with the Clearasil. This group will soon learn that AC/DC is not classic music, and their albums will gather dust while more sophisticated music is played.'

But wherever AC/DC performed, airplay followed. Even when they couldn't get their hands on new material, radio announcers proved resourceful.

'When I received the Australian version of *Dirty Deeds*, Atlantic got a little upset and said they were working *High*

Voltage,' remembers Bill Bartlett. 'It took them long enough. They, in so many words, wanted me to back off from AC/DC because it did not fit into their master plan. Of course, I could not do that. It was difficult to back off from *Dirty Deeds* after I played it on the radio.'

Says Tony Berardini: 'I went to our local import music store and grabbed *Dirty Deeds* and began playing "Jailbreak" as an import. The listeners loved it.'

$$\not\!\!\!4$$

In 1977 Peter Mensch, who two years later as an employee of Leber-Krebs would supplant Michael Browning as manager of AC/DC, wrote a university thesis called *An Exploratory Study Of The Effects Of Radio Airplay And Advertising On Record Sales*. The equation was simple: 'Support of a tour by a record company will demonstrate to radio program directors that the artist is important to the company and thus might have something to offer their audiences . . . unless the product is promoted by the record company, it won't get airplay.'

But Nick Maria says the number-one challenge for the Australian band was visibility – literally, stock in record shops. Once they had visibility the rest followed. And touring achieved it.

'Visibility, having them in the stores, was difficult when they had no airplay,' he says. 'They stayed on the road forever. I don't know how they did it, but they did it.'

Larry Yasgar recalls having to chase their music around the country.

'Wherever they got airplay I had to follow it,' he says. 'I'd have to get stock into the various markets. If a record went on [the air] I had to make sure it got into those stores. A lot of times we'd give the singles away for nothing just to get a sense if the record was going to happen based on airplay.'

Steve Leeds was behind promotional tours for bands such as The Rolling Stones and Led Zeppelin at Atlantic. When things were starting to happen for AC/DC, as he saw it, it was Texas where the loudest racket was being made on the airwaves.

'Texas was the market that first really embraced AC/DC in the United States,' he says. 'A little station in Texas started playing AC/DC: KMAC/KISS in San Antonio. Bill Bartlett was an early supporter but the real support was in San Antonio. San Antonio is a very blue-collar town. It's where the Alamo is. KMAC/KISS was appealing to a working-class male and I think AC/DC was something they understood. A lot of the hard-rock bands had their first initial success in Texas, particularly San Antonio. Florida was another place. *Redneck rock*. The South embraced that hard-rock sensibility.'

Yasgar, for his part, pinpoints the Midwest as the crucible of the AC/DC liftoff.

'AC/DC to me started in the Midwest,' he says. 'Cleveland. Detroit. Chicago. That was a big rock area for us. In fact, with all our records we would concentrate on the Midwest. That's where the concentrated airplay was.'

⚡

One look at AC/DC's US summer tour dates for *Let There Be Rock* shows how important those working-class and 'redneck' areas were to the rise of AC/DC: Texas, Florida, Missouri, Illinois, Ohio, Wisconsin, Indiana and Michigan, with New York and California at the tailend. In the winter, the band did a bunch of dates in Tennessee, West Virginia, Pennsylvania and North Carolina.

After seeing Dropkick Murphys in Boston, I drive down to Tennessee via Connecticut, New York, New Jersey, Maryland, Pennsylvania, Virginia and North Carolina and cut back to Massachusetts via Kentucky and West Virginia. AC/DC is rarely off the radio, even in the rural backroads. Nashville, incidentally, is where AC/DC would part ways with the manager who'd got them to the States – Michael Browning – in September 1979. It was the last time he'd ever see the Youngs.

John Wheeler, the lead singer of Hayseed Dixie, a 'rockgrass' band from Nashville that shot to fame (and the top of the country charts in Australia) in 2001 with *A Hillbilly Tribute To AC/DC*, an album of covers, first heard AC/DC on the radio around the age of 10 and remembers that 'it just sort of jumped out of the speakers – it was on about 12 times a day – then *Back In Black* came out and I don't think the radio played much else for the next two years'.

He insists Nashville's reputation as a country-music town is erroneous.

'Nashville actually isn't particularly country. It's known internationally for that musical style, but only because there is a branch of the music industry there that cranks out a cookie-cutter version of "country" music. Most of the local people in Nashville are no more interested in, say, Tim McGraw or whichever is the latest country "hat act" than they are in any other American city. There are more rock and pop radio stations than country ones.

'There are always more blue-collar people in any city than white-collar ones; this is the case everywhere in the world. In Nashville and the South, the same people who loved Lynyrd Skynyrd and Hank Williams Jr also loved AC/DC. If you went to a Hank show in the 1980s, half the audience would be wearing AC/DC T-shirts and vice versa.'

Music is important in the American South because the reality of daily life can be pretty humdrum compared to the big cities on the East and West Coasts. But smalltown America is the real America. The waitress who's seen better years wiping down the counter in the café. The Creedence song on the radio. The young girls in flipflops and NFL sweatpants catching up for gossip on the street. Listening to country music on the road, it strikes me that the themes are pretty much constant: being reassured that all you need to be happy with your lot is a tin roof over your head, a porch to drink beer on, a beautiful woman in your bed and mud on the soles of your shoes. AC/DC's music reassures in the same way. It elevates you by breaking down life to some pretty basic requirements: sex, drink and rock. Wherever you live, whatever your background, the intended effect is the same: to make you move with the rhythm, to forget your troubles. It's arguably why, more than any other rock band in the world, AC/DC connects with 'real' people.

They achieved that lofty status not only through graft and talent, but through the investment of time and money on the part of the people the Youngs entrusted with making their career happen. In most tellings of the AC/DC story it's those people who tend to get short shrift.

'With AC/DC we had to really put the money in,' says Greenberg. 'That's what we did. I think probably one of their big breaks was opening for Aerosmith and a couple of other big bands after they went to Leber-Krebs. It really helped. There was no MTV during those early days. The only way you could break a band was to just put them in that van and ship 'em around.'

David Krebs concurs on that point.

'I think that's true. But our management philosophy was if you loved Aerosmith there were other artists whose music we represented that you would love, so Ted Nugent broke off from Aerosmith, AC/DC broke off from Aerosmith or Nugent, Scorpions the same. We had a really good knack for picking great live acts and we tried to make sure that our support acts did not blow away our headliners or we could not do this.'

Krebs was at the Rainbow in March 1977, the same night as

Doug Thaler, and instantly wanted to sign the band. He got it straight away; as you do when you're more of a Rolling Stones and Ten Years After man than you are a sucker for The Beatles. Krebs was in the business of music with a harder edge and AC/DC fitted the bill. When he approached an initially 'receptive' Browning on behalf of Leber-Krebs to offer a co-management deal, he got turned down.

'I was foolish,' he laughs, stirring a coffee in a booth at Three Guys, a Greek diner on New York's Upper East Side. 'You know how you re-examine things you did?'

Krebs's mistake, it appears, was his involving a third party. Browning blames Peter Mensch, who was at the summit with Krebs, of talking out of school and for white-anting his relationship with the band.

'It fell apart because the guy who was going to run with them, Mensch, went back to the group and mouthed off about what went down at the meeting, so the confidentiality went out of the equation,' says Browning. 'I think that got in the way of us being able to do a deal.'

Sighs Krebs: 'I should have made a deal with him then.'

Though short of an alliance, Leber-Krebs got AC/DC dates supporting his bands. The Australians were about to hit rock music's biggest stages.

'I thought they were fabulous,' says Krebs. 'I just loved the band. I tried to help them by putting them on some of my tours. It was good for them because I had two major headliners [Aerosmith and Ted Nugent], so from a standpoint of touring I ensured the fact that they could have the right exposure.

'The move [to Leber-Krebs] eventually happened. In the course of that Aerosmith tour Peter Mensch became friendly with them, they had a falling out with Michael Browning and they wanted to sign with us for worldwide management if we established an office in London that was run by Peter. The real day-to-day manager of AC/DC was Peter Mensch.'

⚡

One of the enduring legends of the band is that they got their break by blowing the by then severely drug-addicted Aerosmith duo of Steven Tyler and Joe Perry off the stage, destroying their confidence, bruising their egos, and the rest was history.

But Steve Leber disagrees: 'No one could really destroy Aerosmith. They were a great band – they really were sensational – and AC/DC broke because of Aerosmith. Because of Aerosmith's popularity, they rose, and because of Aerosmith allowing them to be the opening act. I wouldn't say they *killed* Aerosmith but AC/DC had their own personality, their own excitement. It was different than Aerosmith's.

'By the time the guys broke, really, Bon was gone. They brought in Brian Johnson and he really wasn't as good as Bon. I wouldn't say as good. Brian was a *different* kind of lead singer. I would say the big difference is that AC/DC is led by a guitar player, Angus Young. And Aerosmith is led by a lead singer, Steven Tyler. Angus is probably one of the all-time greatest, if not *the* best lead guitar player in the world because he has personality besides having the ability to play. He's special and unique compared to other guitar players out there. Angus was one of a kind. *Is*. Not was. *Is* one of a kind.'

So was Aerosmith pissed off that AC/DC were so good?

'I wouldn't say pissed off. Just *aware*. They didn't throw them off the tour. They also didn't do any other tours together. But they broke them. And so did we.'

AC/DC, contends Krebs, also benefited from a privileged time in music history: the days before expensive videos with high production values and record-company pressure of having to come up with hit singles every release.

'If you come from the 1970s,' he says, 'you come from a philosophy of this kind of music, which is: "I like to have one hit single every two albums." In the 1980s, with the advent of MTV and giant advances for groups like Aerosmith, it's four, five hit singles. It's a whole different mentality. How many hit singles did AC/DC ever have in a pop sense?'

Well, none that broke the top 10 on the *Billboard* Hot 100. Aerosmith had eight; *nine* if you include their 1986 reprise of 'Walk This Way' with Run-DMC. The highest position AC/DC ever reached was #23 with 'Moneytalks' in 1991, though they've since gone to #1 three times on the Mainstream Rock charts with 'Hard As A Rock', 'Stiff Upper Lip' and 'Rock 'N' Roll Train'.

'Jailbreak' never did any real business as a single, only on the 1984 EP that was cynically recast in the liner notes to the 2003 reissue as 'a testament, a salute to AC/DC's tenth anniversary'. It ended up going platinum. All of which, of course, made their coming world domination even more remarkable.

5

AC/DC

'Let There Be Rock' (1977)

If Atlantic didn't know what to make of *Dirty Deeds*, they were right to be scared out of their wits with *Let There Be Rock*, an album that was recorded in a matter of weeks in early 1977 and sneerily delivered by AC/DC to their truculent overseers at 75 Rockefeller Plaza with unmistakable intent.

Let There Be Rock and its volcanic title track consigned much of the swing of *High Voltage*, *TNT* and *Dirty Deeds* to the scrapheap. Wherever AC/DC ended up in the annals of rock history, this album would stand for all time as an expression of their unrivalled might as a guitar band. Its buzzsaw electricity demanded that Jerry Greenberg and his dithering pals in New York stand up and take notice.

But they were taking a big gamble.

'AC/DC's music *was* difficult,' says Steve Leeds, at the time Atlantic's head of album promotion. 'It was the weirdest sounding thing; the weirdest thing on the musical spectrum. It just didn't sit with anything. It was loud, noisy rock 'n' roll. It was stripped down and the production was very austere. It wasn't slick. It was raw.

The vocals – Bon was like, *growling*. And it was *filthy*. She's got the jack. He's got big balls. It didn't fit in. It was atypical. Vanda & Young always pushed the envelope. With Flash and the Pan, Cheetah, AC/DC, even "Evie" by Stevie Wright, these were things that were *atypical*.

'All of AC/DC's songs had that repetitive, hard-rock rhythm, with Bon screaming over it. It was different. It didn't fit in with what was going on at the time. *Bagpipes!* There are no bagpipes on the radio, even today. George and Harry were fucking geniuses. They figured it out. Conventional wisdom says, "You guys are crazy."'

But having seen AC/DC at Fabrik in Hamburg, the man who mattered most – Greenberg – was now a believer. Asked if he was happy with *Let There Be Rock*, he says: 'Oh yeah, absolutely. Absolutely.'

$$\lightning$$

In June that year *Let There Be Rock* was released in the United States (albeit with 'Crabsody In Blue' missing) and Greenberg's *touring, touring, touring* edict was followed to the letter. By the end of July AC/DC was playing its first show (tickets $5.50) in the United States – as support for Canadian band Moxy at the Armadillo World Headquarters in Austin, Texas, having been lured there by promoter Jack Orbin. He'd heard the band played on radio station KMAC/KISS by Lou Roney and the late Joseph Yannuzzi (aka 'Joe Anthony'). In a 1978 feature, *Texas Monthly* magazine hailed KMAC/KISS as 'the champion of hard-rock radio and the last vestige of true progressive-rock programming in Texas'.

The next night the band played San Antonio, then Corpus Christi and Dallas.

'Those were the good old days for the music industry,' says Orbin. 'Lots of good bands being played on AOR stations. However, AC/DC always stood out as something special. Perhaps it was the raw rock 'n' roll beat that they drive home so well. At any rate, Lou and Joe played them and I wanted to promote them immediately. They were destined to become popular from the outset. Moxy was also a San Antonio favourite. However, AC/DC even back then played second fiddle to no one. How could they?'

Orbin won't have a bar of Jacksonville's claim to breaking the band.

'Jacksonville? Where is that? San Antonio has the reputation and the history. It was the breeding ground of some of the best, if not the very best, hard-rock bands ever. San Antonio broke all the strong hard-rock bands: AC/DC, Rush, Judas Priest, Trapeze. That's why San Antonio has the label of "Heavy Metal Capital of the World" and my company helped break them. The bands broke out of San Antonio and we used that fact to help promote them in other cities, especially in Texas. These bands all were new and upcoming but were also the cream of the crop of hard rock back then, so after the initial promotions, once they played in front of a decent audience, they exploded. Rightfully so.'

But Mark Evans never got his chance to play with AC/DC on an American stage, having been dumped from the band in May; Cliff Williams played those Texas shows. *Let There Be Rock* was the last album he'd record with AC/DC. He was only 21.

'It was a real disappointment,' he says of missing out. 'Probably on the same scale as getting the flick from the band. It was an upsetting time. It was a whole bunch of things. When you're in a band like that it's pretty much like being in a professional football team. You're just moving around to all these different grounds or gigs and you're just taken care of and you don't have to think of anything other than playing the gig. So once you're outside that sort of thing, it's like a divorce. Not only does your employment change but because you're living with the guys in the band your whole lifestyle changes. It was a wrench.'

Evans flew from London to Melbourne and straight into a charity gig where George Young and Harry Vanda were making an appearance. There was a domestic pilots' strike going on and the ex-Easybeats pair had ridden in the back of a limo all the way from Sydney.

'I remember George's exact words,' says Evans. 'He said, "Listen, you know, things happen. I wish it were different. But it's *not*."'

It was an interesting meeting for another reason; coming not long after the Reading Festival in 1976, where George had given Evans a ferocious dressing-down after a lacklustre performance.

'I've got a lot of time for George,' he says. 'I took [what happened in Reading] almost like a medal. He got stuck into me like how he got stuck into his brothers. So I didn't really take that badly. In Melbourne George actually said, "You've got to come and play bass for Stevie Wright." That was when Stevie was still very much inside the [Alberts] building. At that stage he'd started missing gigs [because of his addiction]. George wanted me to go straight into that. Not much later I was approached to join Rose Tattoo.'

At Alberts, Evans subsequently bumped into George at Studio 2 while recording with Finch (aka Contraband). He'd turn up to sessions to find the tuning on his bass had been fiddled with overnight: George had borrowed his guitar.

Does he think George had anything to do with his sacking?

'I don't think he would have been directly involved,' he says after taking about six seconds to formulate a response. 'I'm surmising here. I don't think he would have had any great issue with it.'

In fact, Evans says he is still on good terms with George and the last time he saw him they 'had a great chat and get on really well, still'.

In his autobiography, *Dirty Deeds*, there's a photo of Evans flanked by Ted Albert, Brian Johnson, Malcolm Young and Phil

Rudd, looking at a platinum record backstage at the Sydney Showgrounds in February 1981, almost four years after he'd been cast aside, the wounds still fresh. The pathos is so thick it's almost painful to behold. How did he feel?

'I felt good at that time,' he says. 'That was a bit of a funny night because really that night was the first time I'd ever seen the band play except for the Station Hotel [in Melbourne, 1975] when they were a four-piece and I first joined them. It was strange. The actual gig had been postponed twice because of wet weather so there was a bit of an unusual build-up. It was the band's first gig back in Sydney without Bon, so it was a very poignant night. But the relationship between us – I think you can tell by the way Malcolm is and the way Phil's looking at me, and Brian – we were all happy to be there. We were all very close up until that point.'

Up until that point.

Some time afterwards Evans launched a legal action over unpaid album royalties against Alberts and AC/DC that dragged on for years and was eventually settled out of court. The terms of the settlement preclude him from speaking about it in detail but he does say: 'It took a long time and it was good to get a resolution.'

In 2003, the year Evans was denied induction into the Rock and Roll Hall of Fame despite being initially invited to the ceremony with other band members, Malcolm Young ripped into him in an interview with *Classic Rock*.

'Mark actually got picked by our manager,' he told Dave Ling. 'We never wanted him; we didn't think he could play properly. We could all hold our own, and so could [AC/DC bass player in 1974] Rob Bailey. What we thought was that when we'd kicked on a bit more we could override the manager and get in a good bass player.'

It was a disgraceful comment and demands dismantling: if Bailey were so capable, why, as Tony Currenti has said, did George Young play bass on most of the songs on *High Voltage* and Bailey

'Bon [Scott] got some of his performance characteristics from Stevie,' says former Rose Tattoo guitarist Rob Riley. Stevie Wright responds humbly: 'I find it hard to believe because he was so good that I admired him.' Wright's three-part 1974 epic, 'Evie', written by Harry Vanda and George Young, was a runaway hit in Australia but didn't take off in America.

COURTESY OF TONY CURRENTI

JESSE FINK

AC/DC and Stevie Wright session drummer Tony Currenti takes a cigarette break at his pizzeria in Penshurst, Sydney. Currenti played most of the drums on 1975's *High Voltage*. He taught himself how to play drums by bashing whatever he could find with spoons. INSET: Currenti (CENTRE) as a child in Italy.

DICK BARNATT

Bon Scott (LEFT) in London, 1976, with AC/DC manager Michael Browning (CENTRE) and the routinely misidentified Australian radio personality Ken Evans (RIGHT), program director for Radio Luxembourg and formerly of pirate stations Radio Caroline and Radio Atlanta.

American radio's first champion of AC/DC, Jacksonville's Bill Bartlett (CENTRE), with fellow DJ Lee Walsh (LEFT) and visiting 2JJ Sydney station coordinator Ron Moss (RIGHT). Moss headed 2JJ when Holger Brockmann played 'It's A Long Way To The Top' on radio for the first time anywhere in the world. And Brockmann didn't just play the song once. He loved it so much that he played it *five* times in a row.

Mark Evans fitted so well aesthetically and musically with AC/DC but was dramatically sacked by the Youngs in 1977, just before the band's first tour of the United States. 'It's like a divorce,' he says. 'Not only does your employment change but because you're living with the guys in the band your whole lifestyle changes. It was a wrench.'

Designer Gerard Huerta with the AC/DC logo commissioned solely for the US release of *Let There Be Rock*. He has not received any royalties for the logo's subsequent use on other AC/DC albums or in AC/DC merchandise.

COURTESY OF TOM HUERTA

COURTESY OF TOM HUERTA

The original artwork, which was inspired by the letterforms of the Gutenberg Bible. Says Huerta: 'It is the only piece of lettering I have done that is made entirely of straight lines.'

All eyes on the 'atomic microbe' during the recording of *Live From The Atlantic Studios*, New York City, 1977. ALSO PICTURED: Atlantic promotion executive Judy Libow (THIRD FROM LEFT AT FRONT), radio program director and future MTV founder Robert Pittman (RIGHT OF LIBOW), AC/DC's US publisher Barry Bergman (BEHIND BON SCOTT, IN GLASSES), Atlantic promotion executive Perry Cooper (BEHIND ANGUS YOUNG) and Philadelphia DJ Ed Sciaky (RIGHT OF COOPER).

In New York, 1977, with two giants of Atlantic Records: marketing and promotion executive Michael Klenfner (LEFT) and co-founder Ahmet Ertegun (CENTRE). Klenfner, widely regarded inside Atlantic as the band's champion, would get fired over his resistance to Mutt Lange as producer of *Highway To Hell*. Ertegun was a crucial player behind the US success of the INXS-Jimmy Barnes cover of The Easybeats track 'Good Times'.

One of a treasure trove of seldom seen AC/DC images from the *Powerage* sessions in Sydney, 1978, never before published in book form. FROM LEFT TO RIGHT: Malcolm Young, music journalist and later record-company executive Jon O'Rourke and Angus Young.

'Malcolm no doubt was the leader of the band,' says *Powerage* engineer Mark Opitz. 'George had had his day with The Easybeats. Not strongly, not overtly, but you could feel during *Powerage* Malcolm was starting to stake his ground a bit [in the brothers' pecking order].'

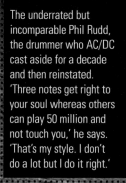

The underrated but incomparable Phil Rudd, the drummer who AC/DC cast aside for a decade and then reinstated. 'Three notes get right to your soul whereas others can play 50 million and not touch you,' he says. 'That's my style. I don't do a lot but I do it right.'

Phil Rudd (RIGHT) lights a cigarette for George Young during the sessions for *Powerage*, considered by aficionados to be AC/DC's best album. As a bass player George is 'a little bit similar to how Ronnie Lane was with The Small Faces', according to Mark Evans. 'Very loopy and very notey, but he always picks the great lines.'

Mark Opitz (LEFT) with Harry Vanda recording *Powerage*. Says Opitz: 'In a way it was AC/DC's *Sgt. Pepper's*. When we came to do *Powerage*, George, Harry and the band did serious rehearsals at Studio 2 in Alberts. George playing bass with the band just out in the studio, Harry and me in the control room.' Opitz later produced the INXS-Jimmy Barnes cover of 'Good Times'.

LEO GOZBEKIAN

Possessed! Angus Young with Tony Berardini, the DJ who broke AC/DC at KTIM in San Rafael, California, and at WBCN in Boston. Berardini MCed their gig at Paradise Theater, Boston, 1978.

On stage at Royal Oak Theater, Michigan, 1978. 'Angus and Malcolm both play off each other so well that it almost sounds like one massive wall of power,' says Rhino Bucket's Georg Dolivo.

TOM WESCHLER

ROBERT ALFORD

'[Bon] was the best,' says Steve Leber of AC/DC's legendary and much-missed singer, here pictured at Cobo Arena, Detroit, 1978. 'When he was alive there was nothing like it.' Could AC/DC have got as big without him?

Ex-Atlantic president Jerry Greenberg believes he was instrumental to AC/DC's success: 'I supported them not only with coming down from the presidential office to the troops [and telling them] that they needed this band but also by writing the cheques. AC/DC were very heavily in the red before they finally broke.' Greenberg was also behind the push to hire Mutt Lange.

The man who signed AC/DC to Atlantic in 1975, Phil Carson, playing bass with Robert Plant. 'AC/DC saw me as their ally in much the same way that I was treated by Led Zeppelin,' he says. 'AC/DC wanted that personal contact with the guy at the label who really had decision-making capabilities that could change their lives.'

ROBERT ALFORD

Publicity-shy AC/DC manager Peter Mensch (LEFT) with Bun E. Carlos and Robin Zander (HOLDING POOL CUE) of Cheap Trick and Bon Scott in Germany, 1979. AC/DC sacked Mensch after the Monsters of Rock concert at Castle Donington, England, 1981. He now manages Metallica and Red Hot Chili Peppers.

JESSE FINK

SIDE ONE
1. DIRTY DEEDS DONE DIRT CHEAP
2. LOVE AT FIRST FEEL
3. BIG BALLS
4. ROCKER
5. PROBLEM CHILD

SIDE TWO
1. THERE'S GONNA BE SOME ROCKIN'
2. AIN'T NO FUN WAITING ROUND TO BE A MILLIONAIRE
3. RIDE ON
4. SQUEALER

Rocker—Studio version. Live version previously released on Atlantic SD 19212—
'If You Want Blood You've Got It'

Problem Child previously released on Atco SD 36-151— 'Let There Be Rock'

All selections recorded in 1976

COLOR TV

The 1981 US version of the long-shelved *Dirty Deeds Done Dirt Cheap* conspicuously missing 'Jailbreak', a song deemed 'too horrific for teenage consumption'. Released after *Back In Black* and before *For Those About To Rock*, Phil Carson considers the timing of its exhuming 'one of the most crass decisions ever made by a record-company executive'.

A rare photo of Mutt Lange with AC/DC, Paris, 1981. FROM LEFT TO RIGHT: Brian Johnson, Malcolm Young, David Thoener (IN GLASSES), assistant engineer Mark Haliday and Lange. 'It was a privilege and honour to work with AC/DC and Mutt, and I will forever be grateful,' says *For Those About To Rock* engineer Thoener, who went on to win two Grammys for his work with Santana.

Thoener with Johnson. 'I never worked with AC/DC again because I never got a call,' he says. 'That's something an engineer/mixer gets used to. Even though you can work on a record that sells millions, it doesn't mean you'll get a call the next time they record. In a year's time there's a new "hot" guy that people want to check out.'

Rose Tattoo were 'more primitive and raucous than AC/DC' but Jerry Greenberg couldn't break Australia's tattooed wild boys in the United States. FROM LEFT TO RIGHT: Rob Riley, Pete Wells, Greenberg, Dallas 'Digger' Royall, Angry Anderson and Geordie Leach.

An AC/DC pinball machine in Chinatown, New York, 2013. The Youngs' musical output has dried up but Gerard Huerta's logo and the band's catalogue continue to produce rivers of gold.

Brian Johnson pretends to strangle Perry Cooper while Ellen Young, Angus's wife, offers her hand. Says Renée Cooper, Perry's daughter: 'AC/DC and my father were really tight. After Bon died, my dad and Brian became best friends. When Bon passed, they found the emergency-person-to-contact card and it was my dad.'

Angus in full flight during the unstoppable *Back In Black* era. Comments AC/DC's longtime film and concert director David Mallet: 'Pink Floyd is about a spectacle. Each song, each number in concert has a different type of spectacle. AC/DC is about the same spectacle every time. Called Angus Young.'

AC/DC performs on their *Black Ice* tour in Sydney, 2010. 'I don't think AC/DC are capable of changing their format because they have no desire to,' says Australian rock singer and Young family friend John Swan. 'It's a work in progress. As long as my arse points towards the floor, AC/DC will be AC/DC and they will never be anything else.'

walk away disgruntled, soon to be sacked? You only need to watch early videos of AC/DC – such as the clip for 'It's A Long Way To The Top'– or listen to a bootleg of a live performance of 'Jailbreak' to appreciate how wonderful Evans really was and how well he suited the group, aesthetically and musically.

Worse, Malcolm also took a cheap shot at Dave Evans. No matter what you think of AC/DC with self-proclaimed 'badass' Evans out front – and few have kind words for that incarnation of the band – no one deserves to be ridiculed in the manner in which Malcolm spoke of their first lead singer: 'The day we fucking got rid of him, that's the day the band started.'

Dave Evans is bemused by it all: 'I don't know anything about it as I don't follow them at all. Malcolm is still resentful that I was so popular, especially with the female fans. He never had a girlfriend the whole time I knew him. He was always pissed off that [drummer] Colin Burgess and I always had plenty of female company. As far as Malcolm was concerned they were all molls. He was quite bitter about it.

'He was glad to get rid of Colin and myself. If he still has resentment after all these years and his success then let the public judge his behaviour . . . he was always a hater and seems to still be. People usually put others down to try to make themselves bigger in the eyes of other people. It usually is a sign of insecurity.'

⚡

To his considerable advantage, Cliff Williams looked even *more* like a Young than Mark Evans did – and he could play a bit. But the replacement of Evans (and other band members before him) at least firmly debunked one myth about the Youngs. For all their talk of 'no bullshit', how the band looks is important. It's just a less obvious form of bullshit.

Was image a consideration in his being replaced?

'I don't think it was image that was the problem,' says Evans. 'I think the change between Cliff and myself was fairly seamless. I've had people send me videos, saying, "This is you in England." Some I've watched two or three times and gone, "Fuck." The only thing that sets you off [on my difference with Cliff] is the bass. There was quite a similarity.'

Evans says he never even thought about whether his replacement was better than he was. They became friends and the pair lunch together when Williams is in Sydney. Did Williams ever express to Evans how he felt about taking over the role from him in the circumstances?

'That never came up. We never spoke about that. Basically because it didn't really matter. I'm sure he didn't think and I know I certainly didn't think it was relevant.'

Did Evans ever wonder to himself, 'Hang on. Why the fuck did you guys replace me? What's Cliff offering that I'm not?'

'That's interesting. Honestly, I've never thought about that.' He pauses. 'Because of the way Angus and Malcolm are and the way they do things, it was so damn final when it happened. It wasn't a surprise; it was a shock. It's like a death in the family. It just goes *bang*. And you go, "Well, okay, there's nothing I can change about this." So it's not worth revisiting. There's really nothing you can do about it. If I were to ask, "What's Cliff got that I haven't got?" I think that would only come forward if you were thinking, "Well, how can I get back in?" or "What can I do to change this at all?" Because of the finality of it and the large bucketful of relief that came along with it, it was just like, "Oh, okay, fine."'

But in Williams the missing link had been located, according to Mark Opitz: 'They wanted someone who could really hold down Phil Rudd, and Cliffy did.'

'Phil's four-on-the-floor style with little embroidery is the root of it all and Malcolm's rhythm playing is at its heart,' argues

Phil Carson, who famously played bass with them on stage in Belgium in 1981. 'When Cliff joined the band, the rhythm section completed the ultimate puzzle. As an ex-musician myself, I know how difficult it is to bury one's ego for the good of the band and those three guys did exactly that. To this day, if you watch an AC/DC concert, the rhythm section does what it's supposed to do. It gives space to Angus and to Brian, and the result is an overwhelming juggernaut.'

Says Tony Platt: 'Cliff is the perfect bass player for AC/DC because he does the job. He's a great bass player. Quite underrated in a lot of respects because it isn't easy to do what he does and keep it absolutely solid. He's a great singer as well, so he helps out hugely with the backing vocals. And of course he looks the part.'

Adds Rob Riley, with typical forthrightness: 'Fuck me. Cliff Williams, well, he drops right in with Mal and it's all simple and accessible. Nice, solid and fucking stompy.'

⚡

In August 1977, AC/DC went to Florida where, thanks to Bill Bartlett, Jacksonville had already been conquered. But the Australians had bruised a few egos, none bigger than those in Lynyrd Skynyrd. The popular tale is that the two bands were great mates, hanging out at the local group's compound in the backwoods, Skynyrd even inviting AC/DC for a ride on their private Convair CV-300 – the same plane that crashed killing Ronnie Van Zant, Steve Gaines and Cassie Gaines and three others that coming October.

Yet Bartlett has another story.

'AC/DC was so big in Jacksonville that they *outsold* Lynyrd Skynyrd,' he says. 'I'd known Skynyrd since I was 13 years old, as I went to school with several of the members of the band. I remember at the time that Ronnie was not all that happy that they had been upstaged by this Aussie band.

'One night, I made a statement on the radio that AC/DC was outrequesting and outselling hometown boys Lynyrd Skynyrd. Ronnie immediately called me up on the radio and said he was coming out to "talk" to me. He came to the station and I showed him the sales data and request data that I collected and he was baffled. His last words to me that night were, "AC/DC *huh*?"'

With Atlantic now right behind them, American audiences beginning to fall under their spell and their most exhilarating album yet under their belts, AC/DC's long way to the top was rapidly shortening. But, according to Riley, it was mostly credit to Alberts not Atlantic.

'They were the rock company of Australia and that's where AC/DC got their liftoff,' he says. 'They had support from Alberts that gave them the ability to go on tour, relentlessly, all through England and Europe.'

Interestingly, Chris Gilbey, who arrived in Australia from England in November 1972 and started working for Alberts in January 1973, says that while the company's commitment to AC/DC was substantial it wasn't because Alberts had a mission to be the rock 'n' roll record label from hell.

He evokes an image of Alberts that is at odds with its reputation as the Mordor of Australian hard rock, recalling how when he turned up in a cheap but elegantly tailored Penang white suit, about to head up their publicity and marketing, the offices were 'all oak panels and elderly ladies walking softly across deep pile carpets, keeping as quiet as they could' and 'like a gentleman's club: leather overstuffed chairs, bookshelves, an antique tooled leather desk'. It was largely Gilbey's industry and his versatility – he'd recorded three singles in his own right in England with a band called Kate, would go on to manage The Saints and produce The Church's first album – combined with the creativity of Vanda & Young and the passion and deep pockets of Ted Albert that gave AC/DC that initial liftoff. Gilbey would leave Alberts in 1977.

'I happened to arrive in Australia when Ted was trying to get the business energised and I think I provided the street smarts and energy he needed,' he says. 'George and Harry arrived back in the country around the same time. They hadn't been able to cut it in London and came back to Sydney to make a fresh start. They convinced Ted to fund them in a little eight-track studio that they built at one of their homes, I believe. They had a bunch of unfinished songs in their heads, and then started recording. They kept very much to themselves. But why wouldn't they? The company then was so 19th century, it was ridiculous.

'Alberts wasn't run on corporate guidelines. It was a small business. But that was paradoxically its strength. So there were several nodes to the business: there was Ted, who was the rich uncle who wrote the cheques, and who had a genuine love of the music business, because he just loved it. He kept his father happy; he was a very straight-laced old money scion. Then there was Brian Byrne, the chief financial officer, who would have preferred that the record label be discontinued because it was a drain on cash. But he had to indulge the whims of the younger son of the family. Then there were the two older brothers, who both became lawyers and who said that they gave the music company to Ted because he couldn't get a proper job.'

But, in the end, old money and rich fathers besides, what pushed AC/DC over the line was the work ethic of the Youngs: sheer graft and unrelenting determination.

'Those fucking blokes, they really did put in the hard yards,' argues Riley. 'That and the fact their music was so accessible to normal people is what put them on the map. That persistence. It's incredible. The rest is history. They got out there and did the hard yards with good catchy songs and Bon Scott, who had a cheeky grin and a fantastic ability to charm people. They had an amazing thing going, which got the ball rolling.'

⚡

It's a good point by Riley about Scott's charm. Were it not for Scott's force of personality, startling showmanship, vocal delivery and lyrical contribution, AC/DC most likely wouldn't have become the titanic stadium band they are today. Not just because the long-dead, much-loved singer, frequently regarded as the most charismatic frontman of all time (and undoubtedly worthy of being spoken of in the same breath as Mick Jagger, Freddie Mercury, Robert Plant and Jim Morrison), made up for whatever social skills the Youngs might have lacked. Rather, their set list would be very thin. Most of what AC/DC performs today in concert was co-written by Scott during the six years he spent writing what he called 'toilet poetry' for the band. He was a clever writer as much as he was the waking nightmare of every father with a beautiful teenage daughter.

As Mark Gable puts it: 'I will always go back to AC/DC's early albums to listen to that raw energy and absolute fun that they must've been having. Bon Scott's lyrics were amazing. If you want genius lyric writing then just read out the lyrics to "Let There Be Rock".'

Certainly, as true originals go, Scott likely will never be surpassed: a hard-drinking, substance-abusing, book-reading, poetry-writing, groupie-shagging, asthmatic, wild-eyed, square-chested, snaggle-toothed Fagin to the scamps that made up the rest of the band.

'Bon Scott's high-waisted flares and Sharpie haircut were definitely cringe inducing to a teenager in tight Levis and cowboy boots,' says Radio Birdman guitarist Chris Masuak, who first saw AC/DC on Australia's *Countdown* TV program in 1975. 'Still, there was something likable about him. He was kind of cheeky and tough, despite his questionable dress sense. And those early clips gave me the impression that they were a kind of novelty act. I slotted Angus in his school uniform in the same bag as Skyhooks, who I loathed more than words could convey.'

But AC/DC proved to be no novelty act, thanks largely to Scott, who gave the band an identity, edge and singleminded purpose that their previous singer could not.

'He was the best,' says Steve Leber. 'When he was alive there was nothing like it. He and Angus were amazing.'

The impact on the band's fans was just as strong. The awful manner of Scott's demise in 1980, his exceptional body of work (created in such a short space of time) and the good vibes that trailed in his wake like magic dust have long combined to enthral not only the band's tens of millions of hard-core fans but rock journalists, biographers and directors.

'One of the greatest rock singers in the history of popular music,' says Phil Carson. 'He was a charismatic performer who lived the life.'

And one who didn't tolerate pomposity, no matter the levels of society in which he moved. Kim Fowley recalled dining in an expensive Sydney restaurant with Scott, Harry Vanda and George Young in the late 1970s: 'Bon reprimanded the waiter for being rude to his teenage girl dinner date, who didn't know how to order from the fancy menu.'

⚡

The reclamation of Scott as a modern folk hero started back in 1994 with Clinton Walker's still-to-be-bettered biography of the man, *Highway To Hell*, and probably reached its pop-culture apotheosis in the 2004 Australian movie *Thunderstruck*. Featuring a pre-*Avatar* Sam Worthington, it's about four young men who travel across the Nullarbor with the ashes of their dead friend (Worthington's 'Ronnie') on a pilgrimage to the singer's gravesite in Fremantle. When it was released in the United States, *Variety* magazine said the 'under-representation of AC/DC music will disappoint audiences seeking an Oz equivalent of *Detroit Rock City*'. It not only disappointed audiences. It bombed for all sorts of reasons, not least that it wasn't a very good movie. But in Hollywood at an Australia Day party in 2013 I met one of its stars, the Australian actor Ryan Johnson, who played 'Lloyd'. According to Johnson, when the producers asked Alberts if they could briefly use AC/DC songs they were told it would cost $250,000 . . . *a song*. The director, Darren Ashton, won't be drawn on the figure for the three songs that were eventually used.

'It wasn't so much about the money for AC/DC but about the content of the film,' he says.

But if that were really so, why charge at all? Hollywood studios can easily afford that sort of coin, but not struggling indie filmmakers. What do AC/DC's Australian handlers care if there's money to be made?

Rumours have circulated that Alberts also refused to allow the band to be used as characters in the film. The band members' faces are darkened and obscured in the concert that opens the movie. In the one scene featuring a character referred to as 'Angus', only the back of his head is seen. Ashton did not respond when I asked if this stipulation was indeed true.

Each year brings whispers of another tribute to or commemoration of Scott, most of which never achieve realisation. Vince Lovegrove, Scott's former bandmate in The Valentines, was killed in a car accident in northern New South Wales in 2012. His daughter Holly confirms that he was writing a 'movie script on Bon pre-AC/DC' and though her father and the Youngs never got on they had been 'extremely generous to us since he died'.

There has been the *Bonfire* box-set release. There's Bonfest in Kirriemuir, Scotland, where Scott was raised as a child before leaving for Australia and there is a campaign to erect a bronze statue in his memory. (He was born in nearby Forfar.) Perth television screened a documentary called *Bon Scott: A Tribute* in 2006. A feature film project called *Bon Scott* received seed money from the Australian government in 2011 but was purportedly knocked on the head by Alberts. During the writing of this book, a stage show called *The Story Of Bon Scott: Hell Ain't A Bad Place To Be* was due to open in Melbourne; a Sydney producer was trying to get *Bon: The Musical* greenlighted by the Youngs; and an American film production company was trying to drum up investors for *Bon Scott: The Legend Of AC/DC*, a biopic of Scott's final days in London, to be filmed in (of all places) South Carolina. Lawyers representing AC/DC and the estate of Bon Scott later sent the producers cease-and-desist letters.

What else is there to say about his story? Not much.

What hope do all these projects have when the AC/DC brand is protected so ferociously by the Youngs? Very little.

Why so much resistance to celebrating the band's greatest icon?

Alvin Handwerker, AC/DC's manager, is said to be of the view that Scott is ancient history and Brian Johnson has been the lead singer for the lion's share of the time the band has been around: the focus should be on Johnson. If that is so, it's remarkably shortsighted, if not stupid, and takes AC/DC's audience for idiots.

There isn't a part of the world where what Scott has come to represent – living life by your own rules – doesn't entrance people. He stands for a positive message even if the circumstances of his death were atrocious. In death, like so many rock stars before and after him, he is far more appreciated than he ever was when he was alive.

That AC/DC has gone on to become even bigger without him, despite the fact that for 30 years the Youngs have had an ordinary lyricist in Brian Johnson or simply done away with him altogether and shared lyric-writing duties between themselves, is extraordinary. Johnson stopped writing – or was asked to stop writing – in 1988. The Youngs have handled everything since, either because they thought they could do it just as well or better, a desire for complete creative control or, as their critics will tell you, outright greed.

In *Why AC/DC Matters*, Anthony Bozza writes: 'As the '70s gave way to the '80s, it was an unplanned but impeccably fitting aesthetic shift for the band. Johnson's blunt, observational, often nonlinear lyrics suited the ADD-addled, video-saturated times ahead, whereas Scott's lyrical storytelling suited a more organic, gilded age of rock and roll.'

Or he simply wasn't as good.

$$\lightning$$

Let There Be Rock marked a young Mark Opitz's first introduction to production. He had been working in Sydney as a local artist label manager for EMI, Alberts' distribution company, but got sacked for what he calls 'stupid, erroneous reasons'. Harry Vanda and George Young took him on as an apprentice producer.

'I was there at the transition of AC/DC's sound from sleazy pop-rock to rock,' he says. 'I can remember the very first time I heard the song "Let There Be Rock"; that was the first major change, that one song. That was *it*. That was the indicator. I don't think the album *Let There Be Rock* totally pointed overall to the change but the song did. Because it had that intro, it had the feel, and it wasn't a spoof on girls or a rock love song, so to speak, like "The Jack" or "Whole Lotta Rosie". The lyrical content had changed as well.

'In the early days, knowing George and Harry on the first albums, they would have been stuck right in. They'd almost be *writing* the songs. Malcolm would come up with a riff and then they'd just be like, "Okay, let's do that, let's do that and let's do *that*", and of course in those days Malcolm and Angus would have gone along with it because they'd be thinking, "Yeah, that's working, it sorta *sounds* like us." I guess it wasn't until that maturation of *Let There Be Rock* and then having a couple of American tours under their belt and starting to feel good about themselves that, like most bands, the process of one and one equalling three started.'

'The closest to it was Ted Nugent,' says Doug Thaler of the album and its title track. 'From 1975 to '77, Ted was the hardest rocker on the scene and AC/DC came and just upped that by a little bit. It was power rock. But it wasn't noise rock. It had form. It was played tightly.'

And that is what makes it like nothing AC/DC has done before or since. Right from the clack of Phil Rudd's sticks, 'Let There Be Rock' is full throttle. The Youngs' guitars – the hammer of Malcolm, the bolt of Angus – are so ferocious they smoke. The rhythm section undulates beneath them like the quick breathing of a man who's had his chest slashed with a knife. The music is so intense, for once even the teeth-gnashing Scott seems superfluous to it all. When there is some respite from the onslaught – drums, bass and vocals keeping the Youngs at bay like snapping dogs on a chain – it starts all over again . . . and then again, until it enters what Clinton Walker accurately describes as 'a realm of pure white noise'. 'Let There Be Rock' is a band pushed to its playing limits but not missing a beat. It is six-and-a-bit minutes of beauty, chaos, precision and primal fire.

Mark Evans is also convinced it was a watershed moment for AC/DC: 'That was when the band really started being the band.'

What about the title track?

'Phil Rudd.'

Right. That's it?

'That's it,' he replies, laughing. 'Brilliant, man. Just like fucking no one else. Brilliant drummer. As much as Charlie Watts is The Rolling Stones, Phil is AC/DC.'

Without question *Let There Be Rock* was the high point of Evans's tenure with AC/DC. But in the 2003 Sony compact-disc reissue with its lavish 14-page booklet and multiple shots of Bon Scott, Angus and Malcolm, there isn't even one clear photo of the bass player. In all of the photos of the band on stage (bar Evans's dark silhouette on the cover, back facing to camera, and one where the headstock and neck of his guitar, a leg and the top of his head is visible behind Scott) he's been miraculously eliminated. Wiped from the face of the earth. Not satisfied with the beating to Evans's ego the first time around, the Youngs appear to have struck again with a vengeance.

In another booklet photo, one from their first US tour, his replacement, Williams, has been cropped out. For the *Let There Be Rock* reissue, AC/DC effectively is a band without a bass player.

What does Evans make of his being omitted?

'It doesn't surprise me all that much.'

Why?

'That's the way it is.'

But there are photos of the band on stage and we can't see you.

'I've got to be honest with you. I didn't even know that [before you told me]. It's not something I pay attention to.'

You weren't aware of that?

'It doesn't bother me one bit. It's a non-issue.'

Cliff's been taken out of some photos, too.

'Well, there you go,' he laughs. 'Really, I'm surprised.'

There's no photos of you. There's no bass player.

'Oh really? Like The Doors?'

In the other reissues, you're there, but in *Let There Be Rock*, it's like you don't exist.

'There you go,' he laughs. 'Was I *really* there?'

Mark Evans wasn't the only person who worked on the album to be denied due recognition. The man who designed AC/DC's iconic logo, Gerard Huerta, saw it used on the US issue of *Let There Be Rock* for the very first time. It was, he claims, a one-off commission specifically for that album.

'I still have the purchase order and invoice for the job,' he says. 'I was paid what was fair for an album lettering job at the time. It was done for a specific album. They used something else for a follow-up album [*Powerage*], then came back to this.'

But ever since it's been used on anything to do with the band. It is a huge part of their appeal, immediately identifiable, religiously worshipped, commercially *extremely* lucrative.

In papers filed in 1996 and registered with the United States Patent and Trademark Office in 2003, a Dutch company called Leidseplein Presse B.V. (a name commonly seen in the fine print of AC/DC products) makes a trademark claim for the logo on such products as 'pennants made of paper and mounted on sticks', 'decals and windshield decals strips', 'corrugated cardboard storage boxes', 'beach coverup dresses' and 'diaper sets'. Similar claims have been made on the name and design around the world. Leidseplein Presse B.V. even successfully appealed to the Trademark Trial and Appeal Board after Angus's well-known caricature of himself as the devil was initially rejected as a trademark.

Who or what exactly is Leidseplein Presse B.V.?

There are few clues but a 1981 article in *Billboard* mentions AC/DC 'was establishing a Netherland [sic] Antilles corporation, Leidesplein [sic] B.V.'. More interestingly, in a typed 2004 letter from Leidseplein Presse B.V. to the United States Commissioner of Trademarks, the name Stuart Prager has been written, in pen, over the top of AC/DC manager Alvin Handwerker. It is signed by Prager.

The letter begins: 'Stuart Prager declares that he is a proxyholder of the managing director of applicant corporation and is authorised to make this declaration on behalf of said applicant.'

In 2004 Prager, of New York law firm Clark & Prager, was AC/DC's attorney. Leidseplein Presse B.V. gives its address in tendered documents as being in The Netherlands, suggesting that if it was originally created in the Caribbean, it had since moved to Europe.

But why a Dutch entity in the first place? One explanation could be tax. Or rather, little or no tax. The very same reason AC/DC had recorded *Back In Black* in The Bahamas, a country with virtually no taxes. It was in AC/DC's interests to stay out of England to avoid 'tax resident' status.

Writes Martin Van Geest, author of the Dutch book *Het Belastingparadijs* (in English, *The Tax Haven*), for Amsterdam magazine *The International Correspondent*: 'Earnings derived from intellectual property such as royalties are taxed at rates close to zero in The Netherlands. This makes it extremely lucrative for artists to transfer a part of their assets, such as the copyright on songs, to a Dutch entity.'

The Rolling Stones is one such act.

'Arguably the most tax-savvy band of all. According to legal documents that were made public a couple of years ago, three band members, Keith Richards, Mick Jagger and Charlie Watts, have channelled over 340 million Euros through their Dutch "headquarters". All in all, they have paid just 5.6 million Euros in taxes on those earnings, or 1.5 per cent. Makes you wonder what their song "Gimme Shelter" was really about.'

And it may possibly account for why the Youngs spend so much time outside of Australia, given its oppressive tax dragnet.

⚡

Even when their records stink, there are still fans willing to fork out $20 for an AC/DC T-shirt because, well, they look really fucking cool because of Huerta's logo. Chicks dig it. Wimps can walk tall wearing it.

Huerta hasn't received a dime.

'No royalties. Although it would be nice to have earned a bit on the merchandising so I can get my last kid through college.'

In Murray Engleheart's biography of AC/DC, the logo is credited to Bob Defrin, Atlantic's creative director, but Defrin only came up with the cover image for the album. The logo, one of the most important and recognisable in music if not design history, was the invention of Huerta, then a 25-year-old from Los Angeles who'd also come up with the lettering for *High Voltage*'s US release in July 1976.

'Bob put together the visual of the band and sky for the cover,' says Huerta. 'Typically he would hire me, as most record art directors did, to produce multiple sketch ideas and then one was chosen for a final. I produced [the AC/DC logo] as finished full-colour artwork, a combination of India-inked outline, colour overlay film and airbrushed gouache.'

For a man who has contributed such an important element of AC/DC's branding, and consequently could be seen to have helped make the Youngs and their record companies a fortune in merchandising sales, you would think Huerta would get a royalty, especially when the logo was designed for one album, not for AC/DC's use for perpetuity. Not so. He only ever got his original commission fee. Nor has he ever had any contact with the band. Not a phone call. *Nothing.* He hasn't got lawyers involved; he's just let it be. The original artwork is stored away in a box in his archives, untouched.

'It was 25 April 1977 when I completed that artwork,' says Huerta, who's also designed logos for Boston, Foreigner, *Time* magazine and Pepsi. 'I was living and working at 210 East 53rd Street in New York City. My studio was a second bedroom and I had been freelancing for a little over a year; this was after a year and four months' employment at CBS Records as an album-cover designer.

'I came to New York right out of school. I had a portfolio that reflected more of a Los Angeles influence, and that included the record business out there. In New York most of the lettering solutions tended to be more conservative or corporate, and my solutions tended to be more experimental, something certainly suited to the record-business art departments that were always looking for something unique.'

Assuming it was purely coincidental, there's a touch of AC/DC's font in Meat Loaf's *Bat Out Of Hell* font by Richard Corben, which was released in October 1977. *Let There Be Rock* was released in June. How did it come about?

'I had produced a lettering design for a live Blue Öyster Cult album in 1975 called *On Your Feet Or On Your Knees*. The cover showed a distorted ominous photo of a church with a limousine in front. It was photographed by John Berg, the creative director at CBS, and with some multiple photo composition and retouching it was great. As I viewed the photo and began sketching, it occurred to me that Gutenberg-inspired letterforms might make an interesting look for this fire-and-brimstone photo. Being influenced by the limo, I combined the letterforms with a car marque metallic bevelled-lettering style and was happy with the result. A couple of years later when sketching up the AC/DC lettering, again the Gutenberg style seemed to work with the art of the band and the dark ominous sky on the cover.

'So the letterforms are based on the first printed book, which was the Gutenberg Bible. You can see many samples now on Google Images, although it took a bit of research in those days.

Gutenberg developed movable type and alternate characters of letters so that his work would replicate the hand-lettered work that scribes produced. This style was certainly German but I think in both cases where I used the type style, the twist in making it a car marque on BÖC or the dimension and tight packing together of the letterforms on "AC/DC" gives it a different context.

'The drawing of the AC/DC lettering, with its less than generous letter spacing and the lightning bolt that is drawn as if it is a letterform, makes it read not as five individual characters but one complete symbol or mark. Its perimeter is serrated and sharp. A traditional "A" is a triangle shape, a traditional "C" is based on an ellipse or circle, and a "D" is a combination straight and curve. All of these letterforms have been forced into a perfect vertical and slightly adjusted 45-degree angle. One comment I make about this lettering: it is the only piece of lettering I have done that is made entirely of straight lines.'

And one that has gone on to be almost a cliché. Hard rock and Gothic-style logos go hand in hand.

'I have not found anything predating this style for a band but I could be wrong,' he says. 'I did not intend that it should be the look for certain kinds of rock, as I was just designing what I thought would work for an album cover and a band. But when I saw the Blue Öyster Cult-influenced Spinal Tap logo in the '80s it was clear this look had become the classic rock parody.'

Surely it irks him that he hasn't got the acclamation and financial reward that some would argue he is due? I ask him how he feels about the logo being used on virtually all of AC/DC's albums and merchandise when it was done for a stand-alone album.

'You did these jobs, then another, and another, and so on. There was a break in the use of that art and by that time I was on to other work. You see, that same year, 1977, just a few months later I worked on another four-letter word, the masthead for *Time* magazine, which paid probably 10 times what a piece of lettering for an album did.

'I was moving into other areas and was pretty much out of the record business by 1979. Technically, Atlantic did not own the rights to use it on other albums but I am not one to go after people. Art never paid well enough to even hire a lawyer. It takes too long for what you are paid.

'You can't copyright fonts because you can't copyright a letter of the alphabet. So you do your art and move on. Besides, the effect to my own business of having done that art is difficult to calculate, but certainly positive. For every AC/DC there are quite a few more that are much more beautiful and interesting to me, but didn't have the legs for whatever reasons.'

When you see how big AC/DC have become do you feel a sense of satisfaction that you were part of creating their image?

'In a word, yes,' he replies. 'But one must understand that there are two components to a successful brand identity. One is the design. The second is the exposure. This band is still touring after more than 40 years and you now have generations who have seen and associated the band with this logo. That has more to do with the success of the logo than its design.'

Maybe so, and it says a lot about Huerta that he can show such equanimity having potentially been denied a fortune, but his stroke of inspiration was still a part of the Youngs' success. He deserved more from AC/DC and their record company.

But arguably so do many others in the AC/DC story who have similar tales of lack of recognition or under-appreciation.

For all their wealth, fame and success, that questionable treatment, and the bad reputation that comes with it, is the Youngs' cross to bear – Glasgow mentality or not.

Manhattan, New York, early 2013. I walk down Mott Street from Nolita into Chinatown, a teeming, *Blade Runner*-like warren of supermarkets and pushy old Chinese ladies. Here it's normal to be confronted by buckets of live frogs and hacked crocodile arms, but instead I come across something more exotic: an old-school video-game parlour.

Right out the front is an AC/DC pinball machine.

New York had seen AC/DC play at The Palladium on East 14th Street and legendary punk club CBGB on The Bowery in August 1977, on the same night, but both venues had been demolished and closed down respectively by the time I got there. CBGB had been swallowed up by a John Varvatos store.

Atlantic's Steve Leeds was in the club the night AC/DC played.

'At The Palladium they announced: "For those of you who want more AC/DC, we're going to be over at CBGB afterwards." *Oh my God*,' he recalls. 'I think it was the last time and only time CBGB was clean because the sound just shook all the spiderwebs and dust out of the place. There were lines around the corner. People couldn't believe AC/DC were playing CBGB. It was an abbreviated set but it was so packed. You couldn't move.'

The old Atlantic Studios, where that December AC/DC recorded *Live From The Atlantic Studios* (a promotional-only release for radio stations that was included in the 1997 *Bonfire* box set), are also long gone, though Electric Lady Studios, where guitar and vocal overdubs for *Back In Black* were recorded in June 1980, survives in Greenwich Village.

Live From The Atlantic Studios, introduced by Ed Sciaky from Philadelphia radio station WIOQ, is a classic example of the quiet but important behind-the-scenes work Atlantic did for AC/DC. The key people behind it were Michael Klenfner, who died in 2009, and Judy Libow. The late Perry Cooper, who was in charge of artist relations, is credited in the Wall, Masino and Engleheart biographies with having coming up with the concept on his own. Indeed, in Susan Masino's book he personally takes credit for it: 'I had come up with the idea.'

But perhaps not on his own.

'Perry helped coordinate the events with the artists we selected and was credited as a co-producer with me,' says Libow. 'We sent these albums out to radio and press. It was a series of releases that we initiated as part of the promotion that Atlantic was doing with a lot of these bands. It was great. We would get a different radio station involved. The band would go in. We'd press it onto disc. They would do a broadcast of the show.

'You have to look at these things as having a cumulative effect on a band's career. Everything that we did over the years and the evolution of the band musically, it was like a perfect wave. It all came together with *Back In Black*. The [*Live*] series was very successful. The radio stations loved being a part of it. It really brought the band very close to the process of what we did to help promote their music. They understood the value in it. At the time it was sort of cutting edge because no other labels were really doing that kind of thing.'

Jimmy Douglass was Atlantic's in-house engineer.

'It was one of the greatest experiences of my life,' he tells me from Miami. 'I was the guy doing all the rock stuff. Foreigner. The Rolling Stones. That was me. Working with AC/DC was amazing. The band speaks for itself. And it was before they really broke big. As a matter of fact we had such a great time on that album that when I went to LA I met with [AC/DC] for quite a bit and they were considering me to actually make their next record. We did do a lot of "shit" back then. I'm pretty sure I had one night with them at a club in LA and we saw Blondie.

'They hadn't really created that [Mutt Lange] sound yet. Something happened between my schedule and theirs and it just didn't happen. There was an honest synergy within them that was just pure energy fire. Straight ahead, right up, fastball, *right down the fucking middle*. I'm talking serious heat. I remember the feeling of standing and just looking at the speakers, listening and going, "*Hooooly shit*."'

On radio, though, America was only just waking up to AC/DC's 'pure energy fire'.

'We saw a reaction with every release,' says Libow. 'And the fan base was growing long before radio even got hip to their music in terms of really hitting the charts and getting behind the band musically. It was just a word-of-mouth thing. It was a combination of the press and their live shows. Wherever they played you heard about it. There was a buzz about this band. Even if the radio stations weren't yet playing their music by the time AC/DC came through their market it wasn't long after that they were playing whatever was available at the time.

'If you had a graph, it just kept moving up: the level of awareness, the support that they were getting from radio and the sales that they were generating with their music. It was the ideal pattern you would want to see with any band you're working with. The incline was just straight up. That's how it was once they really focused on the States.'

However, AC/DC still hadn't recorded that breakthrough album to get them over the top. It was about to come in short time but it wasn't to be the one they were expecting.

6

AC/DC
'Riff Raff' (1978)

It's Keith Richards's, Eddie Van Halen's and Gene Simmons's favourite AC/DC album, a good indicator that the Youngs must have been doing something right with their guitar playing. But it was also a triumph for the band's unheralded rhythm section. Says Georg Dolivo of Rhino Bucket: 'Every drummer and bass player I know loves *Powerage*.'

Armed with their best ever collection of songs, the recording sessions for AC/DC's fifth studio album were fuelled by endless cups of tea, a steady supply of Benson & Hedges cigarettes and Drum tobacco, and a ton of ambition to properly crack America outside of the drudgery of touring and make inroads where it really mattered: record stores.

'In a way it was AC/DC's *Sgt. Pepper's*,' says Mark Opitz, defining *Powerage* as a transitional moment for the group. 'When we came to do *Powerage*, George, Harry and the band did serious rehearsals at Studio 2 in Alberts. George playing bass with the band just out in the studio, Harry and me in the control room. Doing rehearsals, basically writing rehearsals, where you have all sorts of riffs. Malcolm was certainly constructing. Angus was too. But you could see Malcolm taking a stronger hand then. They were maturing: songs like "What's Next To The Moon", "Gimme A Bullet", "Riff Raff", "Sin City", "Rock 'N' Roll Damnation". It was different. We rehearsed at night, followed by midnight-to-dawn recording sessions. Eight o'clock in the evenings we'd start. We'd finish early in the mornings, to the point where Malcolm, Phil Rudd and I would hire a tinny at Rose Bay and motor out into Sydney Harbour with a six-pack of beer and a couple of joints and do a bit of fishing while people were catching a ferry to work.

'I'd spend the days testing the Marshall amps till I could find two really good-sounding ones that were the best to record with. They're all sort of different, amps. In the studio, particularly during *Powerage*, it was like a family. It wasn't a normal recording session. It was a project.'

AC/DC having styled themselves as an album band, Atlantic now wanted them to deliver hits, and they were happy to oblige: 'Rock 'N' Roll Damnation' was belatedly cut for that very purpose after the first edit of the album had received a lukewarm response from New York and it was suggested they record a radio-friendly track. But *Powerage* was also the album where Malcolm began asserting executive control.

'Malcolm no doubt was the leader of the band,' says Opitz. 'George had had his day with The Easybeats. Not strongly, not overtly, but you could feel during *Powerage* Malcolm was starting to stake his ground a bit [in the brothers' pecking order].'

Family intrigues put aside, *Powerage* was a high point creatively for the three Youngs, an album arguably superior to the commercially successful Mutt Lange circuitbreakers that followed, *Highway To Hell* and *Back In Black*. After *Powerage*, the boogie and groove largely disappeared. What was left was still great – Lange amplified so many of their strengths – but at the expense of leaching Vanda & Young's deft touches. Out went the handclaps and the maracas and so much of the rawness. The change of singer had an effect too. Bon Scott's cheekiness and fun was superseded by Brian Johnson's heaviness and malevolence.

If you want an aural marker of how much the band altered its sound between 1978 and 1983, listen to 'Landslide' off *Flick Of The Switch* against *Powerage*'s 'Riff Raff'. The songs are both foot-to-the-floor numbers, but don't compare in quality. It's hard to ignore the feeling that something was lost in the changeover, even if the Youngs' good friend John Swan doesn't agree.

'I never teach my granny how to suck eggs, you know,' he tells me. 'Fuck that; I'm not getting involved in that one. To me, it's still the same recipe. The basic content is so fucking strong, it still comes through for what it is.'

⚡

Ever the innovator, and mindful of the positive effect a modicum of aggression had had on the band with *Let There Be Rock*, George played on the cabin fever inside the studio by working everyone up to the point where sparks were flying.

'He'd be like, "Did you see *The Don Lane Show* last night? That *bloody* hypnotist!"' says Opitz of one George's psychological techniques. Dissecting the performance of a guest on a TV variety show might seem unusual, but *anything* was fair game to George when it came to motivating musicians. 'It wound everyone up into a state of angst. Got the adrenalin pumping.'

But there was also a degree of personal anger in the room that the band had already brought in, without George's egging them on.

Anthony O'Grady had kept in touch with Bon Scott while they were touring overseas, Scott writing letters to him. According to O'Grady, by the time *Powerage* was ready to be cut in early 1978, AC/DC weren't as flavour-of-the-month as they used to be.

Let There Be Rock had fizzled in Australia. Cliff Williams had encountered visa problems. Local shows were cancelled.

'They weren't very popular then because they'd been out of the [public] eye; they hadn't had any hits,' he says. 'Molly Meldrum and *Countdown* had gone off them. Bon was not bitter. He was actually very angry about the Australian music industry, which had turned their back on them. AC/DC just weren't on the agenda.'

All well and good, though, for *Powerage*. When the aggression was off the meter, the tape would roll.

Making use of the band's first remotes, Angus would take his guitar everywhere. As is well known, he did the solo for 'Riff Raff' in the control room.

'An *unbelievable* riff,' says Opitz. 'I sat there with Angus for an hour and a half learning it off him. You can trawl the world of AC/DC aficionados and see which album comes up best, and it's funny how *Powerage* has stood the test of time.'

Later, the band took the aggression-first approach George perfected on *Powerage* into their live shows.

'I'd hear stories from Malcolm and Phil about the way they'd sit around on their American tours, backstage supporting REO Speedwagon, and use the same tactic we used in the studio,' says Opitz. 'They'd start ripping, talking about what a shit band REO Speedwagon is: "Let's go and blow them off the fucking stage. Fuck 'em. They're cunts with their fucking wussy, fucking long-haired, pop fucking music. They wouldn't know fucking rock 'n' roll." All that sort of shit. They'd psych each other up in the dressing room, hit the stage and fucking go *bang*.'

⚡

Meanwhile Cliff Williams, now free to record with the band, was a bundle of nervous excitement. This 'definitely helped with the rhythm tracks', according to Opitz. Williams did what he was told and knew his place. He'd learned a few things from the fate of Mark Evans and has largely kept his counsel ever since.

Tony Platt says he heard some of Williams's songs recorded with Laurie Wisefield from Wishbone Ash when he visited the AC/DC bass player's house and home studio in Florida and they were 'fantastic songs; really, *really* great songs', but 'it would have been a difficult thing for [Williams] to do anything outside AC/DC without it rocking the boat'.

In well over 30 years playing with the band but being a non-writing member, Williams, like Phil Rudd and Brian Johnson, has done very little outside it. Typically over such a stretch of time lower profile members of major acts do solo records. Bill Wyman, Ron Wood and Charlie Watts did so while being part of The Rolling Stones. That freedom doesn't seem to extend to AC/DC's non-writing personnel much beyond benefit gigs and the odd guest appearance onstage or in the studio, though Rudd released his first album in August 2014.

Before this surprise announcement, I asked Phil Carson if Angus and Malcolm ever placed restrictions or had control over what the band's other three members did outside AC/DC.

'As far as I am aware, the Youngs do not exert any particular controls on this except to set the AC/DC tone. They have never involved themselves in an outside recording project and everybody seems to follow that line.'

Asked how his own relationship is with them now, Carson plays a straight bat but, controversially, hints at discord within the band over the treatment of Johnson.

'That depends who you ask. In later years, I became particularly friendly with Brian and tried to help him with a musical he had written about Helen of Troy. I still believe there are some superb songs in there, along with a first-class script written by [*Porridge* creators] Ian La Frenais and Dick Clement. We took that one quite a long way, even making a deal with AEG [Anschutz Entertainment Group] at one point, but we never got as far as Broadway.

'While all this was going on, certain things came up regarding Brian's treatment by the band's accountant and the Youngs. I will leave that one alone other than to quote George Orwell: "All men are created equal, but some are more equal than others."'

The band's accountant?

'I am not naming any names.'

For the opening 45 seconds of 'Riff Raff' AC/DC manages the singular feat of sounding like a massing Orc army. When Phil Rudd hits the hi-hat – *one, two, three* – it's the cue for Malcolm's rhythm guitar to come swinging in, Angus's opening riff falling away like a separating rocket, and there's a massive release of tension. Outside of Led Zeppelin's 'Kashmir' it's probably the most *cinematic* introduction to a rock 'n' roll song ever put to tape.

The man who recorded it considers it his favourite AC/DC track.

'Oh, 100 per cent,' says Opitz. 'It just has every element of AC/DC right in it. *Every* bit. The rock element. The lyrical element. The cheekiness element. The complexity.'

And also the tone. Guitar sound is really where AC/DC set themselves apart from other bands. How do they get it?

'Two ways. I had that ability to go and find the right amplifiers. I sat there for a couple of weeks during the *Powerage* sessions with a notebook checking out every fucking speaker in every speaker box with every amp until I found what I felt was the best combination of amplifier and speaker. And then when they were in the studio I was keen to set the Marshall amps – every Marshall amp has a sweet spot in terms of volume – and to have those amps at the proper volumes, not turned down.'

What about the chunkiness?

'Malcolm has got his Gretsch Firebird with supersonic pickups; he's got it on full volume as normal, so he's able to hit the strings really lightly but get a big sound so it doesn't overcompress, because he's hitting the strings lighter and the pickups aren't overloading. And the Gretsch pickups are known for being louder. It just so happens that AC/DC's combination of a Gibson guitar with Gibson pickups and the Gretsch guitar with Gretsch pickups is the perfect combination. The other one's got what the other one hasn't. It's typical to that guitar sound.

'The drums and bass you keep pretty dry and turn up the guitars and Bon can sing in an up register to cut through it. It's a combination of all that, the microphones they use, Malcolm's right-hand guitar and Angus's right hand. That's the major factor.'

But when they took the song on the road, AC/DC was able to summon the same energy, even ratchet it up. In video of their performance at the Glasgow Apollo in April 1978, the same concert that was used for the *If You Want Blood (You've Got It)* live album, Scott conducts Angus like Mickey Mouse in *Fantasia* directing the magic broomsticks. There is a beauty in the arrangement of the stationary Malcolm and Williams at the back of the stage and in the way they only surge forward with Scott in threes (Angus is off in his own world). There's no prancing about. Just straight up and back. On top of their musical tightness AC/DC also have consummate stagecraft. So many other bands have tried to echo this AC/DC aesthetic in their own performance but too often deliver outright mimicry.

In 2010 I saw Airbourne at the Metro Theatre in Sydney and lead singer and guitarist Joel O'Keeffe carried off the whole Angus-Young-getting-carried-off-into-the-audience routine with polished aplomb. He even split a can of Victoria Bitter beer on his head standing on top of a Marshall amp and sprayed it over the audience.

'Airbourne are trying to capture that spirit. But they probably overemphasise a point,' says Opitz, diplomatically.

↯

After eight weeks of recording with mixing involved, *Powerage* was done and dusted.

Everyone involved in the production, which had been done mostly on feel, was pleased with the results, even after it had been sent back by Atlantic for the band to record 'Rock 'N' Roll Damnation'.

'You can hear Vanda & Young in "Rock 'N' Roll Damnation",' says Opitz. 'The hooks. The shakers coming in. Tambourine to get the groove. Which if you notice is just like [John Paul Young's] "Love Is In The Air". They were very big on lots of Motown tricks. Clapping hands. Harry would clap behind George.'

It was a brilliant concoction by Vanda & Young, a song in the spirit of 'Good Times' and 'It's A Long Way To The Top', and went to #24 in the United Kingdom. However, to this day not everyone is impressed by *Powerage*'s only single. In his biography, Mick Wall calls it 'a two-bit piece of head-bopping guff', which is so ungenerous and untrue it's a scandal of its own. Since when is head bopping a crime when it comes to rock 'n' roll?

'AC/DC gets you moving,' says Opitz. 'One thing George Young said to me was, "Always make sure they can dance to it." That wasn't lost on the band. The dance would be a four on the floor. As long as you can stamp your foot, that's all you needed. That was it. No complex twist. Just a straight, dead-ahead, four-on-the-floor rock 'n' roll that connects physically with young guys in particular.'

The man whose opinion mattered most, Jerry Greenberg, thought the whole album overall was 'a little too hard edge' for US radio.

'That was the problem,' he says, bluntly. 'After *Powerage* I was the guy that convinced the band that they should come to America and work with another producer. That was pretty tough because the brothers' brother was the producer of the band.'

Opitz's take is different: 'There was a big change in the songs, which didn't go down with Atlantic well at all. They thought the producers were losing control, which they weren't obviously. They were just giving them their head to find their own groove.'

But Doug Thaler, who visited Sydney during the recording, backs Greenberg: 'When I went down to the studio in '78 the albums didn't sound quite as great as they might have. The music was great, the performances were great, but the sound was *juuuusssst* not quite what it needed to be.'

In any event, heads rolled. The fallout from the failure of *Powerage* was immense. AC/DC sacked their manager, Michael Browning, and Vanda & Young were replaced by Eddie Kramer, who was forced to make way for Mutt Lange.

Browning didn't want to be drawn too much on the switch that would kill his relationship with AC/DC, insisting he'd already said enough about it in other books. As Clinton Walker wrote in 1994: 'Thicker than water though blood may be, Malcolm and Angus were also extremely ambitious . . . [they] assuaged their guilt at George's sacking by blaming Michael Browning. From this point on, things would never be the same again. What was once a defensive insularity now degenerated into fully blown paranoia. It was an atmosphere of fear and loathing that would escalate for years to come, and only exacerbated Bon's growing sense of dislocation.'

Yet Browning is happy to boast: 'It was the choice of producer where it went pear shaped until I managed to rectify that and hire Mutt Lange.'

By 1983's *Flick Of The Switch*, however, Lange too was gone. Continued Walker: 'The production credit the album bore, to Malcolm and Angus themselves, was merely the tip of the iceberg of a purging the pair had effected throughout the entire band and its infrastructure. It's a classic syndrome: the successful campaigner who fears his own troops. But Malcolm and Angus never trusted anyone anyway. They sacked practically everybody: Mutt Lange, who had artistically engineered their breakthrough; drummer Phil Rudd; Peter Mensch, who himself had usurped Michael Browning; even de-facto official photographer Robert Ellis was ousted.'

When I tried to speak to Ellis, who toured with AC/DC at their peak and produced some of the best images of the band, he struck a sour note: 'Everyone closely associated with the Youngs knows their attitude and closed ways. Anything you and I say can be mere speculation. As is most of what is in the biographies and books so far. I read the Phil Sutcliffe, Murray Engleheart and Mick Wall books. I reckon all are only adding to the mystique. There is plenty of space for the real story, but only [the Youngs] can tell it, and they have no intention of ever doing such a thing. Email me what you want to know from me. I will consider it, and give you some reply.'

So I did just as I was asked. But he responded with an outburst: 'I am not convinced this is a project I want to be any part of. Another fan perspective, and another outsider view of "what really went down" is just not interesting.'

Ellis's pomposity surprised me. I will never claim *The Youngs* to be an account of 'what really went down'. As David Krebs said to me in Manhattan, managing a rock band or writing about a rock band is like *Rashomon*. There are so many versions of the truth. Ellis himself is not writing the definitive biography. Who is? And would the Youngs, if they cared to write their life stories, produce the 'real' story? Would they acknowledge the hurt they have caused so many people? What, exactly, is *definitive*? Is it even possible to be definitive?

I think not. So the band's chroniclers try to patch together what they can from what came before or whatever they can obtain themselves through their own investigations. Even if the result of those labours is an approximation of the truth, there are stories worth trying to tell and to get right – such as the shabby treatment of Michael Browning.

Most tellingly, before he died in 2005, Perry Cooper, one of the band's closest allies, told Walker: 'Michael [Browning] gave his all for that band. But they're as tough as nails, these guys.'

'It was hurtful,' Browning admitted to the same author, 'and what made it more hurtful was that over the years, everyone, me included, with the Youngs and AC/DC, tends to get written out of history. It's like you never existed.'

Phil Carson has only praise for Browning and the band's original champions at Alberts: 'Michael and I plotted every step of the way of the early development of the band. I still have the greatest respect for George Young and for Harry Vanda too. They were doing such a great job in the studio; I really left them to it and they delivered the goods. I also had a great relationship with Fifa Riccobono and Ted Albert. Ted was the guy I would call, along with Michael, to get Alberts to foot the bill for promotional events about which Atlantic were dubious. It was a truly terrific relationship and between us we made it work.'

Opitz was another band luminary to never work with the Youngs again.

'It's really weird we haven't put the same combination back together again, but that's the way it goes.'

Or at least in the closed-off world of the Youngs.

Atlantic's hiring of Mutt Lange changed everything for AC/DC. But how he came into their orbit and who can take credit for introducing him to the band is probably the most unchallenged story in AC/DC lore. Existing published accounts are either erroneous or don't really scratch the surface of what happened, and it's another story that needs to be retold from a different angle because it was a marriage of musicians that changed the course of so many lives, not to mention the history of rock. Without Lange and without the input of two other very important but unheralded players behind the scenes, AC/DC might not be kicking on today.

It all started with Doug Thaler. In 1976, two years before *Powerage*, he had got involved with an English band called City Boy, who happened to be produced by Lange and were managed by Lange's managers, South Africans Ralph Simon and Clive Calder. City Boy had supported AC/DC on one of their first shows in the United States, a December 1977 gig at the Capitol Theater in Flint, Michigan, and right before AC/DC's *Live From The Atlantic Studios* performance in New York. Thaler was involved in the arrangement.

'City Boy had a minor hit in the States in 1979 called "5-7-0-5" but they hadn't really sold any great numbers of records over three releases with [record label] Mercury,' he says. 'They had this great track called "New York Times". It came out later in 1979 and just *shit the bed* – it did nothing.

'I became very close with Clive. And I had a client in the late '70s, a Southern rock band called The Outlaws, and I contacted Clive and said, "Clive, do you think Mutt would be interested in producing The Outlaws?" Of course The Outlaws, who were arena headliners at that time, weren't interested in being produced. They were interested in snorting as much cocaine as they could get their hands on. So Mutt did an album with them [1978's *Playin' To Win*] and they didn't really get their act together and write the songs that they should have.'

Enter the formidable frame of Michael Klenfner. A huge man who'd got his start doing security for late San Francisco AC/DC promoter Bill Graham, he was part of the stage crew at Woodstock, worked as music director and disc jockey at WNEW in New York and rose through the record business, first at Columbia and then Arista, to head Atlantic's marketing and promotion department by 1977, reporting to Jerry Greenberg.

Outside of AC/DC, Klenfner was an important figure in the careers of The Grateful Dead, Boz Scaggs and Bruce Springsteen, among others. He's best known (even if no one can put a name to his face) for a memorable cameo appearance – written especially for him – right at the end of *The Blues Brothers*. He's the fat guy with the thick moustache playing the president of Clarion Records ('the largest recording company on the eastern seaboard') who bails up Jake and Elwood Blues backstage during their big concert at the Palace Hotel Ballroom and offers them a record contract while they're trying to escape from the cops.

'You guys were hot,' he says, grabbing them by their shoulders and about to hand over a brown paper envelope stuffed with $10,000. 'You were great. Insane. I've gotta record you!'

In 1978 Klenfner's influence on AC/DC had already returned handsome dividends: a hit with 'Rock 'N' Roll Damnation' in England, the *Live From The Atlantic Studios* promotion, and concert bookings on both coasts, where his personal connections came into play. Now he was right behind the push for South African Eddie Kramer to supplant Vanda & Young and flew to Sydney to break the news to the Australian pair that they were history.

Kramer was best known for his work with Jimi Hendrix, Kiss and Led Zeppelin.

'I didn't dig Eddie Kramer's work,' says Thaler. 'I didn't think there was anything special about what he did. And I got hold of Clive Calder and I said, "Clive, do you think Mutt would have interest in working with AC/DC?" I just thought it would be a great choice. He was starting to hit his stride as a producer and I'd already given him a project, The Outlaws. I was curious to see if he would even be interested since [AC/DC] were much harder than anything he had done to that date.

'So I put forward the idea of Mutt working with the band, as I knew George and Harry were open to other ideas to help push them over the top. When Clive said that Mutt would be interested, I passed the suggestion on to Michael Browning. It really wasn't my place to do much more than that. I may have suggested Mutt to someone at Atlantic as well; I just don't clearly recall. As City Boy's agent and AC/DC's agent all I could really do with respect to producers was make suggestions and that's what I did. I believe Clive was already in talks with Ahmet Ertegun and Jerry Greenberg about a deal between Atlantic and Mutt.'

This is confirmed by Greenberg, who says the first time he heard the name Mutt Lange was inside Atlantic.

'Yes,' he says. 'It was one of the guys in my A&R department: John Kalodner. Kalodner wanted to sign City Boy.'

But Greenberg also says he maintained a direct line of communication with Browning.

'Oh, all the time. All the time.'

Did Browning ever mention Lange?

'*Um*, he may have. I'm not sure. I will tell you that I was the guy that Browning had to come to quite often for what we called in those days "tour support" to keep the band alive.'

Phil Carson recalls the chronology of events clearly.

'Jerry brought Mutt into the fold via an album that he had produced for an Atlantic group, City Boy. The album got some pretty good airplay, but never made the grade. Jerry and John Kalodner both thought that Mutt had something special to offer AC/DC.'

Meanwhile, Klenfner had got his way with Kramer. But the sessions, first in Sydney and later in Miami, collapsed in acrimony between the producer and the band. Kramer didn't understand their methods. They didn't like him. The Kramer disaster is part of AC/DC legend. As Thaler describes it: 'When that experiment blew up, the shit hit the fan.' Even with Kramer's production pedigree, it wasn't working.

Mark Opitz had been seconded to work with Kramer while in Sydney.

'Malcolm saw through Eddie pretty quickly,' he says. 'Didn't like the idea. He was like, "Fuck you", because he's that kinda guy. Didn't like being told what to do.'

It didn't improve when they shifted to Florida.

'I got a phone call after a week or two [of the Kramer sessions] from Angus [in Miami], and he said they were going home,' says Greenberg. 'They couldn't work with Kramer any more. I said, "Sit tight. Give me a couple of days. Just sit there and enjoy the sun." I was ready to sign City Boy and the producer was Mutt Lange. The production was incredible. I called Clive Calder; I got him on the phone and I told him about AC/DC. I said, "Listen, they're in Miami, can I get Mutt to come over and produce the band?" He said, "I'll put him on the next plane", and history was made.'

So how does Kalodner fit in?

'Kalodner wanted to sign City Boy. I heard City Boy and Kalodner was *crazy* about the production and said, "Mutt Lange: this guy's a great producer; listen to the production", and at that point that's when – I don't care about whose *suggestion* it was – I made the *decision* to call the boys and talk them into Lange and make the deal with Clive. So you can word it any way you want.

'I think maybe [the Youngs] knew who [Lange] was, I don't remember. But I'm sure that somehow Michael Browning was involved at that moment also. Lange came in as soon as Kramer packed up and left. You keep talking to a lot of people you'll put it together.'

It's worth trying to put together because Doug Thaler's, Phil Carson's and Jerry Greenberg's version of events completely contradicts that of Michael Browning in the Murray Engleheart biography of AC/DC, which downplays Thaler's involvement, saying only he 'played a role in securing Lange's services from Atlantic's end' and that Browning was 'sharing a house' with Calder and Lange and took a call from a distressed Malcolm Young in Miami. Virtually the same account appears in the Clinton Walker, Susan Masino and Mick Wall tomes, but in Masino's book Browning is 'visiting' Calder and Lange and in Wall's book Browning is sharing with Calder and Browning's business partner, Cedric Kushner.

Says Browning in Walker's *Highway To Hell*: 'I was at that stage based temporarily in New York. I'd met some people who'd invited me to stay with them, one of whom was Mutt Lange's manager, Clive Calder. I got the phone call from Malcolm, and I got off the phone, and Mutt was there, in the apartment, and I said, "You've got to do this record." At the time, Mutt had really only done City Boy, The Boomtown Rats, but I happened to think he was incredibly talented. So within a couple of days they agreed to do the next record.'

Or as he puts it in Engleheart's *AC/DC, Maximum Rock & Roll*: 'I just turned round to Mutt, virtually as I had Malcolm on the phone, and said, "Mate, you've got to do this record." That was it.'

And again in Wall's *AC/DC: Hell Ain't A Bad Place To Be*: 'I just didn't stop. I just hammered them and by the end of the night I'd convinced Clive and Mutt to do it. I called Malcolm back and said, "It's cool. I've got Mutt Lange" . . . so that's how the whole thing with Mutt Lange started.'

Wall writes, dramatically, 'It was to be a game-changing decision for all involved.'

But from the testimonies of Thaler, Carson and Greenberg it would appear that isn't exactly the case. And, crucially, Clive Calder's former partner Ralph Simon seems to support them.

In a 2011 interview with celebrityaccess.com he told music writer Larry LeBlanc: 'I remember [Clive and I] getting [Lange] AC/DC in 1979. We suggested to AC/DC that they needed to improve their backing vocals. Make it a little more commercial, but without losing their edge. It was a big fight to get them to do that on *Highway To Hell* but it proved to be correct.'

Yet Browning won't have a bar of alternative versions: he maintains it was he and he alone who came up with the idea and that Thaler is wrong.

'No, that's not correct,' he says. 'He's big-noting himself.'

He insists his mentioning of Lange to Malcolm Young was the first AC/DC had ever heard of City Boy's producer.

'Absolutely.'

Had you heard of Lange from inside Atlantic before you suggested his name to Malcolm?

'No, the idea didn't get to Atlantic until I presented it to them.'

And you got the introduction to Lange through Calder?

'Through Clive, yeah.'

The most AC/DC themselves have said about the affair was contained in an interview with *MOJO* magazine in 1984. According to Malcolm, he was unhappy with Kramer and told Browning: 'This guy's got to go, otherwise you're not going to have a band.'

He went on: '[Browning] did a bit of wheeling-dealing and got a tape to a friend of his, Mutt Lange . . . we told Kramer, "We're having tomorrow off, we need a break", and we went in and wrote nine songs in one day and whacked them off to Mutt. He got straight back and said he wanted to do it.'

Thaler holds to his story that Lange was raised with AC/DC and Atlantic well before any Malcolm SOS to Browning.

'Oh, *absolutely*,' he says. 'I never acted behind Michael's back. I felt it was my responsibility to counsel and advise him as best as I could for the sake of AC/DC. We never acted in opposition to each other. While I maintain that I got the ball rolling with putting AC/DC together with Mutt, I simply was playing a role on the team. We were all working together for one common purpose – to get this band's career over the top as we all felt it should be.

'There was a South African promoter that lived in New York that I was very close with at the time, Cedric Kushner. Cedric lived in a luxury apartment building on West 58th between 5th and 6th Avenues. Clive Calder lived in England but had begun making more frequent trips to New York by 1978. Cedric was in talks with Michael Browning about joining with him to co-manage the band. And Clive used to stay at Cedric's apartment. Clive and Cedric were born in South Africa and bonded over that fact. And I'd go over there and we'd sorta hang out.

'Michael got an apartment about a block away from Cedric, on West 58th between 6th and 7th. Michael and his wife, Julie, had stayed with me at my apartment for a couple of weeks in '78.'

Before he died in 2015 I asked Kushner to give his version of events.

⚡

Cedric Kushner was briefly co-manager of AC/DC with Michael Browning and made his name promoting acts such as The Doobie Brothers, Fleetwood Mac and The Rolling Stones. He was best known as a boxing promoter and had not spoken about his time with AC/DC before this book.

Kushner, a lampooned figure in previous books about the band, almost as much as Michael Klenfner, told me he had been 'happy to turn' his good friend Clive Calder on to AC/DC and was 'very disappointed that they ended up leaving me'. Without his input, he says, Calder would not have met Michael Browning.

'Michael was staying at my place, we all became friends; this was also at a time when the band had a hard-on for Michael,' he said. 'They wanted to bail out of the relationship. That relationship had gone its course. Peter Mensch was romancing them. I don't think Michael put the band in touch with Mutt Lange. I think the fact that Clive Calder and Ralph Simon were friends of mine – they were representing Mutt – made a very good situation. That gave them more of an opportunity to spend some time with Michael. That helped bond that relationship.'

So did he believe Mutt Lange-to-AC/DC was an idea that suddenly came to Browning?

'No. That he woke up and said, "Gee, I'd love to get a good producer?" No, *no*.'

But he conceded it was 'quite possible' Browning picked up the phone to Malcolm Young in his apartment and suggested Lange, which is corroborated by Malcolm's own statement on the matter.

Thaler agrees: 'Absolutely possible and probable – I simply wasn't privy to that call between Michael and Malcolm. The story of the phone call at least seems consistent with what I had been trying to engineer for several months.'

Did Kushner believe the Calder-Lange connection with AC/DC predated that conversation?

'I believe so.'

Kushner also said he never once suggested to Calder that Lange produce AC/DC, even though he was involved in a business relationship with Browning. The Australian, sensing that Mensch was circling, had entered into a partnership with Kushner, but instead of solidifying his hold on the band it had blown up in his face.

'I wasn't thinking that far ahead because I didn't think that Browning was going to last that long,' said Kushner. 'Everyone likes to take credit and I don't claim to take credit.'

Had he contemplated taking over the band from a weakened Browning?

'I wasn't thinking that way. I was thinking more along the lines that it would just be an overall strengthening of my presence in the music business. My objective was just to raise my profile.'

Kushner, like Greenberg and Carson, fully backed the Thaler story and even said AC/DC's humble American booking agent personally introduced him to Calder. And through Calder, he met Lange and Simon. One night, he went out to dinner with Calder and Simon in London.

'By the end of dinner I felt like I'd known these guys for a long time.'

They got on so well Kushner offered them the free use of a room in his two-bedroom apartment in Manhattan, the same apartment where Browning says he took the phone call from Malcolm.

'Michael stayed at my place on a few occasions,' said Kushner. 'Clive was a good friend of mine that I introduced to Michael. And they ended up doing a deal for the publishing. Mutt was managed by Clive, so when we all sat down obviously Mutt had a very good reputation. It wasn't too hard to sell him. Atlantic were very much in favour of Mutt doing the album. Obviously Clive was. Mutt was excited about it. It was a good situation.'

Was Lange actually living with him at any point?

'No.'

The Browning-Kushner management of AC/DC lasted all of six months and today Browning says it was 'a mistake . . . I needed the money'.

There was no love lost between the two men.

Says Browning of Kushner: 'He was just an absolute total mistake all round.'

Kushner, for his part, recalled going to Roundhouse Studios in London, where AC/DC recorded *Highway To Hell* with Lange, and picking up a 'bad vibe'. Thaler remembers it being literally frosty, which wouldn't have helped the mood: 'I went to a rehearsal hall where AC/DC was writing and practising. It was cold. The place wasn't heated and they had a kerosene construction space heater on to keep warm.'

'It became obvious to me that Browning was in serious trouble,' said Kushner. 'Sometimes you know you're in trouble. You don't need someone to tell you.'

But Browning puts down the Youngs' coldness in London to their antipathy towards Kushner: 'The group didn't want to know about him. I appointed a co-manager they hadn't approved of and subsequently didn't like. In management there are ups and downs. It was certainly a tough period, just having changed producers . . . I wasn't their most popular person at the time. But it was the Kushner thing that basically took it over the top. It was a mistake.'

'They were a very tough crowd, AC/DC, tough guys to manage,' conceded Kushner. 'Rough and ready. They were guys that did what they wanted to do. They wanted to call the shots.'

But they were about to meet their match.

7

AC/DC
'Highway To Hell' (1979)

What is it about this song that makes it so much more powerful than anything else AC/DC had written or produced up to that stage of their career?

Is it the unforgettable chorus? Is it the opening power chord that builds to become a mountain of sound? Is it the production? Is it the good-time lyrics? Or is it the backing, almost baying, vocals that simply *erupt* when they arrive in the mix?

'That's one of the things that first caught me when I heard it,' says Mark Evans. 'Most of it is Bon. You can hear Malcolm coming through a bit. But you mostly hear Bon, which I found really odd, because it was like, "What's *that*?" But hey, listen. The proof's in the pudding. To me personally it's their best album.'

In his book *Highway To Hell*, Joe Bonomo has a shot at divining its secret: 'An effortless, head-rocking, arms-elevated, smile-lifting chorus so appealing and fun and full of filthy guarantees, and so layered with harmonised, gang-bellowed vocals that you feel surrounded at a smoky party.'

John Wheeler of Hayseed Dixie has his own theory: 'It's the

perfect rock lyric. There are eight lines [in each verse] and a chorus, which is just the same line over and over, not counting "Don't stop me!" That's pure genius: to write something so economical that *absolutely* says it. A lot of bands have a "sound", but when you strip the sound away and just play the song solo on an acoustic guitar there isn't much actually there. That's not the case with "Highway To Hell". That song works whether it's played by a rock band, a bluegrass band or a brass marching band.'

But Tony Platt, its mixing engineer, puts it down to something more primal.

'It's very spiky and angular,' he says. 'But that gives you the punch. Just a damn good rhythm. Very simple and very straight-forward. It's just that stripped-down openness of the rhythm.'

Whatever it is that makes 'Highway To Hell' undoubtedly one of the top half dozen in the Youngs' songbook, it's the single that not only broke AC/DC in the United States as a radio-friendly band but forced AC/DC's haters – and there were still many of them in 1979 – to stop dead in their tracks.

'When the clip for "Highway To Hell" popped up on TV I had to sit up and pay attention,' says Radio Birdman's Chris Masuak. 'The production was tough but polished enough for my "superior" sensibilities and the guitar sounds were awesome. I went out and bought the record and had my first twinge of regret and guilt for being given a valuable guitar lesson almost too late. AC/DC didn't rate in our camp but I'm glad that I finally *got* them.'

Tony Platt worked on four AC/DC records: *Highway To Hell*, *Back In Black*, *Flick Of The Switch* (as co-producer with Malcolm and Angus Young) and the soundtrack album to the film *AC/DC: Let There Be Rock*, which is contained in the *Bonfire* box set.

The Englishman had been introduced to Lange through a mutual friend called Adam Sieff, who went on to become Sony's director of jazz for the United Kingdom and Europe, and found someone who appreciated his pedigree: Lange wanted an engineer who was completely across the 'fat' British rock sound and Platt, fortuitously, had worked with its foremost exponent: Free.

Their storied guitarist, Paul Kossoff, had not only left AC/DC in the lurch when he died on them before they were due to support his band Back Street Crawler in 1976 but left an indelible imprint on Malcolm Young's tone. Free's 'All Right Now' had been covered live by AC/DC in 1974 and, as Phil Sutcliffe points out in his biography, 'the opening guitar figure of "You Ain't Got A Hold On Me" echoes Free's "Wishing Well", with a lead solo by Malcolm' on the original Australian version of *High Voltage*.

'When I heard what Lange was doing on *Highway To Hell* I thought, "Oh, this is a step up,"' says Platt. 'Some of the rawness had been refined a little bit where it needed to be but it hadn't been overrefined or lost the energy. "Highway To Hell" is probably the one song that owes most to "All Right Now" in its construction. There are all sorts of things that come to bear [on a recording]. The desk that it was mixed on was the same desk that "All Right Now" was mixed on. So there's a certain tone that comes from that. The recording process is kind of a compromise at every step of the way because microphones are not quite as sensitive as ears in a lot of respects. And your brain processes sound in a particular way. And when you squeeze sound down wires all sorts of things happen to it.

'So really the job of an engineer and a producer is to try to reduce the amount of *compromise* that's being applied. Now you can either do that by kind of chasing your tail with it or you can say, "Well, let's turn this into a creative process." So then by choosing microphones, consoles, pieces of equipment and all those sort of things that address the compromises that you're faced with [you can] actually turn them to your advantage in one way or another.'

Terry Manning, who's also engineered for Lange, agrees choice of gear and equipment and even the room where the music is recorded has a massive effect on the resulting sound of an album.

'There is an influence,' he says. 'It is true that whatever equipment you use and the way you utilise it will have an effect. But by far the biggest influence is the musicians and the sound that they are able to generate from the very beginning. And then second to that is the philosophy of the people recording it, in this case Tony and Mutt. A very big factor, too, I think, is the room itself because that's one thing that was always so great about Compass Point: both studios, but especially Studio A, just had a really, *really* good room sound. You can also hear it on "Addicted To Love" by Robert Palmer. The way things just sort of *pop* out.'

Continues Platt: 'When you have a band like AC/DC who've got a very distinct sound, what you're actually trying to do is not screw that up. You're actually trying to get that across as faithfully as possible and, at the same time, if you can possibly do it, *enhance* it in ways that will make it sound larger than life so when it comes across on a record you come back to this thing of having the visual enhancement of imagining the band playing right in front of you.'

This is *Highway To Hell*'s great triumph. Lange achieved something Vanda & Young could not. He makes you *see* the music: the Youngs' small fingers digging into the strings, even the *grooves* on the strings. The sound is that delineated.

'What Mutt wanted to do was to capture some of that British rock essence, the *fatness*, rather than have the edginess that you got from American rock,' says Platt. 'So, having worked on those sort of things, I knew it was a matter of not having loads of layers of guitars and things like that.

'It was about creating a sound where you felt you could actually picture the room with the band playing in it. There's a certain amount of visual aspect that you need to conjure up with the sound. And it was a little tough to do with *Highway To Hell* because it hadn't been recorded in a way that enabled that to happen easily. So when I was asked to go back and do *Back In Black* I'd already got in my head, "Well, I want to do this slightly differently."

'So there's even a movement from *Highway To Hell* to *Back In Black* in terms of opening that space and making it much more accessible. It's the sort of sound where you can envisage [the band] in the room but at the same time you can dive into it and rub it all over yourself. You've got to be able to *see* the strings humming to feel it.'

It's a testament to what a good job Lange and his team did on *Highway To Hell* that other producers use it to test their studios.

'When we were recording ZZ Top's *Eliminator*,' says Manning, 'Billy Gibbons and I would start every morning by listening to a cut or two from *Highway To Hell* over the studio monitors, cranked up loud. This always got us revved up, in the mood for *our* rock 'n' roll.

'Mutt wants something to be as professional and as able to translate to more of the world as possible, and maybe being "polished" is a part of that, but he has always pushed the boundaries of technology, especially in that era, probably getting to certain ways of making things sound bigger, better, tighter and more compact than most people were doing at the time.'

For example, on *Back In Black* Platt and Lange used Angus Young's live radio set-up to send his guitar to different amplifiers in different rooms, creating a sound so unique that when they wanted to change a part of one of the solos during mixing and the radios weren't available, matching the sound was very difficult. For the mix of *Highway To Hell*, Platt also fed the guitar into the studio room in order to give it a 'roomy' feel.

'Mutt was a terrific influence on AC/DC and a complete perfectionist,' says Phil Carson. 'He got the very best out of AC/DC's studio performances.'

In 1981, before working on *For Those About To Rock*, the album that marked the end of his association with AC/DC, Lange (again with Platt in tow) produced Foreigner's *4*, containing the superlative radio smashes 'Waiting For A Girl Like You' and 'Urgent', which went to #2 and #4 respectively in the United States: his biggest hits to that date. Jimmy Douglass, AC/DC's engineer on *Live From The Atlantic Studios* and considered for the *Highway To Hell* producer's seat before Lange stepped in, worked on Foreigner's first album.

'I was totally blown the fuck away by *Highway To Hell*,' he says. 'I wouldn't have made the record like that. I didn't see that [coming]. It was really retro Zeppelin to me, as I saw it. They fucking nailed it. When I heard it, I was like, "Wow, that's amazing." They were so powerful and so dynamic I didn't see that as the direction they were going to take. The genius of Lange was that he went back and made something that we'd heard already and just made it fucking better.'

Mario 'The Big M' Medious, Atlantic's legendary promotion executive who worked with Led Zeppelin in the early '70s and was once described by *Rolling Stone* as the 'hottest promo man in the music biz', seconds Douglass: 'AC/DC picked up where Zeppelin left off. They had the energy and mindblowing, must-play-loud sound that made them some bad mamajamas. I loved AC/DC.'

Lange, a fine musician in his own right, didn't impose his imprint on the band but extracted the best he could from them without having them mutiny.

'He was someone who loved hooks, and loved chord constructions,' Ralph Simon told Larry LeBlanc. 'He always used to stress that you have the principal hook and then you have four hooks in counterpoint flecking the major hook.' He was also 'very much into The Eagles [sic] and The Eagles kind of sound' and was 'so talented' that 'he is probably the closest shoe-filler to Quincy Jones'.

A rare insight into Lange's approach in the studio was given in a *Billboard* interview in 1998 by Trevor Horn, the great British producer of Frankie Goes to Hollywood, Grace Jones and Seal. Horn's exacting, lush production places him comfortably in the same perfectionist category.

'Mutt Lange once said to me, "You get a band, you get them in a rehearsal room to do the songs, you rehearse them, you get them in a studio, you set them up, you go into the control room to listen, and it sounds like rubbish. That's invariably what happens. After that, it's a question of how much tenacity you have and how far you want to go." I think he's right.'

The Youngs, as much as they grumbled about Lange's painstaking ways, would have known they were in the presence of someone truly gifted. Michael Bolton, one of Lange's most commercially successful acts, calls him 'a mystic among producers – a serene, sage-like Obi-Wan Kenobi'.

'He never really stamped *his* sound on those guys, like he did with Def Leppard and Shania Twain,' says Mike Fraser. 'He's definitely got a sound to him. *Highway To Hell* and *Back In Black* still sound like AC/DC to me. Mutt's really good at *defining* everything. He helps bring that out either in the arrangement or the sound structure of the songs. But it was always there with AC/DC; it's just a matter of how you're presenting it. Mutt's such a Type-A guy, so attentive to detail, so he makes sure that comes out. Mixing his stuff for *Iron Man 2*, I have to say, *boy*, was it ever recorded well. You can almost just push the faders up and it was there.'

Says David Thoener, who mixed *For Those About To Rock*: 'I'd agree with Mike. Mutt always knows what he wants and hears it in his head, so it's just a matter of time to get the artist to perform exactly as Mutt hears it in his head. Sometimes that's bar by bar if necessary. He has more patience than anyone I've ever worked with and doesn't settle.'

Thoener, a New Yorker, remembers spending a lot of time with Lange 'on a mobile truck parked outside The Rolling Stones' rehearsal room' at Quai de Bercy, Paris, recording what would be Lange's swansong album with AC/DC. He'd been working with The J. Geils Band on *Freeze Frame* when he got the call in June 1981 to come to France to work on the *For Those About To Rock* sessions. Another J. Geils Band album, 1980's *Love Stinks*, was a Lange favourite.

'I thought I'd be done with J. Geils long before my August departure date. I was working 14 hours a day seven days a week and finished the last mix of *Freeze Frame* on a Saturday, slept on Sunday and got on a plane to Paris on Monday.

'It was a big stone room, as I recall; quite a challenge. We worked from 10 am to midnight six days a week in Paris finishing the recording, then flew to London. I had off the day we flew to London and started mixing the next day six days a week 14 hours a day for a little over a month. By the time we were done, I was toast.

'We spent five days mixing the song "For Those About To Rock" even though I felt we had it after the first day. It was only 24-track analogue but Mutt didn't give up until all his ideas had been addressed. Yes, he is a perfectionist. I believe that's why all the artists he's worked with have amazing-sounding records. Every song he's involved with is a work of art. When you work with Mutt, as an engineer you just try to keep up and do your job to the best of your ability. He is always several steps ahead.'

That obsessive zeal to get it right, no matter how long it takes, required forbearance not only from AC/DC, who were used to getting in and getting out in the shortest possible time frame, and Lange's overworked assistants but also from the project's paymasters: Atlantic. They were happy to stand back and let the eccentric producer do his thing.

'I was told that he really didn't like anybody in the studio,' says Jerry Greenberg. 'So we honoured his wishes. I was used to being in the studio, sitting there watching Jerry Wexler and Tom Dowd record Aretha Franklin. I'd walk in and I would *see* the genius of Wexler and Dowd. Mutt Lange, all I could do was *hear* the genius. But *Highway To Hell* was a much sharper, much more well-produced record obviously than what we were getting with Vanda & Young.'

And what AC/DC's American record company got for that patience, investment and tough decision making was everything they had been waiting for all along: a hit.

⚡

I spent months trying to work out ways of contacting Lange to get his memories of working with AC/DC, but to no avail.

'It's a self-perpetuating thing,' says Tony Platt of Lange's aversion to speaking about the past. 'If you actually make enough money out of one album to be able to relax on the next album and not put up with the compromises, make sure that the album's made right and the people that are marketing it do their job and all of those other little things that go towards making hit albums, you're going to make another hit album. You then litter that with the huge amount of talent that Mutt has as well, and you've got a major success.

'He has no real need to promote himself in any way, shape or form. So he's in a very fortunate position of not having to talk to press to promote himself and not having to step in that minefield that is doing interviews and being misunderstood and misrepresented.'

Platt suggests one interview that Lange did for a major American magazine sowed the seeds of some disharmony with AC/DC and put him off doing press forever.

'The interviewer said to him, "So what's it like going from working with AC/DC to working with Foreigner?" And what Mutt said was, "Well, they're kind of two different bands, really, because AC/DC's songs are riff-based and Foreigner's songs are melody-based." A perfectly reasonable response. But the reporter actually wrote it up as: "Well, it would be nice to get back to some melodies." You can imagine what happened. Angus and Malcolm were, "What the *fuck* is this?" And of course it all had to be explained. So you get burned a couple of times like that and it's no wonder you go away and say no.'

But there is another explanation for Lange's Greta Garbo impersonation.

David Thoener told Daniel J. Levitin for the book *The Encyclopedia Of Record Producers* that Lange's motives were ultimately egotistical: 'His philosophy is to be very low-key about the music business, not to do interviews . . . he told me, "Don't let anyone know what you think. If you don't do interviews, there's kind of a mystery about you. No one really knows what you think or why you think it."'

Thoener never worked with Lange again after *For Those About To Rock*, or with AC/DC, which he admits was 'a tough pill to swallow', though 'it's the nature of the business and I've come to accept it'. No one could fault the man's mixing or the majesty of songs such as the title track and the closer, 'Spellbound', which calibrates the power of AC/DC so awesomely it's like a sort of rock Valhalla. However, in 1984 he went to Amsterdam to work on

Def Leppard's *Hysteria* with Meat Loaf's producer, Jim Steinman. Steinman was sacked, Thoener took over, 'but then the drummer [Rick Allen] got in a car accident, which put the record on indefinite hold'. Losing an arm does that. When they were ready to record again, Lange came on board and Thoener's work was shelved.

'As far as I'm aware, everything I did was redone. I got a "thank you" on the credits after working 12 hours a day for three months. The last time I saw Mutt was in LA when he was mixing The Corrs' [2000 album] *In Blue* with Mike Shipley.'

Thoener had his own revenge, of sorts, winning two Grammys for Santana's *Supernatural*, which went 15 times platinum, three million more than *Hysteria*. Does he think Lange's aversion to the media is ultimately to his detriment?

'Mutt has an opinion about that aspect of a career and I understand,' he responds. 'I can't say that's the way I should have conducted my career, in retrospect. I listened to him and for many years I never spoke about anything. I've had my career for almost 40 years and I've experienced an incredible amount of history I've never spoken about.

'We used to hang quite a bit, go to dinners. He is a terrific guy, one of the nicest producers I've ever worked with. I have tremendous respect and admiration for him. He and Clive Calder had approached me back in 1980 about becoming a part of their production team and I foolishly passed, something I have regretted since that day. I recently watched a movie about Phil Spector and in it he makes a comment that he was the best producer in the world. I think Mutt has a claim on that statement.'

In the only interview with Lange known to exist from recent times, a short email interview with a fan site in the 1990s, he was asked if he stayed in any contact with bands he had worked with: 'No. We have separate lives. Some of them believe I was a merciless tyrant in the studio and obsessed with absolute perfection with each song. Some of those albums took several years to complete. They've seen enough of me for one lifetime.'

⚡

Mutt the Merciless went on to record two more albums with AC/DC but *Highway To Hell* was the end of the road for three of the band's most important contributors: Michael Klenfner, Michael Browning and, most prominently of all, Bon Scott.

Atlantic's larger-than-life marketing and promotion walrus, Klenfner, the man who above all others worked tirelessly inside the company to get AC/DC to the top, was to pay dearly for his stubborn faith in Eddie Kramer and resistance to Mutt Lange.

'Clive Calder actually got Michael Klenfner fired from Atlantic over the whole Kramer thing,' says Doug Thaler.

'That's true,' says Jerry Greenberg, of the story that Klenfner bailed up Calder when the pair met by chance in a New York club and complained about Lange having displaced his man, Kramer. A mortified Calder called Greenberg. The next day Klenfner was out on his ear.

'When the [AC/DC] guys called me and told me they were getting rid of Eddie Kramer, and I suggested Mutt Lange, they said okay. And that particular night, first Klenfner came into my office and basically called me a jerk. I mean, how would you like it if one your employees walked in and told you that you were a jerk? And you're making a mistake? And you don't know what you're doing? So he rambled on and on, but I let that slide. Except that night he bumped into Clive Calder and he told Clive the same thing: "Mutt Lange shouldn't be producing this band, he's the wrong producer; Jerry Greenberg doesn't know what he's doing, *buh buh buh buh*."

'So Clive called me up and said – because at the time we were negotiating for City Boy – "Listen, I can't give you City

206

Boy." I said, "What are you talking about?" He said, "Well, your senior vice-president grabbed me at this club, told me that we were making a mistake with Mutt Lange" and he really went on and on and on and "I can't do business with Atlantic then". I said, "Clive, you don't have to worry about that. He's leaving the company tomorrow." So he goes, "Really?" I said, "Yep." And I fired Michael the next day.'

I tried to corroborate this account with Calder but was given a firm no by the office of Neil Portnow, the president/CEO of The Recording Academy, the Los Angeles home of the Grammys: 'The response we received was that the projects you mention took place more than 30 years ago, and he will not be in a position unfortunately to be of any assistance.'

Calder, who started out in A&R for EMI in South Africa, was ranked by *Forbes* as the 521st richest person in the world in 2012 and #1 on the *Sunday Times* Rich List of Music Millionaires the same year, ahead of Sir Paul McCartney. He got his first big payday selling the Zomba Group, which he founded with Ralph Simon in 1975, to BMG for almost $3 billion in 2002. Simon and Calder had earlier split in 1990 over an 'ethical disagreement' and, in Simon's words, it 'did not finish on a good note . . . Calder's ego had just gotten out of control'.

Despite Simon's criticism, Greenberg defends Calder as 'one of the all-time, great, *great* record men', and Cedric Kushner went further: 'He's probably the most successful entrepreneur in all of the music business in the entire world. A very brilliant guy.'

As for Klenfner, Greenberg says he gave him the option of announcing that he had resigned rather than been fired.

'His answer to me was: "*Fuck you*. I want everybody to know you fired me." And I told him to leave the building, which he did.'

In January 2013, Klenfner's collection of rock memorabilia, most of it from his years at Atlantic, was auctioned in Bloomfield,

New Jersey. A cherry-red Gibson SG signed in silver pen by Brian Johnson, Malcolm Young, Angus Young, Phil Rudd and Cliff Williams sold for $860. Angus had even drawn a caricature of himself and signed it 'To Klef'. A *Powerage* tour jacket went for $176. A fire sale: an unfitting fate for the treasured possessions of a man who'd given so much of his best years to AC/DC, even if he had got it wrong over Lange.

Michael Browning nominates Klenfner as the most important figure inside Atlantic for AC/DC. Again, it's a surprising sentiment given he is so unflatteringly portrayed by the band's biographers.

'He shouldn't be,' says Browning, who can take credit for being one of the very few people who has previously sung his praises, having done so in the Wall biography – even if the English author couldn't return the compliment to Klenfner and spell his name right. 'He was one of the great supporters.'

I ask Klenfner's widow, Carol, how her husband felt after what happened at Atlantic. Does she think he was unfairly treated?

'Michael was always a fierce advocate for what he believed in and not afraid of speaking his truth and stepping on toes, so he was aware that going with his gut had ramifications,' she says. 'And he paid the price at Atlantic. I remember how upset and devastated he was about the selection of Mutt Lange as producer. He was passionately committed to the band and thought they could be huge. He loved them. He saw something special in them early on and fought tirelessly for them like a lion.'

Browning himself was the next to be axed, Peter Mensch of Leber-Krebs becoming the band's new manager in July 1979. In 2014 Browning released a book about his time with AC/DC.

'Michael was a good guy that saw the raw potential of this band and worked his ass off to deliver them,' says Doug Thaler, who has more charitable things to say about Browning than Browning does about him. 'He got shoved out before the big payday and that is a shame because he brought them right to the threshold of huge international success, which is no small feat.'

Then, last of all, there was Scott. He died alone, out of it, lying back and covered by a blanket in the front seat of a Renault 5 in London in February 1980, six months after the release of *Highway To Hell*. One beautiful but flawed soul lost, millions of words written, and are we any closer to the real truth about who he loved, what he lived for, and how, let alone why, it ended? There are some compelling theories, the most sensational involving heroin. But can it ever be known? Is there a definitive truth? Or was David Krebs right? Is the AC/DC story just another *Rashomon*?

I've started to think it is.

Allan Fryer was at his home in Adelaide, South Australia, when he got the call from George Young to come to Sydney to audition for the vacant position in AC/DC. At the time he was lead singer of Fat Lip, soon to be renamed Heaven, a leather-clad hard-rock band of Frank Stallone clones that would go on to sign with Michael Browning. Mark Evans joined them briefly in 1983. When AC/DC's former bass player finally got to America for the first time, touching down in Los Angeles, his old bandmates were playing at The Forum.

'I just [said to myself], "*Ohhh*, another one of those weird coincidences, Mark; well done,"' he laughs.

'They were big shoes,' says Fryer of the ones he was in the running to fill.

But there was no question in his mind about going. He flew to Alberts in Sydney and ended up singing on a bunch of AC/DC tracks stripped of Scott's vocals.

George, by Fryer's account, was happy with the audition and told the singer not to say anything to anybody. Fryer went back to

Adelaide. Yet the music press in England prematurely broke the story he'd landed the gig as AC/DC's new singer. The calls wouldn't stop. He remembers sitting on his sofa in Adelaide, staring at the buzzing phone, thinking, 'Wow, shit.'

Nothing official, however, had come through from Vanda & Young, Alberts, AC/DC or their new management company, Leber-Krebs. So Fryer, assuming no news meant no thanks, signed on with Browning: he wanted a record deal and a chance to get to America.

Anecdotal evidence abounds that much else was going on. There was Stevie Wright's assertion that George offered him the role. Promoting his autobiography, *Who's Crazee Now?*, Slade's Noddy Holder claimed in 2000 he'd turned it down. Other names linked to the vacant job included Marc Storace of AC/DC soundalikes Krokus and Gary Holton of Heavy Metal Kids. More recently there was the left-field suggestion made by Moxy guitarist Earl Johnson in *The Austin Chronicle* in 2008 that Buzz Shearman, the band's singer, was approached. AC/DC had supported Moxy at their first American gig in Texas in 1977. (Shearman died in a motorcycle accident in 1983.) Others closely associated with the band also had their own ideas about who was the right fit.

Mark Opitz was one: 'When the unfortunate news came through about Bon I just assumed, "Swanee's got a gig now." At that time he was clearly the best male singer in Australia. He even had the edge on John Farnham with that big, pure, full voice he had; a real rock voice. He was Glaswegian. You couldn't have got a better fit. He was a ten-pound tourist, just like the rest of them. I thought that would be it. That he was a lay-down misère.'

But John Swan was by his own admission 'out of control' on alcohol and cocaine.

'That was what we did to be *in* control,' quips Swan, who has been sober and clean for over a decade.

In his view the band didn't need another Scott; they needed someone who could hold it down night after night. Even though Swan was an honorary member of the Young family, 'the reality is the phone call didn't come from the boys, so I know that to be the reason; that's what it is'.

He reflects: 'One of the things we do have in this industry is a lot of loyalty from people who love you no matter what you do wrong. And that's the boys. The lads were making a business decision. I was told at that time I had about six months to live.'

Ironically, he'd support AC/DC when they played in Australia a year later.

⚡

Meanwhile, over in England, Angus and Malcolm Young were conducting their own exhaustive auditions, with two singers standing out.

Terry Slesser, formerly of Back Street Crawler, got a call from Mutt Lange's then wife, Olga, asking him if he'd like to sit in with the band in Pimlico. He'd also heard separately that Ahmet Ertegun personally wanted him to join AC/DC.

Slesser had drunk with Scott at the Marquee and Speakeasy clubs 'many times' and was introduced to the Youngs through Coral Browning in 1976, around the time Paul Kossoff died mid-flight from Los Angeles to New York of a drug-related heart attack.

Like Tony Platt, he believes it was 'very evident' that the Youngs were influenced by Kossoff's guitar playing, which probably accounted for their interest when Scott died.

'Not many could cope with the minimalist way Koss played,' he says. 'Most players copied the speed-freak guys. Hence you ended up with Steve Vai, Joe Satriani, Yngwie Malmsteen and other similar drivel. It's easier to twiddle than feel it for real.'

Says Phil Carson, who worked with Free: 'If you listen to early Free tracks, particularly "All Right Now", you can hear a lot of the space that Paul put into his playing. [Free's drummer] Simon Kirke also epitomises the no-frills, four-on-the-floor approach to drumming, so there must have been a certain Free influence on the Youngs.'

Then there was Geordie's Brian Johnson. Scott had previously mentioned Johnson to the Youngs and Lange put his name forward on a list he put together with Platt.

'This was pretty much a foregone conclusion,' says Carson. 'The band had met Brian in Newcastle and Bon had told them that if anything happened to him, here was their replacement.'

To this day Slesser believes he was still in with a shot, but let the chance slip.

'It was down to Brian and myself. But my audition recordings on ReVox [an open-reel tape recorder] had not actually recorded. Malcolm asked if I would like to do them again, and at the time I wasn't keen on redoing the whole thing and sort of allowed the opportunity to pass me by. I did offer to return if they still hadn't found anyone but meanwhile Brian came in after me and no doubt blew them away with his voice, humour and enthusiasm.'

Says Carson: 'This was a decision in which I totally deferred to the Youngs. They knew how their band should sound and they made the right decision. The move, of course, changed Brian's life, but at the same time injected new blood into AC/DC. I was simply a facilitator at that point and, along with Peter Mensch, made sure that the administrative details caused no glitches. Bringing in Brian was solely a decision made by the Youngs.'

In Fort Worth, Fryer is still scratching his head.

'It wasn't really explained [why I didn't get the gig],' he says. 'I've heard different things. Our similarities; that I was too close to

Bon. You take Journey and that guy from The Philippines [Arnel Pineda] who sounds like Steve Perry. *Identical*, you know what I mean? Some bands go down that road. Judas Priest when Rob Halford dropped out and Tim 'Ripper' Owens got the gig. You'd close your eyes and think it was Rob singing.

'I really wish I had a tape of some of the stuff I did for Alberts but I know that wasn't to be expected. The only thing I can really tell anybody is that it was just the real deal. We did so much good stuff, like "Whole Lotta Rosie". George and Harry were ecstatic. They were happy as a pig in shit and were going to give [the tapes] to Angus and Malcolm in London. They loved it. Down the road it came about [George and Harry] really wanted me in the band. But, you know, [Angus and Malcolm] went with Brian.'

Even though Fryer had the backing of Leber-Krebs, who he'd go on to sign with after eventually parting ways with Browning.

'Heaven was virtually the last band they did before that organisation started to break up after history-making things,' he says. 'David and [his assistant] Paul O'Neill wanted me in the band. They wanted me in AC/DC. That was another reason why Leber-Krebs signed Heaven, apart from doing the [1985] *Knockin' On Heaven's Door* album. To this day David swears black and blue that he would have had me frontin' AC/DC.'

'Absolutely right, no question,' says Krebs. 'Brian Johnson was the antithesis of Bon Scott as a singer. I thought Allan Fryer was very much in the tradition of Bon Scott.'

Steve Leber is less committal and insists the decision wasn't his and Krebs's to make anyway: 'David *may* have suggested that during that time. We were all looking for a lead singer. But [the Youngs] picked their own person.'

Ultimately, Fryer puts his rejection down to politics.

'There was bad blood between Michael Browning and the Young brothers, to hit the nail on the head. They didn't like

Michael. I was naïve. Michael wanted to get [Fat Lip] and sign us. And once we'd signed on the dotted line, it was virtually my death notice with the Youngs.

'When they played with Brian on the *Back In Black* tour, I got together with Brian and everything was cordial. In LA I met up with Angus and Malcolm down at the Rainbow [Bar & Grill in West Hollywood] one night, when we were playing, and the very first words out of fucking Angus's mouth, he goes [*adopting a knuckle-dragging Scottish accent*], "So you're still with Browning, are *ya*?" There was *really* bad blood between Browning and AC/DC. I think it's known history. It took me so much heartache getting out of my contract with Browning. He was like a moray eel. Once he got his jaws on you, that was it. It took a lot of dollars.'

But Mark Evans dismisses the notion that the Youngs hated Browning.

'No, that's not true,' he says. 'I'm not sure where Allan would have got that from. But I know there was always a very healthy wariness of all management because the folklore was George and The Easybeats got burned by Mike Vaughan.'

Management, he says, was viewed inside AC/DC as a case of 'Who's going to take us to the next step?' and adds: 'Management ultimately would have been very, *very* disposable.'

Like a lot of people involved in the rise of AC/DC.

The choice of Brian Johnson as Bon Scott's replacement proved to be a shrewd one by the Youngs. It was a decision that stood in stark contrast to the one made by INXS, who many years later dealt with the death of their own resident 'gypsy', Michael Hutchence, spectacularly poorly.

AC/DC got it right for one simple reason: they didn't piss about. After the death of Scott, they released a new album full of great songs that their new singer made his own. Not only would it remake the band in terms of image and sound but it gave them a platform for the next 30 years of playing live. INXS didn't cut that big new record, that statement they needed. They couldn't settle on a replacement and kept playing live shows thinking people were going to be all right with the fact that Hutchence wasn't there. They weren't. It took eight years for them to record a new album with a new singer.

No replacement vocalist has given a band a better second act than Johnson did for AC/DC. Not even Sammy Hagar with Van Halen for the near 11 years he lasted.

But not everybody was convinced by the change.

'Johnson, he's got a higher voice, but with Bon at least you could understand the lyric,' says Stevie Wright. 'Bon was more like me, and Brian wasn't. Bon was clear in his diction. With Johnson, I thought, "Oh no, this is terrible. I can't understand his diction." He came [not far] from where I come from in England. And I couldn't understand him and he couldn't understand me.'

Johnson's vocal cords also really only held out for five years. Three decades on they sound feeble, constricted, like a tight little fist, muted and phlegmy. Or as Mick Wall describes it adroitly, 'cindered'.

Mike Fraser, though, takes an alternative view: 'For *Black Ice*, Brendan O'Brien was the producer. While we were tracking the songs and working on solos, Brendan would take Brian to another room to do vocals. Brian was in tiptop shape coming in to do the record. He loves racing cars as a hobby and because of a busy racing schedule prior to the recording we caught him at a peak. Brendan did an awesome job bringing out the best of Brian as well and really pushed him.'

Maybe so. But in the *Back In Black* and *For Those About To Rock* era, Johnson's prime, the man was so on fire he was Ghost

Rider. He's been using a teleprompter for live shows. AC/DC's most recent live album, *Live At River Plate*, was almost unlistenable at times because of his vocals.

But there are other factors that need to be considered. Johnson is closing in on 70. The AC/DC singer revealed in 2009 he'd been diagnosed with Barrett's Syndrome, a condition caused by chronic reflux that can lead to vocal-cord inflammation and dysphonia. As a learned doctor friend explained: 'Pathologically it is defined as squamous metaplasia of the distal oesophagus. Metaplasia of the oesophagus does not cause vocal-cord problems. What affects the voice is actually the underlying condition of severe, chronic gastroesophageal reflux.'

It's a condition that also affects Journey's Arnel Pineda. So is Johnson paying for 30 years of screaming like a banshee, smoking cigarettes and drinking ale?

'Environment. Age. Reflux. All of it. Cumulative.'

That he survives and hasn't been fired by the normally ruthless Youngs, then, is something of a miracle: testament to his good nature and enduring popularity not just with his bandmates but the music-buying public. AC/DC are a much bigger band with Johnson out front than they ever were with Scott. They could easily go down the road taken by Journey with Pineda and get themselves a younger clone of their best singer. But commendably they have stuck by Johnson.

Rhino Bucket's Georg Dolivo is a fan: 'Bon was always a hero of mine but hats off to Brian, who must have balls of steel to be able to front that band for so long.'

'Brian Johnson is more streety and not the singer that Bon was, but he's as much a part of AC/DC as anybody,' says Rob Riley. 'Bon was only there for six years. Brian's been there for 30. The Youngs made a good choice. They keep making great records.'

Ken Casey from Dropkick Murphys agrees: 'Bon was an icon.

Commanding stage presence. You listen to one song, you say, "I want to hang out with that fucking guy." Same for Brian. To be able to step in and fill those shoes; boy, I give that guy all the credit in the world. Their legacy is immense.'

Or, as Tony Platt points out, 'Brian's got the most difficult job of all of them. He's still managing to *kind of* get the notes. It's a really tough call to get there. But they don't have to persuade anybody now, do they?'

They most certainly don't.

8

AC/DC

'Back In Black' (1980)

B *ack In Black* didn't just signal a darker, heavier sound for the decade that was to follow for AC/DC but stands even today as a signpost of when Angus and Malcolm Young came into their own as musicians. Even, it's not a stretch to say, as men.

Malcolm was 27 years old and Angus had turned 25. They'd changed managers, had to accept artistic and spiritual relegation for their older brother George and lost their lead singer, friend, guide, muse and lyricist. There was a new bloke with a big mop of curls out front and another, altogether odder one behind the mixing desk – someone more demanding and finicky but undeniably more brilliant than anyone they'd ever encountered in the music business.

But after four weeks of recording at Compass Point, west of Nassau on the Caribbean island of New Providence, then 12 days of mixing at Electric Lady Studios in New York City they delivered not only a great album but the best song of their lives: the title track. It remains the most penetrative AC/DC song in popular culture. It's been covered by Santana, Muse, Shakira, Foo Fighters and Living Colour (the latter brilliantly) and sampled in music by Nelly, Limp

Bizkit, Eminem, Public Enemy, Beastie Boys and Boogie Down Productions. Why?

'It's a song that is very important in the history of rock 'n' roll and moving on in life in general,' explains former Guns N' Roses drummer Matt Sorum. 'I always look to that song as the ultimate statement in "never give up". The greatest resurrection of a band in history.'

'Their licks, those themes they came up with,' coos Jerry Greenberg. 'Oh. My. God. It was absolutely unbelievable. I just thought it could be one of the biggest all-time rock records ever and it proved right.'

But not everyone was sure. Atlantic's head of singles, Larry Yasgar, who was on the ground ordering stock for record stores, was worried Brian Johnson wasn't going to take with fans.

'We didn't know if the kids were going to be turned off or what was going to happen,' he says. 'Well, we found out. It didn't matter.'

⚡

'*Highway To Hell* and *Back In Black* really are the seminal albums for the band because so many things came together,' argues Tony Platt. 'The culmination of things at that particular point meant that AC/DC were at their peak at the moment that they had the best set of songs. I would say that the band was at their first peak playing-wise and Mutt Lange was at his first peak production-wise. Plus the overriding factor of having had such a tragic and important death in the band, and with the emotional aspects permeating every facet of the music, there must have been just an amazing perfect storm going on.

'The songs were direct and powerful, the playing was incredibly impactful, nothing was out of place. And the enthusiasm and prowess of Brian Johnson, with his desire to prove himself, cannot be overlooked.'

Even Mark Opitz, who'd had to make way for *Highway To Hell* engineers Mark Dearnley and Tony Platt in the crossover from Vanda & Young to Lange, agrees the Youngs pulled out something special with *Back In Black*.

'*Back In Black*'s very good,' he says. '*Highway To Hell* was okay. But you can see *Highway To Hell* was a transitional experience for them. *Powerage* went, "Okay, that's too far to the left; now we've gotta swing right because the record company wants it and we've got to learn how to do it so we like it." You could see that transformation happening there. If *Back In Black* hadn't worked they would have gone home. That was crucial. A *huge* album. The mere title. *Fuck*. If we're going to do something, it's going to be fucking good. And we're going to do it as best we can, no matter what. And we're going to bunker down with Mutt; he fucking understands us. And you listen to *Back In Black* [against] something like Def Leppard's *Hysteria* – two different records, same producer – and what needed to be done on *Hysteria* didn't need to be done on *Back In Black*, that's for sure. Because these guys could play.'

In the no-frills clips for the title track and five others off the album filmed in one day in Breda, The Netherlands, and directed by *AC/DC: Let There Be Rock* directors Eric Mistler and Eric Dionysius, Malcolm Young is not much bigger than the white Gretsch Falcon he's playing. *Him?* Producing that *unbelievable* riff? Johnson looks like he'd tear your head off in a bar fight. But *that* little guy? He's the one driving all of it. And then there's Phil Rudd, whose desiccated, heavy drumming is eclipsed by the twin guitar work of the Youngs in the AC/DC 'experience' but is as much a part of the AC/DC sound as three-chord riffs and flyaway solos.

In a 1991 interview with German AC/DC fanzine *Daily Dirt*, reproduced in Howard Johnson's *Get Your Jumbo Jet Out Of*

My Airport: Random Notes For AC/DC Obsessives, Rudd says: 'I don't think about making things faster but heavier. A big hit at the right point can improve the song. The trick is the same with all the instruments. Look at the old blues players. Three notes get right to your soul whereas others can play 50 million and not touch you. That's my style. I don't do a lot but I do it right.'

When he left the band for those Martin Guerre years in the 1980s and early 1990s, the band had lost one of its limbs. The Youngs had to shaft him first, though, to realise it.

'Big fucking cement slabs,' says F-word factory Rob Riley. 'One of the greatest fucking drummers that ever fucking lived. He just lays it down. He's absolutely fucking fantastic.'

'Phil Rudd is the heart and soul of that band,' says Mike Fraser. 'He's got really interesting placement of where the cymbals go. It's not always on the one and three or the two and four. He'll do sort of offbeat cymbals, though not a lot of them. So it keeps the drum part powerful and driving but still interesting.'

Sorum maintains the unshowy Rudd has been there so long it's all become symbiotic. It's not the same without him.

'It's really the way Rudd sits in the groove. It's all moving together, although there is a push-and-pull from the other guys that makes it so in the pocket and sexy.

'Phil's a guy that is the ultimate example of meat-and-potatoes drumming while being very musical at the same time. He's not the "Hey, look at me, I'm the drummer" type, which really is what's so cool about Phil.'

As with 'Highway To Hell', a catchy chorus was paramount to 'Back In Black', along with the angular, spiky rhythm.

'It sort of stores up the energy then pumps it out in little spurts,' says Platt. 'The orchestration, and the way that the arrangements are set, every instrument is really doing its part. Nothing's getting in the way of anything else. So when the vocal is spitting out that rhythmic verse the guitars are just underpinning it. They're not trying to be clever in any way. And then when it hits the chorus the riff just *riiiiips* through the whole thing and the riff is as good as the melody.'

Back In Black was also an album where AC/DC happily deployed the benefits of technology to augment their sound and make it fatter and bigger, with the caveat that the tricks used weren't obvious. For *Highway To Hell*, says Platt, the guitars were overdubbed 'quite extensively' and the album was a 'little less live' than its successor.

'*Back In Black* is a very honest, truthful, upfront album and I think it reflects that in the sound. One of the most important things that I remember from working with the Youngs was that you can use effects but don't let them get heard at all. So there are plenty of effects lurking in the background of the albums that I worked on but you're not aware that they're there. They're tucked in behind the natural sounds and they don't impose in the slightest.'

Johnson's vocals, however, were true to his capability. Contrary to rumour there was no double tracking.

'There are some reverbs and some little tweaks and tricks that are sitting there that thicken the vocal out but there's no double tracking. On choruses there are sometimes backing vocals that are singing the same note, the melody notes, the unison notes. Mutt was particularly good at getting those kind of football crowd-type choruses without it sounding like a football crowd.'

Yet most of it was recorded with outdated equipment.

'It's somewhat ironic because the desk that was in that studio at Compass Point at that particular time was an MCI, and it is looked on today as one of the lesser of the period desks,' says Terry Manning. 'But it didn't seem to matter, did it?'

The band that arrived at Compass Point straight after AC/DC was Talking Heads. They were there to cut *Remain In Light*, an album containing one of the most extraordinary songs in pop-music history: 'Once In A Lifetime'.

Equipment didn't matter at all.

⚡

Barry Diament is widely regarded as one of the godfathers of mastering. For Atlantic Records, he was one of the first sound engineers entrusted with a newfangled technology called the compact disc. For a man whose name is synonymous (at least among audiophile geeks) with some of the biggest rock albums of all time (Guns N' Roses' *Appetite For Destruction*, Led Zeppelin's *Physical Graffiti*, U2's *October*, Bad Company's *Bad Company*) his face should be on a few black T-shirts. For AC/DC alone he's created compact-disc masters for *High Voltage*, *Let There Be Rock*, *If You Want Blood*, *Dirty Deeds Done Dirt Cheap*, *Highway To Hell*, *Back In Black*, *For Those About To Rock* and *Who Made Who*.

And mastering is big business. When AC/DC signed to Sony in 2002, the first announcement made by their new record company was that the entire back catalogue would be digitally remastered and reissued. Those 2003 reissues have gone on to shift tens of millions of units. The same catalogue was put through the mastering laundry again when it was made available on iTunes. From an audio perspective, this constant remastering of remasters of old masters can amount to a whole lot of nothing but, with fans as passionate as AC/DC's, it's a licence to print money. In the band's first week on iTunes in the United States in late 2012, there were 50,000 downloads of its albums (15,000 of *Back In Black* alone) and 700,000 single downloads.

Mastering, unlike producing, is a solo, largely thankless activity; Diament didn't work with any members of the band on the AC/DC catalogue when he was at Atlantic. His job, he says, is to look for 'the sonic truth' when he masters an album – rather than 'editorialise or beautify the sound' – in order to keep the original recording and the finished master to as much parity as possible. And it's all about dynamics.

'It is the dynamics that make a record powerful sounding,' he says. 'Dynamics are the differences between the loud parts and the quiet – or less loud – parts. Dynamics determine just how much "slam" the listener experiences in the drums, just how much "weight" there is in the attacks of the bass or in the guitar chords and just how much "bite" there is in the lead guitar solo. One of my prime goals in mastering AC/DC's albums for CD was to preserve 100 per cent of the dynamics in the source tapes.'

As was protecting AC/DC's distinctive 'space' in their music. A job that began with Tony Platt in the recording studio.

'I had room mikes up,' explains Platt. 'I just controlled how much of each instrument was leaking onto the other instruments' microphones. So that when you combine them together, it's what I call "acoustic glue". It enables the sounds to actually feel like they're being played in the same place and at the same time, because of course they are. So it just helps to stick it all together. And that only works if you've got a band who is capable of playing tracks live – two guitars, bass and drums – and can get it right.'

When the tapes got to Diament, the onus was on him to retain that space rather than augment.

'Space is one of those things that can very easily be diminished, obscured or completely eradicated by too much processing, by compression of dynamics or by a less than optimal signal path in the mastering room. In addition to preserving performance dynamics, space and air are important considerations.'

That focus on preservation included some of the incidental sounds from the recording, such as the drag on Brian Johnson's cigarette in 'Rock And Roll Ain't Noise Pollution' and Phil Rudd counting down the beat in 'Back In Black'.

'When we experience a musical performance, it isn't just the instruments in isolation that make up what we hear,' he says. 'The humans playing the instruments and the space between and around the humans and their instruments are all part of the total experience. If the original recording engineer captured these, I would consider them crucial to the whole.'

Unlike some bands, AC/DC also manages to be powerful without being teeth-shatteringly loud.

'Some artists have mistakenly been led to believe that raising the level encoded on their CD – making the record itself "hot" – makes their recording cut through more on the radio. In fact, the opposite is true: radio compressors tend to clamp down even more on this type of record, resulting in rather wimpy sound rather than powerful sound. It would seem many record-company executives also believe people buy records because they are loud. I don't know about this as I've always bought records because I like the music. Neither do I know anyone who ever said, "Wow, that record is loud, I've just got to get a copy."

'Making the record itself loud means other aspects of the sound must be compromised. Prime among these are the dynamics – the very place where the slam and power of the recording come from. This is why so many modern masterings have no real energy. In addition, the compressed dynamics lead to a stress response in the listener. No wonder folks aren't buying as many records as they used to. Joe and Jane Average might not be thinking about it consciously but they know their newer records just aren't as much fun to listen to as records used to be and they don't listen to them as many times as they've listened to purchases made years ago.

'In contrast, when the dynamics of the recording are preserved, the listener will have to turn up their playback volume control, especially compared to recordings mastered in the past several years. What a difference. They can turn the recordings way up without experiencing the painful quality a "hot" record engenders. And they can experience the full dynamics, the full slam, weight and power of the music in ways those "hot" records just can't achieve.'

Tristin Norwell, a freelance engineer at Alberts back in the early 1990s who relocated to London to work for Neneh Cherry and Dave Stewart of Eurythmics before becoming a composer in his own right, agrees with Diament.

'The recording purist will always want to capture and reproduce the full width of dynamics of an artist's performance,' he says. 'If you go to a lyrical theatre, and you are in a good one, you will hear an actor whisper when they are being coy, and when they shout they will get the message across without it being distorted.

'Recording music is the same. But the broadcast mediums are very different and therefore reproduction tricks vary depending on the message being sent. Tools such as compression, limiting and "loudness" are designed to exacerbate subtlety, not retain it. They are designed for an inattentive audience who might only ever hear music when they're shopping, so any musical message needs to be rammed down their ears at any given opportunity.

'*Back In Black* works because it's a beautiful technical reproduction of a great performance and of the space in which they are doing it. With Johnson's voice carefully balanced between the air of the room and two great-sounding electric guitars, a drummer and a bass player, all performing with genuine "intent", it becomes a god-sent ear-candy moment.

'Any less dynamic would soften the message, and any more may send a metalhead to sleep. The point is that the quiet bits are as captivating to its audience as the loud bits. This is what an engineer is talking about when he or she talks about "space" – dynamic space. Space that is reproduced by a technical exercise in which we, the listener, get to "feel" a performer.

'Classical music is usually the best example of this for the audio junkie, as it requires massive signal-to-noise ratios for transparent reproduction, but *Back In Black* comes close to this for the hard-rock junkie.'

For all the audio whizzbangery of the AC/DC catalogue, it hasn't always been so sophisticated. Tony Platt recounts a story that during the production of the *Bonfire* box set in 1997, George Young was forced to master the *AC/DC: Let There Be Rock* film soundtrack from old cassettes Platt had lying about. Norwell recalls that before he moved to the UK he was asked by Alberts to archive the entire AC/DC two-inch tape collection.

'I went into Studio 2 one day and found the in-house building maintenance bloke trying to work out why a tape he'd put on the MCI tape machine wasn't rewinding. I asked what it was, and freaked out when he told me.

'It was an original AC/DC tape. It was so old – and a notoriously bad batch of BASF – that it was dropping metal onto the heads. By the time I got there it was half a centimetre thick. The tape was ruined. Fortunately, it was probably only about two minutes of an old outtake, but I hand-wound it back on and sent it off to be rebaked.'

Rebaking is an archiving process by which the tape is restored temporarily to allow just enough time to transfer it to a new reel.

'Anyway, with a heavy heart I turned down the job. I would have spent six months transferring every recording AC/DC had made to that date. I don't know who did it in the end. Hopefully not the mentalist bong-head from the workshop cellar.'

While Alberts might have been sloppy with their archiving, Lange left nothing to chance in The Bahamas. *Back In Black* was as much a career-defining album for him as it was for AC/DC. He had under his belt a bunch of City Boy, Boomtown Rats, Supercharge and Clover records, Graham Parker's *Heat Treatment* and a ream of one-offs for a gaggle of nobodies. Foreigner and Def Leppard were still to come. The only album he produced between *Highway To Hell* and *Back In Black* was the self-titled debut of Broken Home, a side group of the British band Mr Big, with Platt engineering.

It was during *Back In Black* that Platt saw the first clear signs of Lange's tendency to strive for technical perfection at the expense of feel. Progressively, Lange was becoming more of a taskmaster and today Platt is happy he got to work with him on those early albums for Atlantic and not later in his career, when Lange's requirements for an engineer didn't necessarily fit into what the Englishman wanted to do.

But Platt insists he enjoyed working with Lange, learned more under him than he had under anyone else for a long time and owes him a debt of gratitude. They did five albums as a producer-engineer combo before Platt went off to become a producer in his own right. And he gives a valuable insight into what set Lange apart from George Young.

'I think I was fortunate to work with Mutt at that particular point in time because I think I would have found it difficult once he became a lot more of a perfectionist. Mutt is an extraordinary producer. He is absolutely totally unique. His consideration for the artist, his understanding of the construction of songs and melodies and so on is quite extraordinary.

'A lot of people will say you're either going to get a take that feels good or a take that's perfect and the two things don't go together. You're always going to have some mistakes in a take that feels good and a take that's perfect is probably not going to feel that great. His response to that was, "Well, I don't understand why." He thinks it should be: "Let's just keep going till we get it."

'My ethos has always been that most of the music I really like has got mistakes in it but it feels great and it doesn't bother me too much. From Mutt's point of view it bothers him but it probably doesn't bother anybody else. So we would occasionally clash about whether a take was perfect enough for him and felt good enough for me. And most of the time I would try to persuade him by using my skill and expertise to repair things, to do edits. Certainly on Foreigner's 4 that was the case; there was a lot of me editing one note or a bar into something just to make it a perfect take so that we could have the take that felt best.'

It's a depiction that finds no argument with David Thoener and Terry Manning. Both men paint a picture of Lange as a workaholic, someone who can get by on a few hours' sleep, gets to the studio first and is the last to leave, who doesn't take drink or food breaks, who's totally absorbed in the *work*.

'When a band hires Mutt, they are hiring a producer with a *vision*,' says Thoener. 'It's not easy to follow that vision to its finality. He has a reputation for making wonderful records; that takes time and patience. Any band should know that before making a commitment to Mutt.'

Says Manning: 'He's an amazing, deep thinker and a hard worker. One thing that you will hear on occasion from people who have worked with Mutt is that in some ways they can almost get tired of being pushed to perfection. But Mutt never gets tired.'

Angus and Malcolm, used to George's expeditious approach in the studio, are on the record as having been very unhappy about that.

Yet Mark Opitz pays tribute to Lange for achieving something important.

'His job is to satisfy two things: the artist's integrity and the commercial proposition,' he says. 'And that's a very hard thing to do; it's a hard balance to get right.'

No one can accuse Lange of not fulfilling that brief on *Back In Black*, no matter how big a pain in the arse he would become. Especially when so many of its lyrics were reputedly contributed by him. Derek Shulman calls the albums Lange made for AC/DC 'incredible'. Yet the enigmatic Zambian producer would ultimately pay the price for being far too good.

$$\frac{4}{}$$

As it had for the Youngs many times before and would many times again in the future, it all came to a head over money.

At a minimum Mutt Lange was costing hundreds of thousands to turn up to the studio – millions when royalties were factored in. But the money was more than worth it, according to Steve Leber of Leber-Krebs, AC/DC's management company between 1979 and 1982. 'They could deliver on stage,' he says. 'That was never a problem. AC/DC needed something else. It was always management and a producer. Once you have that team in place you *never* break it up. It's like George Martin with The Beatles. Why break it up? AC/DC not only fired Mutt Lange, they later fired us after we broke them.'

Peter Mensch, the one-time tour accountant for Aerosmith who'd taken over from Michael Browning in 1979, was terminated after an August 1981 performance at the Monsters of Rock concert at Castle Donington, England, was ruined by a malfunctioning sound system. But it affected many bands that day; AC/DC's experience wasn't isolated.

Mensch didn't respond to interview requests for this book and has never explained why he thought he was sacked by AC/DC. His only comments on the matter were to Mick Wall, when he said: 'I was never told why I was fired. They called their lawyer, who called David Krebs, who called me.' And to Phil Sutcliffe: 'I was stunned. Till then my shit didn't smell.' Wall comes to the conclusion that Donington was to blame for the band dispensing with their manager: 'Malcolm was in a vengeful mood. Somebody would have to pay; in this case, Peter Mensch.'

By most reliable accounts Mensch was a hard worker for AC/DC: an ambitious manager who was willing to move to London, hang out and be there for the band whenever he was required. He even identified Bon Scott's body in the morgue.

'That was my first job,' he told *The Sunday Times* in October 2012 as part of a profile of his marriage to former British Tory MP Louise Bagshawe. 'I get a phone call that Bon Scott has died and I have to come and identify the body. I say to the rest of AC/DC, "Couldn't you guys go?" And they go, "No, you should go, you're the manager."'

In April 2013, in a spontaneous question-and-answer session with Reddit, he gave an example of how the band tested his loyalty: 'The dumbest request I've ever received was while managing AC/DC. I was in London. They were in Paris. Phil Rudd wanted hot water because his kettle was broken. He called at midnight to ask me to bring over hot water . . . wish I had told him I would charter a flight to bring him a kettle, and billed it back. Needless to say, I didn't go.'

Mensch briefly stayed on with Leber-Krebs but eventually came to an arrangement where he left to form his own management company – Q Prime – with business partner Cliff Burnstein. Def Leppard, a former Leber-Krebs band, was their first signing – with Lange as producer. Over four albums, the union was lucrative: 1983's *Pyromania* sold 10 million copies in the United States alone and 1987's *Hysteria* sold 20 million worldwide.

Today Mensch is a multimillionaire and manages acts such as Metallica and Red Hot Chili Peppers. In February 2013, *Billboard* jointly named him and Burnstein #55 in its Power 100 list of the most powerful individuals in music. He's come a long way from taking late-night hot-water orders from Phil Rudd.

'I credit Peter Mensch for raising AC/DC to the next level,' says Phil Carson, the man who signed them to Atlantic and who enjoyed a close relationship with the Youngs for many years until it fell away. 'I absolutely consider firing both Mutt and Peter was a mistake. Mutt's excellence as their producer was mirrored by Peter's performance as their manager.'

Leber is still upset about the decision and confirms 'money was a factor' and the band was 'set up in a crazy kind of way' with George Young and Alberts, and George may have been a 'factor' in the decision to can Lange.

'It was just crazy. We loved Mutt. We thought Mutt was great. Peter went on to hire Mutt to do Def Leppard and the rest is history. Mutt became a *superstar* producer. The two elements that broke AC/DC were not the lawyers and the accountants who'd later take over. It was the creative forces of Leber-Krebs and Mutt Lange and, most important of all, the guys delivering on stage. They're a great group of guys. I loved every one of them. I was upset when I lost them. Look at all the groups we had: Aerosmith, Ted Nugent, AC/DC, Scorpions. No management company has that many great rock 'n' roll groups all at once.

'I never lost faith in the band. That's the bottom line. I thought they were the greatest band in the world and we were right. I felt they'd always be big but I just felt that they could have been bigger and stronger if they had [kept] Mutt Lange. He was part of that greatness. The band was better with Mutt Lange than without Mutt Lange.'

But though Mensch has never spoken about why he was fired by Angus and Malcolm Young, Leber's old partner David Krebs has an idea.

'Peter had a girlfriend working for the merchandise company who I think came over to Australia to be on tour with him,' he says. 'They objected. They fired him. We took the position that we didn't understand why they were firing him. We had, like, six months left on our contract.'

The man who replaced Mensch, AC/DC tour manager Ian Jeffery, says he has no recollection of any objection to Mensch's girlfriend.

'No, not at all,' he says. 'They thought Peter had stopped having their best interests at hand and was not around enough during recordings in Paris, though he and I made the trip there [from London] every Friday.'

Australia, where AC/DC had played before Donington, hadn't been the happiest leg of the *Back In Black* tour, Mensch's choice of companion aside. Brawls broke out after two shows at the Sidney Myer Music Bowl in Melbourne, where there were nearly as many people drunk on the park lawns outside the venue as there were inside. Police were injured, emergency rooms were overrun, trains and trees were trashed, noise complaints were lodged, 100 people were arrested, and there was talk the bowl would never host a rock concert again. The band copped a big spray in the Australian press, prompting Brian Johnson to hit back at the critics: 'We were warned, we were warned. But even I thought it went over the top.'

$$\text{\textit{ϟ}}$$

It was a period of enormous angst, avarice, spite, bitterness and recrimination but with little point to any of it. Not to mention physical violence. The Youngs have never been shy of a barney, from George headbutting a Cairns good ol' boy in the 1960s (which opens Murray Engleheart's biography), Angus punching Mark Evans or Malcolm decking Phil Rudd. Angus and Malcolm fought over Malcolm's alcohol problem that saw him leave the band temporarily in the late 1980s. The three brothers even had an all-in punch-up over the disastrous show at Reading in 1976.

When I ask Evans why he didn't thump Angus back, there is a long pause.

'I don't know, to be honest,' he says and starts laughing. He concedes, though, he was drunk, out of line and out of order. The fracas had been sparked by a comment he made to Fifa Riccobono. 'I held nothing against Angus for doing that because I brought it on myself. Malcolm put himself in the middle of it, along with Michael Browning, who physically had hold of me. Angus was behind Malcolm. I remember seeing a line through him and thinking, "I can sneak one through you." What stopped me, right at that very moment? I know it was respect for Malcolm, unquestionably.'

So how does Angus punch? Evans flops one of his hands onto my shoulder like a dead fish.

'*Nothing.* Because the guy's tiny. He can't hurt you. There's nothing going on.'

Steve Leber believes Malcolm, a hothead at the best of times, was jealous of the star Angus had become and that jealousy was taken out on the band's management company. In the Wall biography Ian Jeffery says the two namesakes of Leber-Krebs never got close to either Malcolm or Angus and Leber admits to me that 'they didn't like David . . . the reality was that David had a falling out with the band and I came right into it really soon after Peter had left'.

Krebs puts his hand up.

'I didn't have any real chemistry with Malcolm,' he says. 'I was personally handling Aerosmith and Ted Nugent, who were both major bands at that time, and in retrospect I should have handed AC/DC over to Steve, who loved them, but I split my time and took them on and it was an error. They were recording [*For Those About To Rock*] in Paris and I would go over for a week a month, which was a mistake.'

Furthermore, when the Youngs decided to part ways with Leber-Krebs, he didn't stand in their way and do whatever it took to keep them.

'I don't think I tried hard enough. I didn't have the personal relationship to swing it around. I never thought we had the leverage to hold on to them. That was my take on it. When I went over to Paris, it was semi-strained. A lot of internal politics had begun to play with the road manager [Jeffery] who wanted to become the manager and all this other stuff that went down.'

Jeffery, however, rejects that categorically.

'Absolute bollocks,' he says. 'I had no intention of becoming manager.'

Krebs continues: 'I was at a meeting with Peter Mensch and Ted Albert and I made a fatal error when I said to Ted Albert, "You know, Ted, do you think it would [really] be a good idea to give the group back half their publishing?" That went over not well. So you never know what that may have set in motion. I didn't quite realise all the relationships.'

Leber says, however, that in his own case the suggestion he didn't have a relationship with the Youngs is not true. He became friends with Angus. He would go into Angus's dressing room after shows and talk for hours while Angus painted.

'I was very close to Angus. Matter of fact I always believed that Malcolm was – they all were – jealous of the fact that Angus, without singing a note, was the lead in AC/DC. He *is* the lead. There is no AC/DC without Angus. Malcolm was certainly jealous of my relationship with Angus. When I say jealous, Angus used to want to stay at my house. And I don't think Malcolm liked it.'

Jeffery tells me that Leber's biggest mistake was 'thinking because Angus had the shorts he was it all'. A similar comment was made by Jeffery to Wall, in which he charged Leber with thinking Angus was the 'route into the band' and 'didn't have a clue that it was Malcolm that ran the show'.

'Exactly. Absolutely true,' concedes Leber. 'Malcolm was the businessman. I said Malcolm was jealous of my relationship with

Angus – maybe jealous is the wrong word, maybe he was *angered* by my relationship – but Malcolm called the shots. And then Angus would not stand up for me, even though Angus was the one who pursued the relationship with me.

'But I loved the whole band. I really did like Malcolm anyway, even though Malcolm didn't think so. I did. Malcolm was the key to making decisions and basically he didn't want to let me run the band because he thought I would favour, I guess, Angus. But that wasn't true. I really cared about the band, period. I felt they were the best rock 'n' roll band out there.'

He wasn't the only one to misjudge the power of Malcolm.

'Ian Jeffery's right,' says Krebs. 'When I met AC/DC I spent my time talking to Bon Scott. We didn't realise that Malcolm was really the engine. He wasn't a warm person. But that could be cultural.'

Leber is prepared to admit that not working on his friendship with Malcolm was his downfall: 'I didn't play it right.' So much so that he maintains if he'd done it differently and played the Young family's 'politics bullshit' properly by befriending Malcolm the same way he'd befriended Angus, 'I'd still have the band'.

Over 30 years later, he's got some clarity on what he did wrong.

'You know at the time you get so close to something you sometimes don't see it? I didn't realise that Malcolm would be so pissed.'

So pissed that quite possibly the most important relationship AC/DC ever had over their four-decade-long career with any of their management disintegrated.

Susan Masino, who makes considerable hay out of her friendship with the band in *Let There Be Rock: The Story Of AC/DC*, in fact endlessly rabbits on about it, deals with AC/DC's break with Leber-Krebs in six words: 'The band stopped working with Leber-Krebs.' About as much as you would expect from a writer who admits, 'I planned to give them a copy of my new book as soon as it was done. I wanted to make sure they didn't have any problems with it.'

'Malcolm never said a word. He didn't have to. He just fired me,' laughs Leber, but it's a laugh rooted in some sadness. 'Look, let's face it: [Leber-Krebs] broke the band. We broke them wide open. I'm the one that got them to the number-one position in the United States. We broke *Back In Black*. We created the excitement for this band. We did a great job managing them. The issue, if there was any issue that was critical, was that we were outspoken. *We* managed bands. We didn't let the bands manage *us* and we delivered.'

The Youngs' notorious nose for a deal would claim another casualty.

'[The thing AC/DC didn't] realise was that we were getting a decent commission but we paid for our expenses when the band wasn't touring,' continues Leber. 'So if the band didn't tour for two years we still had the expense of running the operation and keeping the excitement going.

'We had huge expenses but the band bought into the idea that Ian could do it for three or five per cent or whatever. It was ridiculous. I break the band, we do an incredible job, we get them to become a stadium band – *stadiums* – and we get terminated because they want to reduce our commission to nothing. Well and truly, no one took them beyond where we took them.'

So if Jeffery was getting five per cent or less, how much was Leber-Krebs's commission?

'A lot more. Let's put it that way. I don't think it should be in books. A *lot* more.'

I put a ballpark figure of 15 to 20 per cent to him. Pretty standard management fees.

'Yeah, standard ballpark, between 15 and 20, but the bottom line is we were reduced to something more reasonable [to AC/DC], but we couldn't work for five per cent. I turned down many groups for that five per cent bullshit. I said, "My time's too valuable."'

For his part, Jeffery says any suggestion he worked for 'three or five per cent', as Leber alleges, is 'absolute rubbish'. He too would get boned and the band would end up being managed by Alvin Handwerker, Leber's accountant. It wasn't so bad for Leber-Krebs, though, because according to Leber they'd done a savvy piece of housekeeping and retained a share of the AC/DC catalogue, including *Back In Black*, 'which paid us handsomely and still does . . . not a bad thing'.

Is this a source of resentment for the band?

'Yep. They have resentment because we own the catalogue. Yeah, *yeah*. Definitely resentment. All of our bands resent the fact we were smart managers and kept the positions in the catalogue.'

So what's his cut?

'Can't say but it was a good situation. But life goes on. I was angry about them leaving me. We did a great job. I was pissed but hey, listen, those things happen. We didn't get the proper recognition for breaking them when everybody else turned their back on them. I always felt that the band kind of, like, didn't appreciate the job we did. It happens a lot. But there's only one time in the history of a band when they really need you – and that's in the beginning.'

So what hurt more? Losing AC/DC or Aerosmith?

'They both hurt. But there's a difference. With Aerosmith, I ripped up their contract because they were heroin addicts and I didn't want to kill them. And they kept on getting more and more money from me but [Steven Tyler and Joe Perry] couldn't get off heroin, Steven especially. I didn't want to see him die. And John Belushi had just died – before that they were friendly – and I realised that Steven was going downhill. I had sent him to many, many institutions. I wasn't going to stay away from three kids and I wasn't going to spend all my time with him. He needed someone who could – and would. So even though Aerosmith owed me five more albums and they had just signed a long-term contract with us I threw them out and ripped it up.'

Krebs backs this account.

'We really threw them out. They didn't fire us. They had gone too far. I had spent over five years trying to cure them, ineptly.'

'Steven later hugged me and appreciated the fact that I'd saved his life,' reveals Leber. 'Because of course, again, they don't like to admit those things. So that one, Aerosmith, I canned them. AC/DC: they canned me – for no real reason – and that pissed me off. If they'd canned me because I was doing a bad job, I could accept that. But don't fire the guy who broke you and did a great job over *money*.

'I'm not bitter about it at all. I laugh about it all the way to the bank because I kept the Aerosmith catalogue and publishing. I kept the AC/DC catalogue. After all these years, I still have it. More than 30 years later I still get money every year and it's a *lot* of money. But at the same time I love the guys. I would have liked to have kept the relationship.'

For tens of millions of reasons.

Says Krebs, matter of factly: '*Back In Black* has outsold the highest selling Aerosmith album two to one.'

AC/DC
'You Shook Me All Night Long'
(1980)

Lyrically, it's the strongest song on *Back In Black*. Musically, despite undeniable flecks of Head East's opening riff in 'Never Been Any Reason', it's become *the* good-time anthem of a band that can't help writing them: a perfect combination of straight-ahead rock and melodic pop that by AC/DC's already peerless standard is so exceptionally radio-friendly it's been covered by middle-of-the-road divas Celine Dion and Shania Twain.

'Just so much going for it. How could any rock song be better?' says Terry Manning. 'It's got a great beat. It's just so incredibly simple. There's so much space around the punctuations that start it off. And then when it all comes together and the chorus starts with the bass coming in and everything, it just rocks. It's rock 'n' roll. Every time I hear it I'm excited by it. I could literally listen to that song a hundred times in a row and not be tired. It keeps you going.'

Yet when Tony Platt presented 'You Shook Me All Night Long' to the marketing team at Atlantic Records at 75 Rockefeller Plaza he was shocked to discover those who liked it were outnumbered by those who didn't. The head of the department dug it but he was in a minority.

'I remember two or three of these marketing guys going, "Nah, I don't see that as a single at all",' he says. 'That's one of the biggest rock singles of all time. So that framed my idea of marketing people within the music industry, that's for sure. It's a song that stands up for itself.'

'Head and shoulders above *everything* else,' agrees Phil Carson. 'It epitomises rock 'n' roll that embodies lyrical humour, along with a musical construction that surrounds a great melody. Hearing it in strip clubs all over the world doesn't hurt either.'

But it's a song that dogs Angus and Malcolm Young like Banquo's ghost. Is it, along with other songs on the record, actually one of Bon Scott's?

⚡

Certainly the best lines (and song titles) on *Back In Black* and their punchy brevity have all the hallmarks of Scott's handiwork and it's very tempting to make a case for it on that basis alone – despite Malcolm's declaration to *Classic Rock* magazine in 2003 that the mere suggestion was 'complete bollocks', the repeated assurances of the band that the whole album is 'a tribute to Bon' and the uncredited but generally widely accepted lyrical contributions of Mutt Lange and even Tony Platt, who says, 'Lots of lines used to get put forward. They just came from *everybody*.'

First up, Angus and Malcolm themselves have confessed that right before Scott died they were working on some songs (barely more than titles at that stage) that found their way onto *Back In Black* and that the late singer had jammed on drums with them in a rehearsal studio on bare-bones versions of 'Have A Drink On Me' and 'Let Me Put My Love Into You'.

It certainly tallies with Doug Thaler's recollection of how the band operated as a songwriting unit around the production of *Powerage*.

'From the early days when I was down there in Australia, I know that what the band did was sit around and come up with titles. And then they would write the song after they had the title to it. "Kicked In The Teeth", onward and onward. And Bon would work on the lyrics. Before they wrote any music or any lyrics they had a list of titles. And then they would figure out what song they could write behind the title.'

More compellingly, though, there are the 'scraps of paper' or 'notebooks' containing lines for songs that allegedly appear on *Back In Black*. Depending on whose version of events you'd rather believe, they were either found in Scott's flat by Ian Jeffery and production manager Jake Berry or left behind at Jeffery's flat by Scott.

I ask Jeffery where they are now.

'I think I still have them somewhere,' he says.

In an interview with *Classic Rock* in 2000 Malcolm further admitted he took possession from Jeffery of 'a note with some scribblings of Bon's' with 'a couple of little lyrics on there' but 'nothing with a title or that would give you any idea of where his head was at'.

Startlingly, Angus contradicts him in the same magazine in 2005. While conceding 'a lot of ideas, choruses, song titles and lyrical snippets were already in place before Brian arrived' he also says 'there was nothing from Bon's notebook' on the album.

'All his stuff went direct to his mother and his family. It was personal material – letters and things. It wouldn't have been right to hang on to it. It wasn't ours to keep.'

The brothers can't have it both ways.

In any case, we know now for a fact that Jeffery claims to be in possession of something that was Scott's. Not everything went back to the Scott family. Which begs the question: if there were lines from those scraps of paper or notebooks on *Back In Black*, why are they still being held by Jeffery?

'Bon used to come round to mine every Sunday for dinner and then [go to the] pub and would quite often leave stuff at my place,' he says. And then he starts backtracking. 'Not totally certain about *Back In Black* but I seem to remember a couple of words, lines [of Bon's being on there]. Maybe not.'

Berry supports Jeffery's account for this book. Speaking about the day he entered the apartment of the dead AC/DC singer, Berry says he didn't see any notebooks in Scott's flat. 'I never saw anything like that. Never saw any books.'

But, all that aside, what really gives weight to the theory that Scott may have contributed to *Back In Black*, even the unforgettable title track, is what was going on in his personal life and his disenchantment with life on the road.

'On the last tour [he did] of the US, Bon was in very bad shape,' says Thaler. 'He was at a point where he'd drink till he passed out and he'd wake up and start drinking again. And the shows were suffering. The guys in the band were getting upset with him because he'd always been more of a leader, but his life had really started to take a bad turn. I think he was depressed. He had an Italian girlfriend named Silver [Smith], who he was living with in Sydney when I came down there in the winter of '78, and a story he told me was that they had a little savings account and she just up and took off and cleaned out their bank account. He wasn't quite right after that.'

Anthony O'Grady has a similar memory: 'Bon was reeling from the effects of age, excess and pressure. But some say he'd written close to half the album that would become *Back In Black*. He'd started out thinking, "Thank God I've got a gig with young rock 'n' rollers and I'm not with old farts like Fraternity any more. I'm 28, or whatever he was at that stage, and I'm hanging out with 17-year-old kids and getting 15-year-old girls and I'm so grateful for this second chance in life."

'But by the time 1978 came around, and he was on his umpteenth tour of America, he was starting to really feel his age. From what Vince Lovegrove was telling me about Bon in 1980 when he met up with him in Los Angeles, the clock was winding down.'

He had started to call old friends out of the blue.

Recalls Thaler: 'I know the last time I spoke with him it was strange. About a week before he died I got a call from him, and he was in England, and he never used to call me from England – I mean he'd call me when he got to the US; when he'd come to New York he'd come over and hang out at my apartment – but I got a call from him and he sounded like he was in good spirits. I said, "You're finally going to the bank." He goes, "Well, I gotta tell you, mate, nothing's changed for me. I'm still rubbin' two nickels together."'

A reading of the lyrics to 'Back In Black' suggests it is not a memorial to Scott but a paean to money, a favourite Scott theme, and even references a Cadillac. The American car is first mentioned in 'Rocker' off *TNT*, but more significantly on *Powerage* in 'Down Payment Blues', a song about being poor. 'Back In Black' is its logical sequel: a song about being rich, of fortunes turning around. In his book *Dirty Deeds*, Mark Evans revealed Scott had wanted to record a solo album of Southern rock, of 'Lynyrd Skynyrd kind of stuff, but really ballsy, something that swings'.

If indeed he'd written 'Back In Black', was it his fantasy of cashing in and perhaps even getting out?

Scott's late mother, Isa, told Lovegrove in 2006: 'He always said he was going to be a millionaire. I just wish he'd been alive to see it and enjoy it, you know? Almost every Christmas, Ron [Bon's real name is Ronald] came home to visit. The last time we saw him was Christmas '79, two months before he died. Ron told me he was working on the *Back In Black* album and that that was going to be it; that he was going to be a millionaire. I said, "Yeah, sure, Ron."'

The line held by the Youngs has never deviated. As Angus told *Guitar World* in 1998: 'The week he died, we had just worked out the music and he was going to come in and start writing lyrics . . . I wouldn't say that he was disgruntled. He was itching to go . . . basically, the music had been finished before he died. The bulk of the tracks were the same.'

The credit on the album is final: 'All songs written by Young, Young and Johnson.'

⚡

Lyrically, a better case can be made for Bon Scott's involvement in 'You Shook Me All Night Long'.

When he got chosen as AC/DC's new singer Brian Johnson hadn't even been to America, let alone toured it with the band, so why was he getting all hot and bothered by his memories of 'American thighs'?

Johnson, by his own explanation, was fantasising about what he hadn't had.

In an interview with a Finnish website (no longer available online), he said: 'We were in [The] Bahamas [recording *Back In Black*], and I had seen a couple of American girls. They were just so beautiful. They were blond, bronzed, tall . . . so I was just using my imagination; what I would do if I could. But Bon had done it all.'

He changed his tune slightly for VH1's *Ultimate Albums*: 'I'd seen them [American women] on the TV. And I'd always wanted to fuck one! They just looked fab. Everything pointed north on them.'

In the same interview Johnson speaks of being possessed by something unexplainable when he wrote the song in his room at Compass Point.

'I was just sitting working on a song and I was a little worried about it being up to the standard of AC/DC and was it good enough and who the hell am I to try to follow in the footsteps of this great poet. He was a great poet, was Bon Scott, not just a songwriter. And something happened to me and I don't like to talk about it. But something definitely happened to me and that's all I'm going to say about it. And, uh . . . er . . . it was good. It was a good thing that happened.'

The tale is expanded in the 2013 book *Louder Than Hell: The Definitive Oral History Of Metal*: 'I don't believe in spirits and that. But something happened to me that night in that room. Something passed through us and I felt great about it. I don't give a fuck if people believe me or not, but something washed through me and went, "It's all right, son, it's all right", this kind of calm. I'd like to think it was Bon but I can't because I'm too cynical and I don't want people getting carried away. But something happened and I just started writing the song.'

Possessed by Scott's ghost? Johnson's a lovable figure but it stretches credulity.

More curiously, Malcolm Dome, a British AC/DC biographer, wrote in *Classic Rock* in 2005: 'I can personally attest that Bon did indeed write some lyrics in preparation for the record, having seen a few sheets myself. This was just a couple of days prior to the man's death, at a venue called The Music Machine in Camden, North London . . . one line sticks in my mind as being on one of those sheets: *She told me to come but I was already there.*'

The best line in 'You Shook Me All Night Long', if not the best line on the whole album.

It's more than enough for Thaler.

'As a comrade in the band, as a good guy, someone that has the right temperament and disposition to fit into the band, Brian Johnson was a great choice,' he says. 'As far as a singer, I thought he was a very strong choice that way. Where he lacked, I think, was that Bon Scott – to my mind, for the kind of music that they did – was a great lyricist. And I don't care who tells me anything different: you can bet your life that Bon Scott wrote the lyrics to "You Shook Me All Night Long".

'It's Bon Scott's lyrics all over the place. As you got further into [AC/DC's career], by the time you got to *For Those About To Rock* the lyrics weren't clever any more. They weren't the tongue-in-cheek tough-guy lyrics like "Whole Lotta Rosie". Bon had a style. Brian couldn't really match that. And by *The Razors Edge* you see that Brian's not even part of the writing team any more.'

Mark Evans is not so sure.

'My idea about it is that there was this crossover of lyrics,' he says. 'I'll underline that I don't know either way. But what I will say is that with Angus and Malcolm, they had a history of writing lyrics before Bon came along. If you go right back to "Can I Sit Next To You Girl" and even "Rock 'N' Roll Singer", that's their lyrics. The lyrics of "Can I Sit Next To You Girl" are great. People think that's a real Bon-esque lyric. That's actually Angus's and Malcolm's writing. "TNT" – Angus used to walk around reciting that; it used to be his catchphrase.

'To me, the lyrics on *Back In Black*, it's not a big stretch for me to think that it's Angus and Malcolm writing them. Because they wrote great lyrics; they came up with a lot of the titles.'

So what about Brian Johnson writing those lyrics?

'I dunno,' he says, fixing me in the eye. 'Has he written much after that?'

⚡

The other eight songs, then?

There was the claim made by Anna Baba, Bon Scott's Japanese girlfriend at the time of his death, that 'Rock And Roll Ain't Noise Pollution' was a title he'd been playing around with and, in the words of Clinton Walker, was 'inspired by the time when the caretaker at Ashley Court [Scott's apartment building in Westminster] complained about loud music late at night'.

In 2005, Walker told Australia's *Rolling Stone* magazine: 'There are trace elements of Scott all over the album; titles and couplets that, if he didn't write, certainly do him proud.'

Consider the lyrics in 'Rock And Roll Ain't Noise Pollution' about taking a look inside a bedroom door and a girl looking 'so good' lying on her bed. It's a natural companion piece to *Highway To Hell*'s 'Night Prowler', with its lines about a girl lying naked on her bed and the protagonist slipping into the room. You can hear Scott singing 'Rock And Roll Ain't Noise Pollution' even if it's another guy, Johnson, getting the words out.

'I think that's where the confusion comes from,' says Evans. 'People look at Bon's lyrics and hear that really cheeky scallywag attitude. And "Rock And Roll Ain't Noise Pollution" really fits that premise. But it goes back to prove my point. People also connect "TNT" and "Dirty Deeds" to that Bon thing. But I know both were ideas from Angus, the actual lyric. He didn't write the whole thing but *TNT/I'm dynamite* and the lyric *Dirty deeds/Done dirt cheap* were all Angus's influence. So, for me, being inside the tent at that point, I do see it flowing on.'

Which would support what the Youngs have said about the song. Malcolm told VH1 in 2003 he and Angus 'bopped it down in about 15 minutes' when they needed a tenth song to round off the album. Said Angus to *Classic Rock* in 2005: 'The last track we completed was "Rock And Roll Ain't Noise Pollution", which

Malcolm and me actually wrote [at Compass Point] . . . we spent a few days writing it in between guitar overdubs and the other things we were doing on the record.' And Malcolm again: 'The song was about London's old Marquee Club when it was in Wardour Street. It was in a built-up area and there was this whole thing about noise pollution in the news, the whole environmental health thing. That's where it came from.'

More recently, though, there was a startling allegation made on Sydney radio by Mark Gable that Scott wrote the lyrics not for just one or two songs on *Back In Black* but for the *entire* album.

'I did get this from the inside,' he tells me. 'My understanding, from several sources of people who were with Alberts back in the day who were close to the band, is that even though Brian Johnson is credited with writing lyrics on *Back In Black*, Bon Scott's estate gets one-third of the publishing royalties. This is becoming more common knowledge throughout the music industry.'

So not just the one song? The whole album?

'Apparently.'

Is that as far as you can elaborate?

'What I was told was that it was the whole album, yes.'

Even Isa Scott supported the Gable story in Walker's 1994 book, *Highway To Hell*.

'They were going to hit the top this time,' she told Walker. 'They called it *Back In Black*. They had to give it a name, you see, but Ron, I think, did all the words.'

Not convinced yet? Oddly, the 1980 vinyl edition put out by Alberts doesn't even have a lyric sheet.

So if Ian Jeffery has the infamous/apocryphal notebooks, and he's on the record as telling Wall that 'a few lines' of Scott's 'are in there' on *Back In Black*, what songs are they?

'Tough one,' he says. 'Can't really remember.'

Right. An odd statement for someone who said in the same book that being sacked by the Youngs was the 'darkest day of my life'.

With time, has that hurt eased at all? How does he regard the Youngs now? Does he stand by his words?

'Was and still is [the darkest day of my life]. I was giving them 100 per cent as I always did. No, it has not eased. I still wish I was with them. I just feel really sad. They were my whole life. They say time is a healer; maybe so. But it does not take away the sadness I still feel every time I hear an AC/DC song. Especially Bon.'

⚡

Yet so much of the *Back In Black* conspiracy theory doesn't wash.

Where Bon Scott's lyrics were known for being naughty, sly and mischievous with accompanying melodies, in the words of John Swan, 'narrated, tugged, pulled and almost spat out with venom', Johnson's lyrics are too frequently the opposite: obvious, graphic and crude. And so many of the songs on *Back In Black* are just that.

If Johnson was possessed by Scott's spirit and managed to write the lyrics to 'Back In Black', 'You Shook Me All Night Long', 'Rock And Roll Ain't Noise Pollution' and 'Hells Bells' off his own bat, then great – all power to him and any royalties that flowed his way. Because that creative eidolon conspicuously deserted him on 'Shake A Leg' and 'Shoot To Thrill'.

Outside those four standout tracks, too many of the other songs on *Back In Black* are steeped in a kind of juvenile chauvinism that Scott, a rogue but one who loved women, was careful not to allow to cross over into outright crassness. That, in all honesty, can't really be said for 'Givin' The Dog A Bone'. (The original spelling in the title – 'Given' – remains on the band's website, though has been changed for some reissues.)

Anthony O'Grady remembers that his early interviews with the Youngs 'tended to degenerate into smutty tales'. He spent some time with them on the road, where what he quaintly describes as 'adventures of the day' were plentiful.

'They were very typically Scottish-Australian and blokish in the sense that they only had time for one sort of girl: and that was the groupie mould, the sort that didn't mind being a possession and thrown around. They would accept groupies from other bands when they were touring in the country and in different cities and they would roll up one of the groupies or a couple of them in a carpet and give them to bands who were coming to Sydney.'

Phil Sutcliffe, who had spent time with AC/DC in 1976, wrote eloquently of the band's view of women for *Classic Rock* in 2011.

'They stand for everything I disagree with about our chauvinist view of the woman's role, yet they're so totally honest, open and funny about it that I got carried away with liking them, and became aware again how life, for all the fine ideals we raise and cling to, insists on turning out like a seaside cartoon postcard. A belly laugh is often the sanest reaction. And that's what AC/DC are into.'

David Mallet, who directed the second 1986 video for 'You Shook Me All Night Long' – featuring a blonde bimbo in black leather astride a mechanical bull – played consciously on this 'seaside cartoon postcard' humour.

'The same humour was in the lyrics and the delivery as was in the videos,' he says. 'I just think the videos were an extension. You call a record *Stiff Upper Lip*, for instance, you can quite easily go away and make a sex-comedy video. When everybody else approaches sex as it's sexy, we approached it as it's funny. I think a very significant part of the "no bullshit" thing [with AC/DC] is that if you look at some of the lyrics and some of the song titles, it's pretty obvious that a comedy video made like that is suitable.

'You go right back to Mae West in the 1930s. Her humour was exactly the same as AC/DC's humour: "Is that a gun in your pocket or are you just glad to see me?" That was Mae West's version of "You Shook Me All Night Long". It was a particular type of humour that was in vogue in the 1980s as indeed it was in the '30s. Nowadays people would jump all over it and say it's not correct or it's not this or it's not that. Normally those people have no sense of humour whatsoever.'

So what is AC/DC's secret?

'It's some sort of musical genius and a totally unique, and I'm glad to say very out of date, sense of humour.'

And 'You Shook Me All Night Long' itself?

'It's an obvious song, it's an easy song, it's an easy chord progression, and yet the way it's played, the little breaks, the way that a bar is split up, not into four, but into about 16, is beyond any subtlety of any other rhythm section that I know. I do not understand it. I don't understand how they are as good as they are.'

Manning also praises it for its simplicity: 'So many other bands, even if they had been able to come up with that song and tried to record it, would have had a lot more "stuff" on it from the beginning. It would have lost the power when everybody came in together.'

⚡

Phil Carson won't have a bar of any conspiracy. He says the very notion that Johnson didn't write the lyrics for 'You Shook Me All Night Long' and indeed the whole album is preposterous tosh.

'All the lyrics on *Back In Black* were written by Brian, with a little gentle nudging by Mutt,' he says. 'As a lyricist, Bon nailed the elements of rock 'n' roll, and there was more than a little humour in his approach to writing. When Brian assumed that mantle, he carried on the tradition. Brian's lyrics embodied the spirit of the band. His lyrics have balls and wit.

'I thought it was something of a disgrace when he was excluded from the writing in later years. He recently played me some new songs he had written. They were far superior than anything that appeared on the last AC/DC album.'

So why, when Johnson would appear to have the faculty to be able to knock together a song about an incident he didn't even witness (1983's 'Bedlam In Belgium', based on a fracas involving a brandished weapon that broke out onstage at a gig in Kontich near Antwerp in 1977, when overzealous and aggressive police tried to shut the band down for breaking a noise curfew), did Angus and Malcolm exclude him from the writing? Was any reason given?

In a 1990 interview with *Kerrang!* magazine reproduced in Howard Johnson's *Get Your Jumbo Jet Out Of My Airport*, Angus claims that he and Malcolm relieved Brian of his duties to help him through some personal issues and free him up to concentrate on giving his best performance. It would appear that the suggestion, made by Johnson himself, that he simply ran out of ideas for lyrics should be treated with some scepticism.

Carson has his own ideas but gives a cryptic, albeit heavy hint: 'I have never discussed the thinking behind this, except to draw your attention to the fact that the people who write the songs get most of the money.'

Who wrote what? Who owns what? Who gets what? How did AC/DC manage to write four of their career-defining songs and the second-biggest selling album of *all time* in the space of a matter of weeks and without their single biggest influence, Bon Scott, yet write only *one* song approaching the same quality ('Thunderstruck') in the following 33 years? No one inside the Youngs' inner circle wants to talk about it – at least publicly – and why should they? Who can prove anything anyway? Does it really matter?

Yet again it comes back to *Rashomon*. One band. So many different versions of an unobtainable truth.

10

AC/DC

'Hells Bells' (1980)

John Wheeler of Hayseed Dixie is in no doubt.

'Maybe the greatest melodic guitar signature line ever,' he says. 'And yet it's not particularly difficult to play. But that's part of its genius. Something doesn't need to be technically difficult in order to be stunning; in fact the contrary is often true. Beethoven's most famous piano piece isn't one of the very difficult sonatas, but rather "Für Elise", which was just a little trill study he tossed off in five minutes so his student, Elise, could practise her third and fourth finger trills. Yet it's so simple and catchy that everybody knows that melody. "Hells Bells" is the same sort of brilliance. You hear it once and it bounces around the inside of your skull for the rest of your life.'

It was certainly a song that American soldier Mike Durant will never forget. Durant was piloting *Super Six-Four*, a UH-60 Black Hawk helicopter, during the Battle of Mogadishu in 1993 when its tail rotor was hit by a rocket-propelled grenade. The chopper crashed in the middle of the city, badly injuring all four crew members on board. Durant broke his back and right femur. He remained trapped in his seat before two Delta Force snipers that had been dropped into the crash site pulled him out. In the ensuing firefight with militiamen and angered locals, they were killed. Durant never saw his crew alive again and was himself beaten with the severed arm of one of his comrades before being taken hostage. The events of the botched raid on Omar Salad and Abdi Hassan Awale, associates of warlord Mohamed Farrah Aidid, chronicled in Durant's memoir, *In The Company Of Heroes*, formed the basis for Mark Bowden's book *Black Hawk Down* and the Ridley Scott film of the same name. In all, two Black Hawks went down, 18 American soldiers died and 73 were injured that day: 3 October 1993.

During his 11 days of captivity before being released by Aidid, American military helicopters circled the city, looking for any sign of Durant, who was being detained in 'a cheap, highway hotel' he called 'Hotel Nowhere'.

My injuries continued to sap a lot of my strength, and I had been dozing again when my eyes suddenly snapped open. The sound of a helicopter flying overhead was louder than before, and in addition to the familiar twirling of Black Hawk rotors, I heard something else. It sounded like some sort of broadcast, as if a large stereo speaker were mounted on one side.

It was probably a propaganda effort of some kind, I reasoned. The helo was flying in a large circular pattern and the transmission was difficult to discern, fading in and out with the wind and the changing position of the aircraft. I looked desperately around the room, wishing I had some way to signal them. Now, as the helo turned again, the thin sound of tolling church bells grew clearer.

Bonggg! . . . Bongg! . . . and then it faded out for a moment as the aircraft made a turn away from my location.

When I heard it again I raised my head. What the hell is that?

It was, of all things, 'Hells Bells'. Durant's would-be rescuers, astonishingly, were playing the opening track of *Back In Black*, trying to find him. They knew AC/DC was one of his favourite bands.

> I sat straight up. My crushed spine sent jolts to my brain, but I didn't even feel it. 'Hells Bells'? Somebody up there was playing 'Hells Bells'? I rubbed my eyes, thinking I must have lost it . . . [but] this was sure as hell no accident! I was not dreaming. The Black Hawk made a roaring turn right above the Hotel Nowhere and AC/DC's earsplitting tune about challenging Satan and his forces of evil thundered into my cell and banged off the walls . . . I smacked my fist into my palm. The Night Stalkers were sending me a message, there was no doubt about it. I had no idea why they were playing that specific tune, but at the time I didn't care – it was music from heaven. Later, I would learn that it was all part of a plan. Suffice it to say that the concept was brilliant.
>
> The Black Hawk moved off and the broadcast faded, but I had blasted out 'Hells Bells' in my bunk at the compound often enough and I knew the words by heart . . . *I hear you, boys,* I thought with an incredible surge of excitement. *I hear you! I don't know what you're trying to tell me, but I'll think about it over and over until I get it!*

Pilot Dan Jollota then started broadcasting Durant's name, assuring their captured comrade that he and his colleagues wouldn't leave without him.

The broadcast and the Black Hawk faded away. I listened hard for a good long minute, but they were gone. Yet I knew that they'd be back. They wouldn't give up. Soon enough, they would find me. Soon enough, it would all be over.

It was quiet again. The children played and mothers called them home. There was no gunfire. I looked over at the small window of my cell. The orange rays of the setting sun were slanting in through the shutters, and in my mind I could still hear Dan's voice and promise.

'We will not leave without you.'

My spirit was soaring, but I quickly wiped the wetness from my cheeks and settled down. I wasn't going to allow the Somalis to witness the heights of my new hope.

As the sun continued to set on that day, I experienced a wave of powerful feelings. But there was one thing I no longer felt at all . . .

Alone.

'I had a broken leg and back,' says Durant, who has also told his unique story to the *Beyond The Thunder* documentary. 'I could hardly roll over. Hearing it did inspire me knowing my friends were out there trying to locate me so that they could launch a rescue mission. I would say it had a psychological effect, primarily. They also had voice recordings from one of my friends. [Dan] was calling my name and saying that they would not leave without me.'

A haunting still of Durant's battered face from a video made by his interrogators ended up on the cover of *Time* magazine and on his return home he was feted as a war hero. He asked AC/DC's attorney if he could use the lyrics of 'Hells Bells' (no apostrophes for AC/DC, cobber) in his book. He was flatly refused.

That was until Brian Johnson found out about it.

'We were just about to give up. Brian found a copy of our request and sent an email to me introducing himself and saying we could use the lyrics for pretty much whatever we wanted. The next day I called his cell and left a message. We were glad to know we didn't need to change the book and I was actually in line at a retail store buying a new copy of *Back In Black* on CD when my cell rang and it was Brian calling me back. He explained he was a big military-history buff and again said we could do what we wanted with the lyrics on this project.'

AC/DC's unfailingly generous singer also helped John Wheeler when he heard *A Hillbilly Tribute To AC/DC*, which contains 'Hells Bells'.

'Cliff Williams hired us to play a party for him the year that the album came out,' says Wheeler. 'I say "hired" because he insisted on paying us even though we tried to insist on playing it for free. I've spoken to Brian on the phone a few times. He actually talked about us a lot to the press in 2001 during their *Stiff Upper Lip* tour in the States. His endorsement rather silenced a lot of the critics who were very much inclined to trash our record at first. I can't thank Brian and the rest of AC/DC enough for being good sports, sincerely.'

AC/DC's new record company, Sony, was less charitable. Hayseed Dixie's name had originally been AC/Dixie but lawyers representing the band forced them to come up with another name.

'AC/DC loved my first record – they were incredibly supportive of it and for that I could not be more grateful. But it was explained to me by "legal people" that [the band doesn't] control the trademark to their own name; rather, it's licensed to their record label. This situation is quite common for bands on major labels; hence situations like Prince not owning the rights to use his own name for performance for several years and going by that wacky squiggle symbol – which looked remarkably like a middle-finger salute to me – for several years.

'Even though I believe we could have won a lawsuit with Sony in court, we would have still essentially lost because it would have cost a fortune that I didn't have. And it wasn't a fight worth fighting. Sony has a team of lawyers on retainer just sitting around looking for something to do every day that might help justify their wages to their employers. I couldn't see any compelling reason to help them do that.'

So he only ever heard from Williams, Johnson and the band's lawyers, not the Youngs?

'Correct. I've never met Angus or Malcolm. Although I know that Brian speaks for the band a good deal of the time in the press, but he doesn't say anything that they don't all agree with him saying when it's tour press.'

⚡

It's an odd thing about 'Hells Bells' but Mike Durant's harrowing experience in Somalia isn't the only time the song, written in memory of Bon Scott according to Angus and Malcolm Young, has been used by the US military as so-called 'acoustic bombardment' in the theatre of war.

'Hells Bells' also makes an appearance in Dexter Filkins's 2008 book *The Forever War*, which opens with the author describing the Battle of Fallujah in 2004 and hearing the song coming from PSYOP (psychological operations) vehicles while 'minarets were flashing by the light of airstrikes', 'rockets were sailing on trails of sparks' and 'bullets poured without direction and without end'. The aim of PSYOP in Fallujah was to drown out the call to arms coming from the mosques. The Iraqis, the thinking went, hated rock 'n' roll.

'A group of marines [sic] were standing at the foot of a gigantic loudspeaker, the kind used at rock concerts,' he wrote. 'It was AC/DC ... I recognised the song immediately: "Hells Bells", the band's celebration of satanic power, had come to us on the battlefield.'

Filkins, a writer for *The New Yorker*, didn't want to be interviewed for this book. But Australian photographer Ashley Gilbertson, who was with Filkins and won the Robert Capa Gold Medal from the Overseas Press Club for his images of the battle, was happy to talk.

'The US military – the Marines and the Army – often uses AC/DC, particularly "Highway To Hell", "Back In Black" and "Thunderstruck",' he says. 'But the first two are the favourites. So I'd been at a couple of battles in which that had taken place. Fallujah was a little stranger than all the rest because the minarets, which are kind of like a belltower in a church where they call to prayer, were playing a call to arms for the insurgents at the same time. So on one side you had the American Marines playing AC/DC and on the other side you had the insurgency playing the Islamic call to arms.

'It was the first night of the actual attack. After that it was really all on foot and the only vehicles we would see were to resupply the Marines. Otherwise it was all house-to-house combat. So when Dexter and I were with 1-8 Bravo and we crossed into the north side of Fallujah that was the last time we had vehicles around us. Of course, we had tanks for the first half-day but they disappeared pretty quickly. So it was all the more eerie. There was white phosphorus coming down illuminating everything. It was the soundtrack to one of the strangest and most unlikely scenes you ever want to be in.'

Why did the US military choose to use AC/DC?

'It motivated the Marines. They love music. It pumped them up. Inside the Humvees it was more American punk-rock and rock but on a PSYOP vehicle the band I can only really remember is AC/DC.

'The weird thing is I actually came to love the band. I used to hate them with a passion. I thought it was bogan music. But now I will actually often put it on in my office [in New York]. It's really bizarre. Now the music motivates me. I feel like PSYOP worked on me. It might not have worked on anyone else but it worked on me. Now I enjoy it. So many of those memories are not happy so I should really despise it all the more. But it has the opposite effect. I think part of it is the fact that I made it home.'

Mogadishu, Fallujah . . . it doesn't end there. In 2009 'Hells Bells' was also revealed as having been highly favoured for interrogation purposes in US military prisons, including the notorious Guantanamo Bay. A Pentagon spokesman called it a 'disincentive' rather than torture.

Which is ironic, given that in a *Rolling Stone* interview with David Fricke in 1980, Brian Johnson made it plain what he'd like to do to reviewers, who were then scathing of the band: 'I'd like to lock 'em up in a cell with AC/DC music for a week. They'll be crying, "Let me out, let me out!" Then I'll put on a week's worth of disco music – and I'll bet you a pound to a pinch of shit they'll be hung by their own belts. With AC/DC, at least they'll come out singing the choruses.'

⚡

With its foreboding tone and dark imagery, 'Hells Bells' was the starting point for more than three decades of a very different AC/DC, one that had only been hinted at by 'Night Prowler' off *Highway To Hell*. The old standby themes of sex, alcohol and rock 'n' roll were rapidly superseded by sex, guns and the National Rifle Association's brand of liberty: 'Shoot To Thrill', 'Guns For Hire', 'Big Gun', 'Fire Your Guns', 'Heatseeker', 'War Machine'. With Scott missing from the line-up, Huerta's sharp-edged logo has never seemed more sinister or militaristic. It's no accident that AC/DC was considered a perfect fit for *Iron Man 2*. Tony Stark's full body armoured superhero is probably the most martial and seriously packing figure in the Marvel Universe.

Explained the film's director, Jon Favreau, before its release in 2010: 'When I was watching AC/DC with my wife and my son and they were playing "Shoot To Thrill" at The Forum [in Los Angeles], I thought, "You know, *this* is how he should show up, right in the middle of this and take the armour off. That's the Tony Stark version of doing things."'

Yet to be fair to the Youngs, who never would have intended for their songs to have such negative associations as violence, torture and death, AC/DC is frequently played at American, Australian, British and European sporting venues and used as entrance or celebration music by athletes and teams.

'It really does go beyond the military,' says Durant. 'I've often remarked at how many times you'd hear "Hells Bells" being played during sports venues over the years. It's just good, hard-driving rock 'n' roll. Not so much today, but in years past, we lived by the "work hard, play hard" rule. I think the band symbolises that same mentality. I've always liked their music and still listen to it today. Like many people, for me it brings back memories of good times and good friends working hard and playing hard.'

Stevie Wright, no Johnson man, even considers it his favourite AC/DC song: 'I love "Hells Bells". The whole thing. The atmosphere. Brian sings really well on it, as he did on "You Shook Me All Night Long". Johnson did some really good songs.'

But is it, as Filkins flippantly suggests, a 'celebration' of Satan? Pull the other one.

∮

While AC/DC has long been harassed by 'God botherers', scrutinised by paranoid loons convinced its name and song titles have hidden codes and nefarious meanings, targeted by Pope

Benedict XVI (in 1996, when he was Cardinal Joseph Ratzinger, he reportedly described their music as 'an instrument of the devil') and unapologetically appropriates infernal iconography and themes in its music, album art and concerts (Angus Young is well known for sticking two fingers above his head while playing live), the band's association with the netherworld is nothing but a harmless lark, a fun prop.

If anything, thematically it's simply a bridge to the album that preceded *Back In Black*.

'"Hells Bells" has ties to "Highway To Hell",' says Joe Matera. 'Bon Scott was singing he was on the road there. Then, with the next release, there's this eerie connection. When you listen to the song there's this bridging of the spirit of Scott and the old AC/DC to the new AC/DC with Johnson: a revitalised band though in no way a better one. Both are the first songs off the respective albums. *Highway To Hell*, the last with Scott. *Back In Black*, the first with Johnson. It's like this connecting thread musically, as it has all the hallmarks of AC/DC though with a new voice.'

As Robert Hilburn wrote in *The Los Angeles Times* in 1985: 'You won't find people at AC/DC's shows wandering around in hooded robes and sacrificing small animals. You'll probably just see 10,000 kids having a good time.' *Back In Black*'s opening track, he goes on, is 'a song about youthful bravado . . . the message is rebellion, not devil worship'.

Tony Platt, who was lumped with the responsibility of recording a four-tonne bell in a church tower in England, only to find it was full of birds that ruined every attempt he made (the bell that ended up being used was custom-made in a foundry), won't hear of it being Satanist either. He follows the Young script: that the whole album was their tribute to Scott and that the brothers' only concerns were to make the songs as good as they could be; good enough that Scott would be proud of them.

'There's no hidden agenda,' he says. 'A good song and a good lyric is one that enables people to make their own interpretations. But those interpretations come from the person who's listening. They're not necessarily the interpretations that were put on it by the person writing it. And the better a song is the more interpretations that can be put on it. It's a very positive thing about a song if lots of people can come up with interpretations, but once they start putting words into the mouth of the writer then I think it's a very wrong thing to do.'

Platt worked for the last time with the Youngs on the cursed *Flick Of The Switch*, as engineer and co-producer, and has had only fleeting contact with them since. After *Dirty Deeds* had been cynically exhumed from the Atlantic crypt and the uneven *For Those About To Rock* had failed to do the business that was expected of it despite going to #1 on the American charts, the critics were sharpening their knives for AC/DC.

'It wasn't the happiest of albums. There were all sorts of tensions within the band,' he says, skirting over Malcolm Young's bust-up with Phil Rudd that saw the drummer abruptly leave the sessions and AC/DC altogether for a decade. 'They were all pretty knackered by that point. It was the album that copped the backlash, really. I don't think it was nearly as bad as a lot of people made it out to be.'

Why did Platt's relationship with the Youngs come apart?

'I don't really know. I've never actually managed to get to the bottom of that. I've always wondered why it's not been a close thing, because I considered them to be good mates. Malcolm and I always got on extremely well, as did Cliff and I. It wasn't just my working with them. I really liked them a lot as people. We had a lot in common.'

Phil Carson is another key figure from that period who can't understand what went wrong for the band with *Flick Of The Switch*. He sheets home the blame to Atlantic's president and Jerry Greenberg's replacement, Doug Morris.

'I thought it was a very good record, too,' he says. 'I am convinced things could have been different if *Dirty Deeds* had been held for a much later release. There is no doubt in my mind that *For Those About To Rock* would have been a much bigger album and the momentum generated by that would have helped *Flick Of The Switch*, and indeed subsequent albums.'

AC/DC, he contends, were never quite the same afterwards.

'After an interim period with their accountant managing their career, the band hired Stewart Young, who is a consummate professional. Unfortunately, even he couldn't undo the damage that Doug Morris and other peripheral people had done.'

Stewart Young wouldn't agree to a full interview though did say the business relationship began inauspiciously but ended up becoming something close and personal. Did he have any misgivings about the band when he signed on to be their manager?

'Yes, I did, and so did they about me,' he says. 'Therefore we started with a trial for three months so both sides could get to know each other. We worked together for around 10 years. I love the Youngs. They are great and always treated me, my staff and my family with the utmost consideration.'

Jerry Greenberg vacated the president's office at Atlantic Records in 1980, around the time of *Back In Black*'s release, when he got a big outside offer to start his own record label.

'I remember when I was leaving we had five of the top 10 albums,' he boasts.

Atlantic's response was to give him an in-house label, Mirage Records, and have him stay on as a consultant. He eventually left for MGM/United Artists in 1985, but not before trying to help another bunch of rock 'n' roll outlaws from Australia break the big time: Rose Tattoo.

They were his fourth signing at Mirage and part of the thinking behind the deal, he says, was to maintain good relations with George Young, Alberts and AC/DC. The response from the American trade press was an odd mix of excitement and bewilderment. *Billboard*, reviewing the US release *Rock 'N' Roll Outlaw* in October 1980, said they were 'more primitive and raucous than AC/DC' and made The Ramones and Van Halen 'seem like the pinnacles of restraint'.

'A great, *great* band,' says Greenberg. 'Unfortunately, we couldn't break them here in America. At that time FM radio wasn't playing a lot of that kind of music. That's why it took so long for AC/DC to happen.'

Rob Riley says that since then the situation hasn't been much better for the Tatts, who now bear little resemblance to the band Greenberg signed all those years ago.

'Rose Tattoo has been ignored by the Australian music business, criminally,' he rails. 'Guns N' Roses coming out and saying we inspired them was a beautiful thing but fucking nothing got done about it.'

Does he see a time when the era that produced iconic Australian bands such as AC/DC, INXS, Men At Work, Cold Chisel and Rose Tattoo will return?

'That'll never come back – at least not in my lifetime. Eighteen- and 20-year-olds on television talent shows: that's the future of Australian music. It's not only depressing but it's fucking disgusting. Back in our day, you wouldn't dare get on stage if you were half-baked or average. You had to be really good. That's why all the stuff you hear back in the old days is really good.'

AC/DC meanwhile, Greenberg maintains, 'didn't feel the love' from Atlantic when he left the company. But in November 1996, while running Michael Jackson's label MJJ Music at Sony, he saw AC/DC again in Melbourne. With the backing of Epic Records president and later chairman David Glew, Greenberg's former general manager at Atlantic and 'a very big supporter of AC/DC', the old stager unsuccessfully tried to woo the Youngs from Warner Music Group, the parent company of Atlantic, Atco and AC/DC's temporary new home, East West. Glew eventually signed AC/DC to Epic, another label of Sony, in 2002.

'To set the record straight, Steve Barnett and I were the ones who made the deal to bring AC/DC and their catalogue to Epic,' says Glew.

Barnett, formerly AC/DC's co-manager with Stewart Young, was executive vice-president/general manager and became president of Epic in 2004. He has since left Sony to head up Universal's Capitol Music Group.

'The reason [we got AC/DC to sign] was Steve's longtime relationship with Angus and the band and his belief in the band,' he continues. 'The catalogue was always and will always be strong. It passes from generation to generation of kids. We repackaged all the catalogue and remarketed the catalogue, which was incredibly successful for the band and for Epic.'

The catalogue. Two words that in modern record-industry parlance have become synonymous with 'cash cow'.

The Wall Street Journal spelled it out plainly in 2002: 'While AC/DC will record new music for Sony, the crux of the deal is the rights to a valuable catalogue of 16 of the band's 18 albums that have been released since the mid 1970s by AOL Time Warner Inc's Warner Music Group. That is somewhat different from many previous megastar deals – such as Sony's 1991 deal with Aerosmith

– which are much more geared toward profiting from new music and don't include an act's prior music.

'Signing AC/DC demonstrates again that, in today's music industry, the past is just as important as the future. Big music catalogues don't often come up for sale. And when they do, record labels eager for market share and revenue growth are willing to pay a high price for proven hits . . . Sony seized on an unusual opportunity. Record companies typically own catalogues of their biggest selling classic rock acts. But in a renegotiation of its contract with Warner Music more than a decade ago, AC/DC got back ownership of their master recordings and has licensed them to Warner Music ever since.'

The controversial Morris, meanwhile, became head of Sony Music in 2011. For a man whose handling of *Dirty Deeds* would have done much to convince the Youngs to leave Atlantic, it's extraordinary that they're now under his purview again. But, to borrow the title of one of their songs, money talks.

Looking back on the years that truly shaped the band – 1975 to 1980 – and saw the Youngs at their most inspired and creative, Jerry Greenberg credits the promotion department at Atlantic as the unsung hero of the AC/DC story. A group of people, led by Michael Klenfner and Perry Cooper, who rallied behind the Australians, even though a lot of their workmates didn't get the band and found them a nuisance because they didn't fit into narrow radio formats. But he saves the last word for himself.

'The whole company really got behind AC/DC,' he says. 'I will tell you, that as the president who had to make the decision when Michael Browning would sit across from me, and tell me he needs $25,000 more to keep the band on the road, and I'd say, "Okay, you got it", I think I was one of the most important people to contribute to their success. I feel very much a part of their success by bringing in Mutt Lange and making that shot happen.

I'm proud of watching AC/DC go from the fucking Whisky A Go-Go to The Forum to a stadium.'

For a guy who says he gave a whole lotta love to and wrote a whole lotta cheques for AC/DC, he hasn't got much back. The Youngs – publicly at least – have said nothing about Greenberg.

But, if it ain't plain by now, that's how these brothers roll.

11

AC/DC
'Thunderstruck' (1990)

In July 2012 an extraordinary news item made headlines around the world: a malware virus had crippled Iranian nuclear stations at Natanz and Fordow by getting their computers to play the AC/DC song 'Thunderstruck' at high volume.

A nuclear scientist at the Atomic Energy Organisation of Iran (AEOI), which was already reeling from attacks by the American- and Israeli-developed Stuxnet and Flame viruses, had sent an email to Finnish IT security firm F-Secure, clearly befuddled about what to do: 'I am writing you to inform you that our nuclear program has once again been compromised and attacked by a new worm with exploits [sic] which have shut down our automation network at Natanz and another facility, Fordo [sic], near Qom. According to the email our cyber experts sent to our teams, they believe a hacker tool, Metasploit, was used. The hackers had access to our VPN. The automation network and Siemens hardware were attacked and shut down. I only know very little about these cyber issues as I am scientist [sic] not a computer expert. There was also some music playing randomly on several of the workstations during the middle of the night with the volume maxed out. I believe it was playing "Thunderstruck" by AC/DC.'

Mikko Hyppönen, chief research officer at F-Secure, wasn't able to establish the email's veracity but was able to confirm it was sent from inside the AEOI and the name of the sender was a known scientist. However, when Hyppönen asked for a sample of the worm, the scientist didn't oblige because, he protested, he wasn't a computer security expert.

Soon the emails to Hyppönen stopped completely.

The AEOI's chief, Fereydoun Abbasi, claimed the story was false but a few months later, a hacker called Unforsaken, a self-described 'huge fan of AC/DC', claimed responsibility on Reddit and said the AC/DC trojan was 'the most thrilling' of his career.

Hypönnen, though, says that it is not possible.

'The claims from Unforsaken are, how should I put this, full of it. Not legitimate at all. Writing a trojan that plays AC/DC could be done by anyone. Getting the trojan *inside* AEOI, especially to a large amount of their machines, could *not* be done by anyone. It would indicate a state-developed attack, most likely from the same source as Stuxnet and Flame . . . so the US and Israel governments. Or it was all a weird hoax.'

Whatever the truth of the matter, going from a New Year's Eve gig at Chequers nightclub in Sydney in 1973 to potentially disabling an Iranian nuclear power plant in 2012 is an extraordinary story arc. But that's how far the Youngs have come. There isn't a part of the world where their music isn't listened to, bought, covered, downloaded, pirated, converted into ringtones or turned into malicious computer bugs.

If a lone hacker or the US and Israel governments were indeed responsible for this act of cyber terrorism, they chose well: if you're going to fuck up the servers of a member of the 'Axis of Evil', do it with 'Thunderstruck'. Out of all of AC/DC's contributions to testosterone rock, it's probably their most muscular song: a mesa of sound that completely belies the physical slightness of the men playing it. Their height – or lack of it – is one of the Youngs' enduring charms. Again, how do guys so small create a sound so big?

'The thumping B chord played by Malcolm provides the foundation for the riff's droning pedal tone and gives the song its modal quality,' says Joe Matera. 'The chords are simple but are a force to be reckoned with. They reflect perfectly the song's title and subject matter.'

'I love the sparsity of it,' says Rob Riley. 'The way it begins with Angus and then Malcolm arrives. It just makes the hairs on my neck stand up. Then Chris Slade comes in, the rest of the band. I get a full fat. It's fantastic. It just rocks like all fuck.'

It's also notable for being just about the last song Brian Johnson ever did where he sounds like he's supposed to and not like a strangled cat.

John Swan, the man who could have taken his job back in 1980, was ironically called in to do vocals on a cover of the song for a Holden vehicle commercial in Australia.

'I'm not kidding you,' he says, 'my throat felt like I had been fucking gargling razor blades for about three weeks. It's really hard work. They take it to a place where it's going to be hard for anybody to emulate.'

Before late Bon Jovi and Aerosmith producer Bruce Fairbairn ultimately got his credit on *The Razors Edge* (again, no punctuation for AC/DC), a lot of the record had already been done at Windmill Lane Studios in Ireland, with George Young helming the sessions.

(In fact, a two-inch multitrack tape of an early version of 'Thunderstruck' was left behind and reported in March 2013 to be in danger of being destroyed after the studio was renovated.) Then George had had to stop working on the album because of family issues and the production shifted to Vancouver, Canada.

Derek Shulman, through his longstanding connection to Bon Jovi, introduced AC/DC to Fairbairn.

'I feel very proud of matching the band with Bruce and producing *The Razors Edge*,' he says. 'To be honest it took a while for me to convince the Youngs that these guys were AC/DC type of people. However, I'm happy to say once they agreed to meet and talk and then record, it went unbelievably smoothly.'

Did he have a feeling it would do for the band what it did?

'As to knowing the album was going to "relaunch" their career, yes. I really did have a feeling that this was a special album for the guys and I couldn't have been happier to work with them to make that happen.'

The experience wasn't so special, though, for Brian Johnson. *The Razors Edge* was the first AC/DC album to carry the Young/ Young credit for every song.

'As Rob said, they "rock like all fuck",' says engineer Mike Fraser. 'This is how AC/DC plays in the studio. Recording AC/DC, while it may be work, is not *hard* work. It's all about making them feel comfortable and being ready to capture them when they fire up. They tend to work very quickly in the studio, so as an engineer you need to be ready for anything at all times.'

It's a far cry from the laboured, torturous sessions they endured under Mutt Lange. But the Youngs – still with George calling a lot of the shots – have navigated themselves to a point in their career where they, and not their record company, managers or producers, make all the decisions. They do few overdubs. They do a lot of single takes. No bullshit.

'The band doesn't really need a producer,' says Fraser. 'But they like to have one there to make sure they're getting what needs to be gotten. Less is more. There are only two guitars, bass and drums in their recordings. None of the guitar parts are doubled and that leaves more room for the vocal without having to make the vocal super loud. They also play their instruments with a lot of dynamics instead of relying on a mix to create the dynamic. This is something that truly makes their sound so distinctive.

'They rarely do more than four takes. But with each take you feel that intensity building and building till finally when you get the right take it's just this onslaught of music. It's just incredible. They have that ability to draw this aggression and angst without being aggressive and angsty. It's like they're playing in front of 60,000 people but you've got three guys in the control room staring at you.'

That stadium effect is obvious on 'Thunderstruck'.

'"Thunderstruck" was one of those songs that just fell into place very easily. Angus's picking part makes that song build like no other. I remember being so pumped up while recording his parts that we were just about as sweaty as he was.

'It's magic. It's got this great sort of build. It's almost like it's holding back, *holding back*, the whole way, but you know it's going to pay off. It just gets you going right away, pumped up. It whips you into a frenzy. It doesn't pay off too early and the whole song is just this build. It's awesome.'

Certainly Angus's opening fingerpicking sortie – one and a half minutes of it before Malcolm arrives – annihilates the memorable intro to 'For Those About To Rock' and has now become almost his signature song.

'To many guitarists, the intro to "Thunderstruck" is to Angus Young what "Eruption" was to Eddie Van Halen,' explains Matera. 'Both sprang out of a playing exercise to morph into a signature and most representative piece for each player. The intro shows the simplicity in Angus's guitar work; yet, like yin and yang, it's underscored by a difficulty. What I mean by that is that during my years of teaching guitar, I've see many guitarists not play it correctly. Most assume it's played completely with the left hand, using hammer-ons and pull-offs – as he does in some live performances – yet in the studio Angus performed it with every note picked individually, using an extremely refined alternate picking technique. It again shows the strength and agility in Angus's playing and also reveals how some of the most loved classics and riffs are usually inherently simple.'

'Thunderstruck' is also the nearest thing to a Scottish Highlands nod in an AC/DC song since 'It's A Long Way To The Top' or 1976 'Jailbreak' B-side, 'Fling Thing'. It served as a timely reminder that this meat-and-potatoes rock band from Australia, which had been completely written off in some quarters as being tired, out of ideas and having had their day, was still capable of coming up with something strikingly brilliant, creative and original.

Qualities David Mallet accentuated in his clip for the song, one of those perfect marriages of sound and vision that encapsulate what is so powerful about rock when it is done right.

'They'd been away,' he says. 'They'd been off the scene for some time. I thought to myself they have to come back with an absolute humdinger of something, and I didn't think it was right to come back with a comedy video like we had done [just four years] before [for "You Shook Me All Night Long"]. I think they had to just come back and redefine what rock 'n' roll music was all about on film. I thought I would like to make the definitive heavy-music video. AC/DC is the ultimate stadium band. Apart from Queen and the Stones, they're probably the only band around who have 10 or 12 songs that are literally anthems.'

Terry Manning likens AC/DC's reliability to a Hollywood star of the 1930s and '40s: Gary Cooper.

'You look at Cooper,' he says. 'He has that same look on his face all the time. He's always stoic. He's always quiet. He delivers his lines a certain way. But it always fits in the plot. It always *works*. In much the same way that Cooper could act with such restraint, yet deliver the movie, deliver the key scenes, deliver the really important lines when needed, AC/DC can stay right where they are comfortable, right in the groove that they love – and invented, by the way – and always come up with something powerful, new and relevant.

'That's a *huge* talent when you're able to do that. Think of it: they had been a band for many years, had "done it all" more than anyone else in the genre, when they came up with the intro guitar for "Thunderstruck". How many bands could do that?'

⚡

Not many.

But not many bands could dispense with the drummer who played on their most popular song so soon after recording it and going on a world tour to promote it. ('Thunderstruck' was by far AC/DC's most popular single download when its back catalogue was released on iTunes in November 2012.)

Yet that's what Angus and Malcolm did in 1993, informing Chris Slade – who'd joined them in 1989 after Simon Wright left to play for Dio/was sacked by Malcolm (take your pick) – that Phil Rudd wanted to come back, was going to have an audition and a decision would soon be made. Disgusted, Slade quit. Rudd rejoined the band in 1994. By late 2014, he was missing again.

The bone-domed Slade, whose unusual stage set-up (featuring two gong bass drums on either side of him) and energetic performances – both in the David Mallet video and live at Donington in 1991 – were such an intrinsic part of the song's power, told French website Highway To AC/DC in 2011: 'I didn't even touch a stick for three straight years.' He used the break from music to take up drawing and sculpting at art school.

Slade ended up forming an AC/DC covers band, Chris Slade Steel Circle or CS/SC. But in 2015 he made a return to AC/DC, taking the seat of the man who had replaced him: Rudd.

Mark Evans saw AC/DC with Slade at Donington and wasn't taken with him: 'I'm probably the worst person to see AC/DC without Phil playing drums because it's so ingrained in my head. It was just like, "What is it?" I'd stop short of saying it sounded like a cover band, it never would, but it was *just . . .*' He trails off.

What about the gong bass drums?

'I was surprised when I even saw those. I wish I'd been at that meeting, you know,' he laughs. '"Fuck 'em off, pal. Fuck 'em off. Where are the fuckin' drums? Fuck 'em off."'

Even Mike Fraser agrees: 'Chris Slade is a great guy and a great drummer but I think he tries to emulate that [Rudd sound] as opposed to just doing it. He was a great drummer for them, though. Great sound and a great look.'

So much greatness and it did him a fat lot of good until Rudd's legal difficulties gifted him another opportunity. For a band who thought they'd got back their best line-up with Rudd, in nearly a quarter century since releasing *The Razors Edge* AC/DC hasn't written a song that comes anywhere near the inventiveness and power of 'Thunderstruck'. Slade was a big part of it.

Was he treated badly the first time around? You could make a case. But the band doesn't give a fuck what anyone else thinks.

So what of AC/DC now?

Barely a week goes by when an announcement isn't made that they've released another commercial tie-in by licensing their logo to a new product or lending their songs to a new Hollywood movie or multiplayer game. It's abundantly clear that the ideas are drying up and it's time to cash in. Like The Rolling Stones, AC/DC in the 21st century is more brand than band.

Even with the arrival of *Rock Or Bust*, musically not a lot is happening – and hasn't for decades – yet AC/DC has always been, supposedly, about the music. Today that is not really the case. And it's not just because they don't have the same machismo or fire in the belly they had as young men. It's not an issue of age. It's not an issue of Malcolm's illness. The sound is still there, as good as it's ever been, but the songs are not.

'I believe when you are younger you tend to have more of a swagger and a chip on your shoulder looking for someone to knock it off,' says Fraser. 'Over the years the boys have always tried to maintain their "sound" but have continued to develop it further and mature it. For instance, on *Stiff Upper Lip* they were going for a more "bluesy feel" than they had on past records.'

Though what use is a 'bluesy feel' if the songs aren't a patch on what they used to be and the singer can't hit the right notes?

Today, AC/DC is largely about perpetuating a fiction. Other bands have good back catalogues. What keeps AC/DC more relevant, fashionable and cool than any other band that has been around for the past 40 years is the fact beautiful young women who men want to fuck and other women want to be – models, pop stars and actresses alike – go on getting photographed wearing their AC/DC T-shirts with Gerard Huerta's perfect logo on the front, and those bevelled edges on the lettering still read out one fundamental word: rebellion. But it's a crock. The AC/DC of today stands mostly for money.

In spirit, too, something seems to be missing. As Clinton Walker wrote so perspicaciously in *Highway To Hell*: 'The earthiness, humour and honesty [Scott] invested the band with, it today only echoes.'

And he wrote that all the way back in 1994.

'It's *okay*,' says Mark Opitz of 21st-century AC/DC. 'Mike Fraser is very good. But it's not fresh for me any more, like it used to be. But that's coming from someone who was there listening to it 24 hours a day when I was working with them. And it was the vibe of the '70s and early '80s that was somewhat akin, not to Beatlemania, but to the pointy end of the cultural revolution. Music *was* the pointy end of that revolution in those days. Music's not the pointy end any more. The cultural revolution is multifaceted: technology, sports, fashion.

'I went and saw AC/DC the last time they were in Melbourne, just went and got a regular seat and checked 'em out, and I didn't get tingles up my spine or anything like that, but then again I wasn't down the very front either. That was opposed to seeing them playing in the '70s at the Bondi Lifesaver with Angus duckwalking up the bar with no shirt on and gashing his leg on a schooner glass, a roadie gaffer-taping it up – all while he's still duckwalking along the bar and getting back on stage – and Bon's cheeky smile. There was nothing corporate about it or anything like that. There was no elaborate stage set. It was just fucking balls-to-the-wall rock 'n' roll.'

Those Sydney days are so long gone that they might as well be another world. On the *Black Ice* tour AC/DC was a Vegas magic act, all smoke and mirrors, an exercise in illusions. That little guy in the school uniform with the Gibson SG is 60. Geordie's old singer still has his cap but beer guts stopped looking good in black singlets a long time ago. He's replaced the singlets with large sleeveless shirts. The other three still have most of their hair but play far enough back on the massive stage that you need to squint to realise they're older than your dad.

The sets are bigger. The crowds are bigger. But so is the fantasy. The fans buying the tickets to their shows are buying a commercialised, Sony-remastered rendition of 'no bullshit'. Has this band that for so long resisted releasing a greatest hits album become a glorified karaoke machine? Has AC/DC become The AC/DC Show, like one of Jerry Greenberg's tribute bands? Perhaps.

But the love and affection is still there because the Youngs remain a totally unique musical force, even if AC/DC is performing the same old songs or remastering them, over and over again. With age, talent doesn't diminish even if creativity has a habit of ebbing away. It just finds new people to appreciate it.

Tony Platt recently worked on a set of vinyl re-releases for the British market and was struck by the power of AC/DC's early records: 'It was very obvious in those early albums that the raw material was very much there. The energy is just phenomenal. It really threatens to throw the needle off the records.

'There are little things that they're particularly good at. The way Malcolm and Angus play unison chords but in different positions. So instead of sounding like a double-tracked guitar it sounds like one really big guitar. The Young family is just a musical bunch of people and they have a really good, open, healthy attitude to making music. They don't complicate things unnecessarily.'

That 'one really big guitar' has changed music and changed lives. Between them George, Angus and Malcolm Young might have stopped writing masterpieces such as 'Evie', 'It's A Long Way To The Top' and 'Back In Black' but very few musicians, even the best of the best, get to write one masterpiece in a lifetime. The Youngs have come up with a couple of dozen, if not more. For that, they will go on enduring, can be forgiven some character faults and are more than entitled to be cut some slack. Whatever it is they do, whatever magic they deal in, it's working.

Says Rob Riley, in his inimitable style: 'No cunt can take that away from them.'

DRAMATIS PERSONAE
'Who Made Who'

TED ALBERT Founder of Albert Productions (Alberts) and producer of The Easybeats. Died in 1990.

BILLY ALTMAN Rock critic for *Rolling Stone*.

JOE ANTHONY Disc jockey for San Antonio radio station KMAC/KISS. Died in 1992.

ROB BAILEY Bass player of AC/DC.

DICK BARNATT Photographer of AC/DC.

JIMMY BARNES Lead singer of Fraternity and Cold Chisel. Solo artist. Brother of John Swan.

STEVE BARNETT Co-manager (with Stewart Young) of AC/DC.

BILL BARTLETT Disc jockey for Jacksonville radio station WPDQ/ WAIV.

TONY BERARDINI Disc jockey for San Rafael radio station KTIM and Boston radio station WBCN.

JAKE BERRY Production manager of AC/DC.

JOE BONOMO Biographer of AC/DC.

ANTHONY BOZZA Biographer of AC/DC.

HOLGER BROCKMANN Disc jockey for Sydney radio station 2JJ.

CORAL BROWNING Sister of Michael Browning. Publicist for AC/DC.

MICHAEL BROWNING Manager and co-manager (with Cedric Kushner) of AC/DC.

CLIVE CALDER Co-manager (with Ralph Simon) of Mutt Lange.

PHIL CARSON President of Atlantic Records (UK). Sometime bass player of Led Zeppelin and AC/DC.

KEN CASEY Lead singer and bass player of Dropkick Murphys.

PERRY COOPER Promotion executive at Atlantic Records. Died in 2005.

TONY CURRENTI Session drummer of AC/DC and Stevie Wright.

MARK DEARNLEY Engineer of AC/DC.

JIM DELEHANT A&R executive at Atlantic Records.

BARRY DIAMENT Mastering engineer of AC/DC.

GEORG DOLIVO Lead singer and guitarist of Rhino Bucket.

JIMMY DOUGLASS Engineer of AC/DC.

PAUL DRANE Film director of AC/DC.

SIDNEY DRASHIN Concert promoter of AC/DC.

MIKE DURANT US Army Special Operations helicopter pilot. American war
    hero.

ROBERT ELLIS Photographer of AC/DC.

MURRAY ENGLEHEART Biographer of AC/DC.

AHMET ERTEGUN Co-founder (with Herb Abramson) of Atlantic Records. Died
    in 2006.

NESUHI ERTEGUN Executive and producer at Atlantic Records. Brother of
    Ahmet. Died in 1989.

DAVE EVANS Lead singer of AC/DC.

MARK EVANS Bass player of AC/DC.

BRUCE FAIRBAIRN Producer of AC/DC. Died in 1999.

BERNARD FANNING Lead singer of Powderfinger.

SNOWY FLEET Drummer of The Easybeats.

KIM FOWLEY Producer of The Runaways and The Clingers. Died in 2015.

MIKE FRASER Engineer and co-producer (with Rick Rubin) of AC/DC.

ALLAN FRYER Lead singer of Heaven. Died in 2015.

MARK GABLE Lead singer and guitarist of The Choirboys.

TIM GAZE Guitarist of Stevie Wright.

ASHLEY GILBERTSON War photographer.

CHRIS GILBEY A&R vice-president of Alberts.

DAVID GLEW General manager of Atlantic Records. President and chairman of
    Epic Records.

GLENN GOLDSMITH Biographer of Stevie Wright.

JERRY GREENBERG President of Atlantic Records and Mirage Records.

ALVIN HANDWERKER Accountant and manager of AC/DC.

ROBERT HILBURN Rock critic of *The Los Angeles Times*.

SAM HORSBURGH Nephew of the Youngs. Son of their sister, Margaret Young.
    A&R manager of Alberts.

GERARD HUERTA Designer of AC/DC's logo.

MICHAEL HUTCHENCE Lead singer of INXS. Died in 1997.

PHIL JAMIESON Lead singer of Grinspoon.

IAN JEFFERY Tour manager and manager of AC/DC.

GLYN JOHNS Producer of The Easybeats.

BRIAN JOHNSON Lead singer of AC/DC.

JOHN KALODNER A&R executive at Atlantic Records.

MICHAEL KLENFNER Marketing and promotion executive at Atlantic Records. Died in 2009.

PAUL KOSSOFF Guitarist of Free and Back Street Crawler. Died in 1976.

EDDIE KRAMER Engineer of Led Zeppelin and Jimi Hendrix. Producer of Kiss.

DAVID KREBS Co-manager (with Steve Leber) of AC/DC.

CEDRIC KUSHNER Co-manager (with Michael Browning) of AC/DC. Concert promoter of AC/DC. Died in 2015.

MUTT LANGE Producer of AC/DC.

LARRY LARSTEAD Film director of AC/DC.

STEVE LEBER Co-manager (with David Krebs) of AC/DC.

STEVE LEEDS Promotion executive at Atlantic Records.

JUDY LIBOW Promotion executive at Atlantic Records.

VINCE LOVEGROVE Lead singer of The Valentines and friend of Bon Scott. Died in 2012.

DAVID MALLET Film and concert director of AC/DC.

TERRY MANNING Co-owner of Compass Point Studios. Engineer of Led Zeppelin and ZZ Top.

NICK MARIA Sales executive at Atlantic Records.

SUSAN MASINO Biographer of AC/DC.

CHRIS MASUAK Guitarist of Radio Birdman.

JOE MATERA Rock guitarist and guitar journalist.

MARIO MEDIOUS Promotion executive at Atlantic Records.

MOLLY MELDRUM Host of Australian TV program *Countdown*.

PETER MENSCH Manager of AC/DC.

DOUG MORRIS President of Atlantic Records. CEO/chairman of Sony Music.

PHILIP MORRIS Photographer of AC/DC.

ANTHONY O'GRADY Rock journalist and friend of Bon Scott.

JOEL O'KEEFFE Lead singer and guitarist of Airbourne.

MARK OPITZ Engineer of AC/DC.

JACK ORBIN Concert promoter of AC/DC.

JOE PERRY Guitarist of Aerosmith.

TONY PLATT Engineer and co-producer (with Angus and Malcolm Young) of AC/DC.

MARK POPE Concert promoter and manager of Jimmy Barnes.

STUART PRAGER Attorney of AC/DC.

JOHN PROUD Session drummer of AC/DC, Marcus Hook Roll Band and Stevie Wright.

FIFA RICCOBONO Assistant to the professional manager, label manager, A&R manager, general manager, CEO and finally executive director of Alberts. Friend of the Youngs.

ROB RILEY Guitarist of Rose Tattoo.

LOU RONEY Disc jockey for San Antonio radio station KMAC/KISS.

PHIL RUDD Drummer of AC/DC.

BON SCOTT Lead singer of AC/DC. Died in 1980.

ISA SCOTT Mother of Bon Scott. Died in 2011.

DEREK SHULMAN Lead singer of Gentle Giant. President of Atco Records.

RALPH SIMON Co-manager (with Clive Calder) of Mutt Lange.

RAY SINGER Producer of The Easybeats.

CHRIS SLADE Drummer of AC/DC.

TERRY SLESSER Lead singer of Back Street Crawler. Friend and bandmate of Paul Kossoff.

MATT SORUM Drummer of Guns N' Roses, The Cult and Velvet Revolver.

PHIL SUTCLIFFE Biographer of AC/DC.

JOHN SWAN Lead singer of Fraternity. Solo artist. Brother of Jimmy Barnes. Friend of Bon Scott and the Youngs.

JOHN TAIT Biographer of The Easybeats.

SHEL TALMY Producer of The Easybeats.

LISA TANNER Photographer of AC/DC.

DENIZ TEK Guitarist of Radio Birdman.

DOUG THALER Booking agent of AC/DC.

DAVID THOENER Engineer of AC/DC.

BILLY THORPE Lead singer and guitarist of Billy Thorpe and the Aztecs. Solo artist. Died in 2007.

STEVEN TYLER Lead singer of Aerosmith.

RONNIE VAN ZANT Lead singer of Lynyrd Skynyrd. Died in 1977.

HARRY VANDA Lead guitarist of The Easybeats. Co-producer (with George Young) of AC/DC, Stevie Wright and Rose Tattoo.

MIKE VAUGHAN Manager of The Easybeats.

CLINTON WALKER Biographer of Bon Scott.

MICK WALL Biographer of AC/DC.

JOHN WHEELER Lead singer, guitarist and violinist of Hayseed Dixie.

CLIFF WILLIAMS Bass player of AC/DC.

STEVIE WRIGHT Lead singer of The Easybeats. Solo artist.

LARRY YASGAR Singles executive at Atlantic Records.

ALEX YOUNG Bass player and vocalist of Grapefruit. Session saxophonist of Marcus Hook Roll Band. Brother of the Youngs. Died in 1997.

ANGUS YOUNG Lead guitarist of AC/DC.

GEORGE YOUNG Rhythm guitarist of The Easybeats. Session bass player, drummer and percussionist of AC/DC. Co-producer (with Harry Vanda) of AC/DC, Stevie Wright and Rose Tattoo. Producer of *Stiff Upper Lip* for AC/DC.

MALCOLM YOUNG Rhythm guitarist of AC/DC. Retired due to dementia in 2014.

MARGARET YOUNG Sister of the Youngs.

STEVIE YOUNG Guitarist of Starfighters and AC/DC. Nephew of the Youngs.

STEWART YOUNG Co-manager (with Steve Barnett) of AC/DC.

MANDAWUY YUNUPINGU Lead singer of Yothu Yindi. Australian of the Year in 1992. Died in 2013.

ACKNOWLEDGEMENTS
'For Those About To Rock
(We Salute You)'

This book wouldn't have been possible without the help, support, friendship, encouragement, generosity, contacts, collected memories and valuable insight of the following people: Rob Riley, Holger Brockmann, Marianne Brockmann, Mark Opitz, Terry Manning, John Swan, Mark Gable, Suzi Dhnaram, Luke Wallis, Stevie Wright, Mark Evans, Chris Gilbey, Ian Jeffery, Tony Currenti, Michael Browning, Greg Stock, Mandawuy Yunupingu, Gerard Huerta, Tom Huerta, Mike Fraser, Bertrand Blier, Rusty Hopkinson, Marc Dwyer, Tony Platt, Allan Fryer, Georg Dolivo, Glenn Goldsmith, Kim Fowley, Joe Matera, Dave Evans, Jack Orbin, Philip Morris, Tom Weschler, Daniel Boud, the estate of Chuck Pulin, Leo Gozbekian, Ray Singer, John Perry, Billy Altman, David Mallet, Terry Slesser, Erin McGuirk, Robert Alford, Ashley Gilbertson, Barry Diament, Chris Keeble, Kerry-Jayne Ryan, Jessica Sartini, Wally Kempton, Chris Bastic, Sidney Drashin, Mark Pope, Doug Thaler, Catherine Milne, Deniz Tek, John Proud, Anthony O'Grady, Phil Jamieson, Mike Rudd, Snowy Fleet, Bill Bartlett, Oliver Fowler, John Wheeler, Stewart Young, David Krebs, Jake

Berry, David W. Larkin, Darren Ashton, Mikko Hyppönen, Derek Shulman, Alan James, Jerry Greenberg, Robert Hilburn, Matt Sorum, Steve Leber, Phil Carson, Sandra Jackson, Tim Gaze, Joel O'Keeffe, Luke Causby, David Thoener, Jimmy Douglass, Mario Medious, Jon O'Rourke, Nick Maria, Larry Yasgar, Jim Delehant, Judy Libow, Steve Leeds, Carol Klenfner, Tony Berardini, David Glew, Ann Glew, Lisa Tanner, Dick Barnatt, Stevie Young, Tristin Norwell, Michael Marley, Cedric Kushner, Ken Casey, Holly Lovegrove, Ryan Johnson, Paul La Rosa, Jordanka Kuzmanov, Chris Masuak, Airlie Lawson, Scott Miller, Glyn Johns, Shel Talmy, Scott McRae, Alison Urquhart, Anne Reilly, Nerrilee Weir, Nikki Christer, Janne Moller, John Richardson, Laura Nicol, Peter Pis, Vanessa Radnidge, Bernard Fanning, Tom Donald, Chris Bruce, Andrew Logan, Renée Cooper, Larry Larstead, Robert Pfeiffer, Shaun Harwood, Michael Hohnen, Patsy Hohnen, Mike Knight, Alan Bailey, Robert Yves, Phil Lageat, Nate Althoff, Colin Nichol, Ken Evans, Larry LeBlanc, Philip Gomes, Rosemary Hanly, Fred Fink and Jan Blum. Special thanks, too, to the authors before me who have recorded their own stories about the music of the Youngs – especially Clinton Walker, Murray Engleheart, Joe Bonomo, John Tait and Mick Wall (plus his small army of paid researchers) – and to Mike Durant for permission to reproduce an extended excerpt from his book, *In The Company Of Heroes*.

And lastly, cheers to The Easybeats, Billy Thorpe, AC/DC, Stevie Wright, Rose Tattoo and Airbourne for giving the world the best Australian rock. It's never gonna die. Never gonna die.

BIBLIOGRAPHY
'Ride On'

BOOKS

AC/DC: Hell Ain't A Bad Place To Be, Mick Wall, Orion Books, London, 2012

AC/DC, High-Voltage Rock 'N' Roll: The Ultimate Illustrated History, Phil Sutcliffe, Voyageur Press, Minneapolis, 2010

AC/DC, Maximum Rock & Roll: The Ultimate Story Of The World's Greatest Rock Band, Murray Engleheart with Arnaud Durieux, HarperCollins, Sydney, 2006

Appetite For Destruction: The Days Of Guns N' Roses, Danny Sugerman, St Martin's Press, New York, 1992

Dirty Deeds: My Life Inside And Outside Of AC/DC, Mark Evans, Allen & Unwin, Sydney, 2011

Get Your Jumbo Jet Out Of My Airport: Random Notes For AC/DC Obsessives, Howard Johnson, The Black Book Company, Pewsey, 1999

Hard Road: The Life And Times Of Stevie Wright, Glenn Goldsmith with Stevie Wright, Random House, Sydney, 2004

Highway To Hell, Joe Bonomo, Continuum Books, New York, 2010

Highway To Hell: The Life And Times Of AC/DC Legend Bon Scott, Clinton Walker, Pan Macmillan, Sydney, 1994

Hot Stuff: Disco And The Remaking of American Culture, Alice Echols, W. W. Norton & Company, New York, 2010

House Of Hits: The Great Untold Story Of Australia's First Family Of Music, Jane Albert, Hardie Grant Books, Melbourne, 2010

In The Company Of Heroes, Michael J. Durant with Steven Hartov, Putnam, New York, 2003

Jimmy Barnes, Too Much Ain't Enough: The Authorised Biography, Toby Creswell, Random House, Sydney, 1993

Let There Be Rock: The Story Of AC/DC, Susan Masino, Omnibus Press, New York, 2006

Louder Than Hell: The Definitive Oral History Of Metal, Jon Wiederhorn and Katherine Turman, HarperCollins, New York, 2013

Sophisto-Punk: The Story Of Mark Opitz & Oz Rock, Mark Opitz (as told to Luke Wallis and Jeff Jenkins), Random House, Sydney, 2012

The Encyclopedia Of Record Producers: An Indispensable Guide To The Most Important Record Producers In History, Eric Olsen, Paul Verna and Carlo Wolff (editors), Daniel J. Levitin (contributor), Billboard Books, New York, 1999

The Forever War, Dexter Filkins, Knopf, New York, 2008

The Soul Of It All: My Music, My Life, Michael Bolton, Center Street, New York, 2013

The 10 Rules Of Rock And Roll: Collected Music Writings/2005–09, Robert Forster, Black Inc. Books, Melbourne, 2009

Vanda & Young: Inside Australia's Hit Factory, John Tait, University of New South Wales Press, Sydney, 2010

Why AC/DC Matters, Anthony Bozza, HarperCollins, New York, 2009

DVD/TV

AC/DC, Back In Black: Classic Albums Under Review, Umbrella Entertainment, Melbourne, 2008

AC/DC, Highway To Hell: Classic Albums Under Review, Umbrella Entertainment, Melbourne, 2009

VH1's Ultimate Albums: Back In Black, AC/DC, Viacom International, New York, 2003

LETTERS/PRESS RELEASES/OTHER DOCUMENTS

'AC/DC', Albert Productions press release, Sydney, 1974

'AC/DC: *High Voltage*', Atco Records press release, New York, 1976

'AC/DC: *Let There Be Rock*', Atlantic Records press release, New York, 1977

Atlantic Records letter to Bill Bartlett, Perry Cooper, New York, 1979

Leidseplein Presse B.V. letter to the United States Commissioner for Trademarks, 'Declaration In Support Of Substitute Specimens', Stuart Prager, New York, 2004

LINER NOTES

Bonfire, Murray Engleheart, East West Records, New York, 1997

'74 Jailbreak, Murray Engleheart, Epic Records, New York, 2003

NEWSPAPERS/MAGAZINES

'AC/DC's Angus Young Discusses Bon Scott And The *Bonfire* Box Set', Tom Beaujour, *Guitar World*, New York, 1998

'AC/DC Celebrate Their Quarter Century', Sylvie Simmons, *MOJO*, London, 2000

'AC/DC Fired Up Over Treatment In Media', Kerry Wakefield, *The Age*, Melbourne, 1981

'AC/DC, Hammersmith Odeon: Concert Review', Clive Bennett, *The Times*, London, 1976

'AC/DC's iTunes Debut Sells 48,000 Digital Albums, 696,000 Songs', Keith Caulfield, *Billboard*, New York, 2012

'AC/DC: Like Comfy Old Shoes That Fit All Feet', Tomi Ervamaa, *Helsingin Sanomat*, Helsinki, 2006

'AC/DC Salvo Levels Sin City', David Lewis, *Sounds*, London, 1978

'AC/DC Shrug Off A Death And Rock On', David Fricke, *Rolling Stone*, New York, 1980

'AC/DC: The Dirtiest Story Ever Told', Phil Sutcliffe, *Sounds*, London, 1976

'Air Raid', Joe Nick Patoski, *Texas Monthly*, Austin, 1978

'A New Rock Star: Proof Of Australia's Oldest Creatures', Simon Benson, *The Daily Telegraph*, Sydney, 1998

'Artists Discover AOR Fickle', Ed Harrison, *Billboard*, New York, 1981

'Atlantic Country: After Some Rough Starts, The Label Goes To Town Big Time In Music City', Chet Flippo, *Billboard*, New York, 1998

'Bands Declare A Truce For Tribute', Patrick Donovan, *The Age*, Melbourne, 2004

'*Back In Black*: The Lyrical Debate', Malcolm Dome, *Classic Rock*, London, 2005

'Court Battle Over Release Of AC/DC Film', John Sippel, *Billboard*, New York, 1981

'Dickensian Conditions In Northern Territory Prisons', Australian Associated Press, *The Australian*, Sydney, 2011

'For Whom The Bells Toll', Geoff Barton and Jens Jam Rasmussen, *Classic Rock*, London, 2005

'Great White Sharks Love AC/DC', Nigel Austin, *Herald Sun*, Melbourne, 2011

'Hells Bell', Philip Wilding, *Classic Rock*, London, 2000

'High Voltage', Vince Lovegrove, *The Australian*, Sydney, 2006

'*High Voltage*: Album Review', Billy Altman, *Rolling Stone*, New York, 1976

'In the Family', Andrew Heathcote, *BRW*, Sydney, 2013

'"*Iron Man 2*" Shoots To Thrill With AC/DC', Geoff Boucher, *The Los Angeles Times*, Los Angeles, 2010

'Kiss, Kiss, Bang, Bang, At Fairgrounds Concert', John Finley, *The Courier-Journal*, Louisville, 1977

'Let There Be Rock: AC/DC @ The "Dillo"', Marky Billson, *The Austin Chronicle*, Austin, 2008

'Malcolm And Angus Young: Interview', Dave Ling, *Classic Rock*, London, 2003

'Marcus Hook Roll Band, "Natural Man": Single Review', Martin Cerf, *Phonograph Record Magazine*, Los Angeles, 1973

'Pop Maven Horn Shows Staying Power As One Of The Industry's Top Producers', Ben Cromer, *Billboard*, New York, 1998

'Sony's Newest Boy Band, AC/DC, Took Stage In 1970s', Jennifer Ordonez, *The Wall Street Journal*, New York, 2002

'The Biggest Tax Haven You've Never Heard Of: Holland', Martin Van Geest, *The International Correspondent*, Amsterdam, 2011

'The Devil You Say? No Way. AC/DC's Message: Rebellion, Not Satan Worship', Robert Hilburn, *The Los Angeles Times*, Los Angeles, 1985

'The Dirtiest Group In Town', David Brown, *Record Mirror*, London, 1976

'The Hits and The Missus', Krissi Murison, *The Sunday Times*, London, 2013

'The Punks Are Out Of Style', Tony Kiss, *The Times-News*, Kingsport, 1978

'The Wild Young Man', Bernard McGovern, *The Daily Express*, London, 1976

'The Young Guns', Jessica Gardner, *BRW*, Sydney, 2011

'*Thunderstruck*: Film Review', Russell Edwards, *Variety*, Los Angeles, 2004

'Top 50 Australian Guitarists Of All Time', Peter Hodgson, Andrew P. Street and Craig White (contributors), *Australian Guitar*, Sydney, 2012

RESEARCH PAPERS/THESES

'Early Myriapodous Arthropods From Australia: *Maldybulakia* From The Devonian Of New South Wales', Gregory D. Edgecombe, *Records Of The Australian Museum*, Sydney, 1998

An Exploratory Study Of The Effects Of Radio Airplay And Advertising On Record Sales, Peter Mensch, unpublished MA thesis, Chicago, 1977

SCRIPTS

Stevie: The Life And Music Of Stevie Wright And The Easybeats, Scott McRae and Ann Petrou, Sydney, 2012

WEBSITES

acdc.com
ac-dc.net
acdc-archives.fr
acdc-bootlegs.com
acdczone.com
albumlinernotes.com
allmusic.com
billboard.com
celebrityaccess.com
classicsdujour.com
discogs.com
45cat.com
forbes.com
f-secure.com
gawker.com

grammy.com
highwaytoacdc.com
johnkalodner.com
metallian.com
milesago.com
mtv.com
muttlange.com
nyeandcompany.com
packagingeurope.com
reddit.com
riaa.com
robert-palmer.over-blog.com
song-database.com
tsdr.uspto.gov
youtube.com

DISCOGRAPHY

'High Voltage'

1
'Good Times'[1]
Written by Harry Vanda & George Young
Produced by Glyn Johns
The Easybeats, *Vigil*,[2] Parlophone/United Artists Records (1968)

2
'Evie'
Written by Harry Vanda & George Young
Produced by Harry Vanda & George Young
Stevie Wright, *Hard Road*, Albert Productions/Atco Records (1974)

3
'It's A Long Way To The Top (If You Wanna Rock 'N' Roll)'
Written by Angus Young, Malcolm Young & Bon Scott
Produced by Harry Vanda & George Young
AC/DC, *TNT*, Albert Productions (1975)[3]

4
'Jailbreak'
Written by Angus Young, Malcolm Young & Bon Scott
Produced by Harry Vanda & George Young
AC/DC, *Dirty Deeds Done Dirt Cheap*, Albert Productions (1976)[4]

5

'Let There Be Rock'
Written by Angus Young, Malcolm Young & Bon Scott
Produced by Harry Vanda & George Young
AC/DC, *Let There Be Rock*, Albert Productions/Atlantic Records (1977)

6

'Riff Raff'
Written by Angus Young, Malcolm Young & Bon Scott
Produced by Harry Vanda & George Young
AC/DC, *Powerage*, Albert Productions/Atlantic Records (1978)

7

'Highway To Hell'
Written by Angus Young, Malcolm Young & Bon Scott
Produced by Robert John 'Mutt' Lange
AC/DC, *Highway To Hell*, Albert Productions/Atlantic Records (1979)

8

'Back In Black'
Written by Angus Young, Malcolm Young & Brian Johnson
Produced by Robert John 'Mutt' Lange
AC/DC, *Back In Black*, Albert Productions/Atlantic Records (1980)

9

'You Shook Me All Night Long'
Written by Angus Young, Malcolm Young & Brian Johnson
Produced by Robert John 'Mutt' Lange
AC/DC, *Back In Black*, Albert Productions/Atlantic Records (1980)

10

'Hells Bells'
Written by Angus Young, Malcolm Young & Brian Johnson
Produced by Robert John 'Mutt' Lange
AC/DC, *Back In Black*, Albert Productions/Atlantic Records (1980)

11

'Thunderstruck'
Written by Angus Young & Malcolm Young
Produced by Bruce Fairbairn
AC/DC, *The Razors Edge*, Albert Productions/Atco Records (1990)

1 Released as 'Gonna Have A Good Time' in the United States.
2 Released as *Falling Off The Edge Of The World* in the United States.
3 Released on *High Voltage*, Atlantic Records, 1976, in the United States.
4 Released sans 'Jailbreak' on *Dirty Deeds Done Dirt Cheap*, Atlantic Records, 1981, in the United States. 'Jailbreak' was released on *'74 Jailbreak*, Atlantic Records, 1984, in the United States.

APPENDIX
'What Do You Do
For Money Honey'

'Books and printed instructional and teaching manuals in the field of entertainment; notepaper; general feature and entertainment magazines; calendars; mounted and unmounted photographs; play and trading cards; road maps; cartoons printed on paper and cardboard; blank and picture postcards; notecards; note pads; greeting cards; adult and children's activity and colouring books; puffy stickers; adhesive stickers; photograph albums; memorandum books; pens; pencils; folders and portfolios for papers; notebook binders; letter openers; memo holders; pennants made of paper and mounted on sticks; diaries; clipboards; book covers; book marks; bulletin boards; erasable memo boards; pen and pencil holders; paper clip holders; paper weights; paper napkins and towels; posters; writing paper and stationery; drawing paper; gift wrapping paper; luminous paper; graphics paper; stickers; paper banners; decals and windshield decals strips; collector decals with display sheets; bumper stickers and strips; plastic water-filled snow globes; memo pads; non-electric erasers; electric erasers; stationery holders; desk sets; colour lithograph sticker books; postcards books; holographic greeting and trading cards; pencil bags; pencil sharpeners; gift wrapping paper sets; decorative gift boxes; comic books; bookmarks; posterbooks; paper signs; paper party signs; paper lawn signs; stamp pads; rubber stamps for impressing illustrated images; check and autograph books; adhesive tape dispensers for stationery or household use; corrugated cardboard storage boxes and corrugated closet wardrobes and storage boxes; reflective paper stock; belts; neckties; suspenders; bandannas; beach sandals; bathrobes; infant and toddler sleepwear; nightshirts, pyjamas and loungewear; beach coverup dresses; diaper sets; toddler short sets; jogging suits; boys short sets; socks; playsuits; coveralls; wristbands; union suits; Henley suits; shorts; pants; slacks; shirts; jackets; referees and umpires uniforms; team uniform reproductions; sweaters; parkas; turtlenecks; mittens; underwear; jerseys; bow ties; headwear and scarves; earmuffs; earbands and headbands; hosiery; rainwear, namely rain ponchos and jackets; footwear, namely shoes, boots and slippers; bath thongs; nylon shells; hats; caps; visors; aprons; cloth and ski bibs; canvas footwear; knickers; wind resistant jackets; masquerade costumes; masquerade masks; blazers; leg warmers; jeans; leotards; workout and sports apparel, namely shorts, jackets, slacks, shirts; clothing for men, women and children, namely bathing trunks, swimsuits, swimsuit covers, coats, dresses, smocks, shirts, jumpers, pullovers, sweatshirts, blouses, nightgowns, socks, trousers, dungarees, tanktops and suntops; belt buckles not of precious metal; and patches for clothing.'

– Goods and services registered under the AC/DC trademark and logo for international classes 016, 025 and 026 by Leidseplein Presse B.V. in 2003 and 2004 with the United States Patent and Trademark Office. Serial numbers: 75982466, 75077335. Registration numbers: 2721830, 2840444.

INDEX

'Up To My Neck In You'